Medical Ministry

Ellen G. White

1932

Copyright © 2021

LS Company

ISBN:978-1-0879-0647-8

Copyright©2021

Preface to the First Edition

How to preserve and to improve health, how to prevent and to treat sickness, are truly living, vital problems in the medical world today. Never before in the history of the human family have these great questions received the earnest, intensive, scientific study and wide publicity that are being given them at the present hour. Medical science in all its ramifications has made marvelous progress during the last half century. It would require a volume to enumerate and explain the discoveries, the development, and achievement, that have been made in this great department of human interest and welfare. The knowledge that has been gained in the exhaustive study of these fundamental subjects has been given to the public in highly scientific and technical volumes, and in simpler form in books, magazines, newspapers, and lectures.

This volume, entitled *Medical Ministry*, is one more valuable contribution to the world's needs in the domain of physical, mental, and spiritual well-being. It is unique in its scope. It recognizes and commends the truly scientific in the causes and treatment of diseases. It places strong emphasis upon the observance of all that relates to the prevention of ailments. And still more, the writer of this volume recognizes that sin, the transgression of divine law, is the primary cause of disease, sickness, and death.

Believing that the transgression of moral law leads to the disregard of physical and mental laws, the writer places very great importance upon obedience to moral law as one of the primary conditions necessary for perfect health. And obedience to moral law, it is urged, can be rendered only through the acceptance of, and union with, Christ, the redeemer of man ruined through transgression. Hence it is claimed that the perfect remedy for the ills of mankind is the combination, appreciation, and observance of the spiritual, the mental, and the physical laws of our being.

It is this wide, all-inclusive scope of instruction set forth in *Medical Ministry* that commends it so highly to the public. This instruction is not technical. It can be understood by laymen. The requirements laid down for spiritual, mental, and physical Health and happiness are so rational that they can be complied with. That which relates to the prevention of sickness is of especial value; for, as an old adage tells us, an ounce of prevention is worth a pound of cure.

The writer of this book, Mrs. E. G. White, devoted nearly seventy years of her very earnest, active life to the gospel ministry. In her youth she was an invalid. In her early married life she battled with a weak heart, with cancer, and with other ailments. At the age of thirty-six she experienced a great awakening on the subject of temperance as it relates to health, to physical and mental efficiency, and to Christian living. The rigid application of the knowledge gained regarding the laws of mind and body brought great relief and restoration to her, and from that time on to the close of her arduous labors, a period of nearly fifty years, she was an earnest exponent of the principles of health and temperance.

In 1865 Mrs. E. G. White made an appeal to the Seventh-day Adventist Church, of which she was a member, to establish a medical institution in which the sick should be given rational, drugless treatment for their ills, and also where they should be given instruction regarding the laws of health. In response, such an institution was established in Battle Creek, Michigan. This undertaking met with great success. The institution grew into large proportions, and for nearly a half century it has been favorably and widely known as the Battle Creek Sanitarium. Through subsequent years many similar sister sanitariums have been established in different parts of the United States and in many other countries of the world.

The Trustees of Mrs. White's Estate, having found in her letters and manuscript files many documents heretofore unpublished which contain valuable instruction for physicians, nurses, sanitarium managers, helpers, gospel evangelists, and Christian workers, believe that this valuable counsel should be sent forth to the public. It is our sincere hope that this volume may prove a great blessing to its readers, and through them, to a great multitude to whom they may minister.

A. G. Daniells

Preface to the Second Edition

Historical Background of the Ellen G. White Writings on Health

The continuing demand for the Ellen G. White books calls for frequent reprinting, and occasionally for new editions also. This volume, issued initially in 1932, is now making its appearance in a second edition. Although the type face and size of page have been altered to bring it into conformity with the popular Christian Home Library size, the text is unchanged and the paging is in keeping with the former printing. Thus the new edition remains consistent with references in the *Comprehensive Index to the Writings of Ellen G. White*.

Medical Ministry was the first Ellen G. White book, compiled largely from unpublished sources, to be issued posthumously. Mrs. White's instructions to her appointed Board of Trustees served as a guide in this work. In her authorization to the board, she provided "for the printing of compilations from my manuscripts." She recognized that in the communications addressed to individuals and to institutions through the years, there were counsels which would be of service to the cause generally.

Medical Ministry has taken its place with other books by the same author, and additional works on the subject of health have followed. Since this is but one link in a chain of books devoted to this important subject, it seems appropriate to review the history of the several Ellen G. White productions, both past and current, which deal with health principles and medical work. This will aid the reader in identifying various publications in print and out of print in this vital field.

Cautions were given to Ellen White in 1848 concerning the use of tobacco, tea, and coffee, and in 1854 light was imparted on the importance of cleanliness and the use of foods not highly refined or too rich. However, not until 1863 did she receive the first comprehensive vision concerning health reform. Of this she wrote, "It was at the house of Bro. A. Hilliard, at Otsego, Mich., June 6, 1863, that the great subject of health reform was opened before me in vision."—The Review and Herald, October 8, 1867. In subsequent visions many details concerning this subject were presented to her, and these visions constituted the basis for the more detailed writing relative to health and the conduct of the health work of the church.

The Primary E. G. White Articles on Health

The first general written presentation made by Mrs. White on the subject of health was in a chapter of thirty-two pages entitled "Health." This appeared in *Spiritual Gifts* 4a:120-151, in the summer of 1864. In this article she set forth in condensed form the great principles given to her in the vision of 1863. This material is available today in the facsimile reprint of the *Spiritual Gifts* volumes.

Recognizing somewhat the magnitude of the task of leading 3,500 Seventh-day Adventists to a full understanding of the health reform message, in 1865 James and Ellen White published six pamphlets entitled "Health, or How to Live." Five of these pamphlets contained sixty-four pages, and one, eighty pages. In each was one article from the pen of Ellen G. White, running under the title, "Disease and its Causes." Appearing with Mrs. White's article was related material drawn from the writings of physicians and ministers, and articles especially prepared by James White and others for these pamphlets. Each was devoted to a fundamental health theme: diet, marriage and home life, the use of drugs, care of the sick and hygiene, child care and attire for children, and healthful dress. In 1899 and 1900, the six Ellen G. White messages were published as a series of continued articles in the *Review and Herald*. In 1958 they were made available as a sixty-nine-page appendix in *Selected Messages*, book 2.

In a more specialized area of early health counsel was the article entitled "An Appeal to Mothers." This was printed in 1864 in a pamphlet by that title. In 1870 James White embodied this as an Ellen G. White contribution to the 270-page *Solemn Appeal Relative to Solitary Vice*. Large portions of this article appear today in *Child Guidance* In the section entitled "Preserving Moral Integrity." The same basic counsels are found in *Testimonies For The Church* 2 and *Testimonies For The Church* 5.

Christian Temperance and Bible Hygiene, 1890

A volume entitled *Christian Temperance and Hygiene* Was published in 1890. The first portion, *Christian Temperance*, was written by Ellen G. White and the second, on *Bible Hygiene*, was compiled from the writings of James White. In the first 162 pages Mrs. White presented basic health principles in more popular and expanded form. Fifteen years later this formed the basis for the book *The Ministry of Healing*. Also all or parts of nine of the eighteen chapters by Mrs. White in the 1890 book were reprinted in 1923 in *Counsels on Health* and *Fundamentals of Christian Education*. The other chapters were closely paralleled in *The Ministry of Healing*.

Healthful Living, 1897

In 1897, while Mrs. White was in Australia, Dr. David Paulson, then working at the Battle Creek Sanitarium, drew together from Mrs. White's writings on health topics then available to him a large number of excerpts and paragraphs, assembling them in topical order. This collection, called *Healthful Living*, appeared eight years before the publication of *The Ministry of Healing*. The volume, 284 pages in length, became a valuable teaching aid, and at least three editions were printed. However, with the appearance of *The Ministry of Healing* in 1905, *The Paulson Compilation* was no longer published. Mrs. White was appreciative of this compiled volume, but of course it did not have the continuity which characterized her books.

The Ministry of Healing, 1905

Mrs. White's well-rounded presentation on the subject of health is made in *The Ministry of Healing*, a 516-page book which she intended for both Adventist and non-Adventist readers, in America and overseas. In preparing its forty-three chapters she drew heavily upon her materials in *Christian Temperance and Bible Hygiene*, though she amplified and rewrote the material. At the time of Mrs. White's death in 1915, this was her only available book on health.

Counsels on Health, 1923

The broad principles of healthful living had been set forth in *The Ministry of Healing*. However, in Mrs. White's articles which had appeared in the journals of the church, in *Testimonies for the Church*, and in certain out-of-print books, were many additional messages. These contained needed instruction regarding health principles, the conduct of Seventh-day Adventist institutions, and the promulgation of the health message. The materials were assembled by the White Trustees in *Counsels on Health*, published in 1923. This 634-page volume, confined to matter which had appeared in print in one form or another, provided a volume of great service to the church and especially to medical personnel.

Medical Ministry, 1932

The promulgation of the health message was for fifty years a topic of major concern to Ellen White. She wrote more in the field of health than on any other single topic of counsel. Many of her manuscript documents, addressed to physicians, institutional managers, nurses, and sanitarium families embody counsels of vital importance. Copies of these were kept on file. Many of the counsels give direction to the medical work. Others, written at crucial times in the development of phases of our medical work, sound warnings. Some were messages written to save a worker faced with special peril. The instruction itself is timeless.

This volume, *Medical Ministry*, is primarily a selection of these counsels addressed to medical personnel and others connected with Seventh-day Adventist medical institutions. The counsels have been drawn together and published so that others might benefit from them. The preface was written by A. G. Daniells, for many years president of the General Conference and one of the trustees chosen by Mrs. White to care for her writings. When the book was first published, Elder Daniells was also chairman of the board of the College of Medical Evangelists.

Counsels on Diet and Foods, 1938

In early 1926 Dr. H. M. Walton, then teaching in the field of nutrition at the College of Medical Evangelists, assembled Ellen G. White materials from published and unpublished sources relating to the subject of diet and foods. This material, prepared in collaboration with the White Trustees, was printed at Loma Linda for classroom use in a two-column, paperbound, 200-page work entitled *Testimony Studies on Diet and Foods*. The materials were topically arranged for ready reference. Eventually the value of a wider circulation of this material among Seventh-day Adventists was discerned. The White Trustees took these materials, dropped out certain items which were repetitious, and supplemented it with new materials from unpublished sources. They also added some sections, and brought out what has proved to be a most popular volume, the 500-page *Counsels on Diet and Foods*. Its counsels, topically arranged and carefully indexed, make the combined Spirit of Prophecy statements on diet readily available for study.

Temperance, 1949

The 300-page volume fittingly entitled *Temperance* sets before the church the full range of counsels drawn from all sources, published and unpublished, bearing on that topic. Three Ellen G. White temperance addresses appear as an appendix. This volume has become a handbook to temperance workers.

Welfare Ministry, 1952

The welfare work of the Seventh-day Adventist Church combines the health work with neighborly deeds of Christian service. In its 350 pages, *Welfare Ministry* Provides Ellen G. White's counsels on these important phases of ministry. Mrs. White's experiences as a welfare worker climax this volume. This, too, is a handbook in its field.

These five currently available volumes, together with portions of *Selected Messages,* book 2, present the full range of Ellen G. White counsels on the subject of health and the conduct of our health work.

Counsels Vital for Today

It is interesting to observe that a century has passed since the attention of Seventh-day Adventists was called to the subject of health through the visions given to Ellen G. White. These counsels have withstood the closest scrutiny of trained scientists. The findings of conservative research workers from day to day add confirmatory evidence to the scientific accuracy of the counsels.

When Mrs. White, a layman in the field of medical science, with a very limited education, began in the 1860's to set forth her views on health, it was natural that some would seek to associate her expositions with the writings of certain contemporary physicians. The suggestion on the part of a few that the opinions of those about her may have been the real inspiration for her writings in the health field, she answered frankly and simply, after referring to the vision of June 6, 1863:

"I did not read any works upon health until I had written '*Spiritual Gifts*,' vols. III and IV, '*Appeal to Mothers*,' and had sketched out most of my six articles in the six numbers of '*How to Live*.' ...

"As I introduced the subject of health to friends where I labored in Michigan, New England, and in the state of New York, and spoke against drugs and flesh-meats, and in favor of water, pure air, and a proper diet, the reply was often made, 'you speak very nearly the opinions taught in the "Laws of Life" and other publications, by Drs. Trall, Jackson, and others. Have you read that paper and those works?' My reply was that I had not, neither should I read them till I had fully written out my views, lest it should be said that I had received my light upon the subject of health from physicians, and not from the Lord."—The Review and Herald, Ocrober 8, 1867.

Again that year as she referred to her writings on the subject of health, she asserted:

"My views were written independent of books or the opinions of others."—Ellen G. White Manuscript 7, 1867.

Certain leading men in our ranks in 1864 commented upon this point in connection with the publication of her article in "*An Appeal to Mothers*." Following her 29-page presentation, certain medical testimony was given. Between the Ellen G. White article and these statements by other writers, the trustees of the Seventh-day Adventist Publishing Association inserted the following significant note:

"We have thought proper to add to the foregoing the following testimonies from men of high standing and authority in the medical world, corroborative of the views presented in the preceding pages. And in justice to the writer of those pages, we would say that she had read nothing from the authors here quoted, and had read no other works on this subject, previous to putting into our hands what she has written. She is not, therefore, a copyist, although she has stated important truths to which men who are entitled to our highest confidence, have borne testimony.

TRUSTEES."

To those who suggested that Mrs. White's writings reflected the conclusions of contemporary medical innovators, one need only observe the conflicting pronouncements of the times and ask, "How would an uninformed layman of that day know what to select and what to reject?" Few of the popular concepts of that day survive, yet Mrs. White's counsels not only stand today, but are reinforced by the latest discoveries in clinic and laboratory.

Objectives and Conditions of Prosperity Unchanged

Great advances have been made in the medical world since the death of Ellen White in 1915. While these advances have brought adjustments in the details of the practice of medicine, they have not outmoded the therapeutic value of "pure air, exercise, proper diet, the use of water," and "trust in divine power," which Ellen G. White enumerated as "the true remedies." While modern methods of rapid diagnosis and treatment of disease have shortened the time patients must stay at a medical institution, and while this has its bearing on the operation of Seventh-day Adventist institutions, the basic principles set forth in the Ellen G. White counsels constitute a safe, workable guide today. Writing reflectively, Mrs. White declared:

"As our work has extended and institutions have multiplied, God's purpose in their establishment remains the same. The conditions of prosperity are unchanged."—Testimonies for the Church 6, page 224.

We can be reassured of the timelessness of these counsels in medical lines. As Mrs. White stood before the General Conference in session in 1909, she said:

"I have been shown that the principles that were given us in the early days of the message are as important and should be regarded just as conscientiously today as they were then."—Testimonies for the Church 9:158.

Principle does not change, though changes in circumstances may make adjustment necessary in the application of some of the principles. Indeed, Ellen White wrote concerning the work at the newly established school in Loma Linda:

"We cannot mark out a precise line to be followed unconditionally. Circumstances and emergencies will arise for which the Lord must give special instruction, but if we begin to work, depending wholly upon the Lord, watching, praying, walking in harmony with the light He sends us, we shall not be left to walk in darkness."—Ellen G. White Letter 192, 1906.

The Testimonies and the Meaning of Words

The significance of certain terms also may change materially over a period of years. However, a careful study of basic principles, as revealed through an accumulation of the counsels, makes clear the intent of the author and thus the proper course of action.

The student of Ellen G. White's health counsels is aware of the frequent condemnation of the use of drugs and the appeal for the employment of simple remedies. A hundred years ago, and for many years thereafter, the remedies employed by physicians were usually those which we know now to be potent poisons. Often the cause of the disease was not known. The germ theory was not yet well established, and treatments usually dealt with symptoms. Anyone familiar with the medical literature of the time is aware of the high mortality rate and of the short life expectancy. He is aware of the nature of many of the medications which were used by physicians. Many died as the result of the use of the drugs prescribed. [Note: for a documented picture illustrating this, see "Story of our Health Message," Chapter 1, entitled "The Times of this Ignorance."] The voice of Ellen White crying out against this disregard of life was not a lone voice, but she spoke from a heart which could feel and a mind enlightened by inspiration.

The careful student will avoid misapplying the references to drugs. Never will he sweepingly apply the condemnation of drugs to tested remedial agencies made available through scientific research. He will find from a review of the Ellen G. White statements, putting line with line and precept with precept, that her references to "strong drugs" and "poisonous drugs" and the use of "medicines which ... leave behind injurious effects upon the system," are qualifying factors which must be taken into account. See the assembled statements on the use of drugs in Selected Messages 2:279-285.

He will find that Mrs. White employed remedial agencies and took advantage of true advances in medical science during the later years of her life. He will observe that her position was neither extreme nor fanatical, but rational and in keeping with scientific findings and a conservative appraisal of those findings. He will observe that through all the Spirit of Prophecy counsels on health, the emphasis is on preventive medicine. There is a call to guard the body, to cultivate simple habits of living, and to take advantage of the restorative agencies available to all.

Medical personnel, as they seek to understand the prevention, cause, and treatment of disease, and as they seek to employ the medical work as the "right arm" of the third angel's message, will find these counsels, warnings, and encouragements of divine origin to be a timely aid.

Contents

Preface to the First Edition iii
Preface to the Second Edition v
   Historical Background of the Ellen G. White Writings on
      Health v
   The Primary E. G. White Articles on Health vi
      Christian Temperance and Bible Hygiene, 1890 vii
      Healthful Living, 1897 vii
      The Ministry of Healing, 1905 vii
      Counsels on Health, 1923 viii
      Medical Ministry, 1932 viii
      Counsels on Diet and Foods, 1938 ix
      Temperance, 1949 ix
      Welfare Ministry, 1952 ix
   Counsels Vital for Today x
   Objectives and Conditions of Prosperity Unchanged xi
   The Testimonies and the Meaning of Words xii
Section 1—Healing Power and Its Source 25
   Nature the Servant of God 25
   Christ the Life and Light 25
   Life by the Power of God 25
   Life of God in Nature 26
   God Feeding Earth's Millions 26
   Kept in Activity 26
   Through Natural Laws 27
   God in Nature 27
   Nature's Message 28
   The Message of Love 29
   Nature Is Not God 29
   The Source of Healing 29
   The Great Healer 30
   A Combined Work 30
   The Holy Spirit Renews the Body 30
   The Best Medicine 31

What the Physician Attempts, Christ Accomplishes 31
Education Better Than Miraculous Healing 31
When Prayer for Healing Is Presumption 32
Provision for Gospel Medical Missionary Work 32
Miracles Not a Sure Evidence of God's Favor 33
When Christ Refused to Work Miracles 33
Reformation to Precede Miracle Working 34
Prayer for the Sick 35
For Further Study 36

Section 2—The Divine Plan in the Medical Missionary Work .. 37
The Majesty of Heaven as a Medical Missionary 37
Understood Through Practice 39
The Purpose of Christ's Humility 40
Disciples of Christ to Represent His Character 41
The Source of Success 43
Types of God's Saving Power 44
The Highest Aim 45
Memorials for God 45
To Reform Medical Practices 45
An Honor to God 45
To Lift Up Christ 46
Christ to Bring Relief and Healing 46
To Awaken Faith in the Great Healer 47
For Further Study 48

Section 3—The Christian Physician and His Work 49
Responsibility for Soul and Body 49
Faithfulness and Perseverance 50
Bringing the Lord's Work Into Disrepute 50
Give Heed to Character Building 51
The Physician's Influence 51
A Pattern of Good Judgment 52
Heavenly Assistants 52
Give God the Glory 52
God the Physician's Efficiency 53
The Peril of Popularity 53
The Physician's First Work 55
To Prepare Souls for Death 56
The Duty of Truthfulness 57

Leading Souls to the Mighty Healer	57
Evangelistic Duties	58
A Deeper Yearning for Souls	59
Take Time to Commune With God	59
To a Young Physician Under Discouragement	59
To a Physician in Perplexity	63
Counsel with Your Brethren	65
Shall Self Rule?	65
A Plea for Brotherly Union	66
A Student of Cause and Effect	67
The Physician as a Sabbath Observer	68
Rest for the Overweary	68
Hiding Self in Christ	70
For Further Study	71
Section 4—Our Medical College	**74**
In the Providence of God	74
A Place to Be Appreciated	75
A Practical Training	75
An Appeal in Behalf of Our Medical College	75
To Provide What Is Essential	76
The Wisest Talent Called For	77
The Classes of Workers to Be Trained	77
To Prepare for Many Lines of Work	78
Women to Be Especially Trained	79
No Compromise	80
Christ's Part and Ours	82
Genuine Missionaries as Pioneers	82
The Medical Student	82
Development of Experience	90
Caution Needed in Encouraging Students	93
A Call for the Best Talent	94
The High Order of the Loma Linda School	94
Who Should Apply	95
Students Should Have Moral Strength	96
Strength of Character Essential	96
Amenable to Authority	96
Mental and Physical Effort Proportionate	96
Educate in the Simplicity of Christ	98

Count the Cost	99
Study Practical Matters	101
Not Amusements, but Consecrated Work	101
Missionary Labor	102
Let Not Truth Be Supplanted	102
Advice to Those Having Limited Powers of Endurance	103
Our Relation to Legal Requirements	104
For Further Study	105
Section 5—Warning Against Spiritistic Sophistry	**107**
Building on the Rock	107
Spurious Scientific Theories	107
The True Higher Education	108
Truth Strengthens the Understanding	109
The Church is Christ's Fortress	110
Exalting Nature Above Nature's God	110
A Right Knowledge of God	111
God Revealed in His Word and His Works	114
Speculation Regarding God's Personality	116
Subtle Theories Regarding God	116
Restraint and Moral Control Destroyed	117
Not a Thread of Pantheism	117
The Issue Foreseen	118
Speculation Regarding the Future Life	119
Deception Regarding Spiritual Affinity	120
A Counterfeit Heaven	121
Neglecting Fundamental Truths for Idle Speculation	122
Honoring Superstition and Falsehood	122
For Further Study	123
Section 6—True and False Systems of Mind Cure	**125**
Happiness and Health	125
Thousands Needlessly Sick	125
Health Through Service for Others	125
Drudgery Versus Healthful Activity	126
Contentment and Cheerfulness	126
Enlisting the Willpower	127
The Holy Spirit as a Restorative	128
Sanctified Mind Cure	128
Indigestion Caused by Fear	129

Inspire the Despondent 130
Counterfeit Miracles 130
Taking Hold of the Eternal 131
Satan's Apparent Miracles 131
Efforts of Satan to Confuse Minds 131
A Dangerous System of Mind Cure 132
Directing the Mind to Christ 136
For Further Study 137

Section 7—Fees and Wages 139
Exorbitant Fees 139
Represent Upright Principles 145
The Percentage Plan a Snare 147
Care in Expenditure 148
The Policy Principle a Dishonor to God 148
Promises for Self-Sacrificing Workers 149
Prepare for Eternity 149
Advice to a Young Physician 150
As the Servants of Christ 153
Heart-Searching Questions 153
Two Classes of Servants 153
A Commendation for Soul Winners 154
Gain That Is Loss 155
For Further Study 155

Section 8—Counsels and Cautions 157
Our Attitude Toward the Lord's Institutions 157
Experience and Wisdom Needed 159
The Minister and His Wife 160
Maintaining a High Moral Standard 161
Like Streams From a Pure Fountain 164
An Appeal for More Sympathy 168
Establishment of New Sanitariums 171
In Wisdom and Equity 173
Counting the Cost 173
Sanitarium Work as a Speculation 174
Move Carefully 177
Honor Through Lowliness 178
Disadvantages of Large Institutions 179
Danger in Separation From the Gospel 179

No Compromise	181
For Further Study	182
Section 9—The Management of Sanitariums	**183**
A Noble Work	183
Essential Qualifications for Management	184
Willing to Take Counsel	186
Unnecessary Debts	186
Not With Outward Show	187
Simplicity in Furnishing	187
The Ministry of Trials	188
Men of Discernment Needed	189
Moderation in Rates	190
To an Inexperienced Manager	191
Consideration for an Injured Worker	191
Be Kind to the Lowly	192
Sanctified Dignity to Be Preserved	193
Experienced Workers Needed	194
Wholly Devoted to God	194
The Selection of Workers	195
Sanitariums and Education	195
Gentleness in Discipline	200
In the Place of a Father	202
For Further Study	206
Section 10—Opportunities for Ministry In Hospitals and Sanitariums	**207**
Restoration Through Reformation	207
Opening Fast-Closed Doors	208
With Tenderness and Wisdom	209
Learning to Work as He Worked	209
Give Heed to Soul-Winning Effort	210
Daily Efforts in Soul Winning	210
The Workers Needed	212
Promptness in Meeting Appointments	212
Promptness and Efficiency	213
The Privilege of Ministry	214
A Winning Influence	216
Consecrated Nurses	217
For Further Study	218

Section 11—The Sanitarium Family 219
Christians to Be Light Bearers 219
To Send Forth Light and Knowledge 219
Training for Various Lines of Work 219
Put On Christ 221
Regular Bible Instruction for Nurses 222
Laying Our Burdens at His Feet 222
In the Daily Round of Duties 223
Imitate God's Perfect Ways 224
A Sacred Responsibility 225
Chosen for the Work 226
Harmony Among Workers 227
Qualifications of the Matron 227
A Woman of Experience 227
To Exalt the Word of God 228
To Bring Comfort and Encouragement 228
Consideration for the Thoughtless 228
Dealing with the Unreasonable 229
The Dull Student 231
Attitude of the Instructor 231
This World Not Heaven 232
Cultivate an Atmosphere of Praise 232
Neatness and Order 232
Gossip 233
Rejoice in the Lord 233
The Observance of the Sabbath 234
The Physician Not Exempt 235
At the Peril of the Soul 236
Sabbath Work 236
The Tithe 237
An Opportune Place for Backsliding 237
Build Harmoniously 237
Changed Into the Divine Likeness 238
For Further Study 240

Section 12—The Prevention of Disease and Its Cure by Rational Methods 242
Prevention of Disease 242
Early Teaching of Physiology 242

Educate the Sick	243
The Law of Faith and Works	247
Combat Disease by Simple Methods	248
Hygienic Principles	248
Seeds of Death	250
Thousands Might Recover	250
What We Can Do for Ourselves	251
Instruction for Missionaries	252
Sunlight, Ventilation, and Temperature	252
Nature's Great Medicinal Resources	252
Healing Power in Outdoor Life	253
An Elixir of Life	254
Awaken Faith in the Great Healer	256
For Further Study	257
Section 13—Medical Missionary Work and the Gospel Ministry	258
A United Work	258
To Open Doors	259
An Effective Instrument	261
Encourage the Workers	261
The Worst Evil	262
A Means of Entrance to Hearts	262
Earnest Appeal to Physicians	262
Many Saved From Degradation	263
The Poor Not to Be Neglected	264
Labor for the Wealthy	264
The Value of Medical Work	266
What the Missionary Nurse Can Do	267
Efficiency and Power	268
An Example of Healing and Soul-Winning Work	268
A Blended Ministry	269
Physicians as City Evangelists	269
A Twofold Service	270
Sent Forth Two and Two	270
Cooperation	271
Not by Proxy	272
The Distinguishing Sign	272
True Charity	272

The Atmosphere of Love	273
Sowing and Reaping	273
As He Is Perfect	274
Zeal and Perseverance in Medical Missionary Work	277
In Excellent Company	278
A Revival Will Come	278
For Further Study	278
Section 14—Teaching Health Principles	**281**
The Gospel of Health	281
The First Work	281
Educate in the Laws of Life	281
The Science of Self-Denial	282
Counsel to a Sanitarium Physician	282
How to Present the Principles of Healthful Diet	283
Labor Lost Without Instruction	284
Educate, Educate, Educate	284
Deeds of Ministry	285
Teach Self-Denial	285
Hygienic Restaurants as Schools	287
Instruction in Homes and in Schools	288
Cooperation With Other Temperance Workers	288
Educate the Poor	288
Purpose of Health-Food Work	289
Like the Manna	289
The Lord Will Teach the Obedient	290
Instruction in the Art of Cooking	290
United Action Necessary	290
Incentives to Activity	291
Tolerance for Others' Opinions	291
Teaching Extreme Views	292
Good Cooking a Science	292
Many Will Be Rescued	294
For Further Study	294
Section 15—Diet and Health	**295**
Important Principles	295
Sanctification and Self-Mastery	297
Show the Value of Health Reform	297
To the Glory of God	297

Appeal to a Physician	299
Appeal to a Minister	301
An Appeal to Parents	302
Making Dyspeptics	303
Eating Too Frequently	303
The Two-Meal Plan	304
Perseverance in Overcoming	304
Pray for Moral Courage	305
Suggestions for Sanitarium Diet	306
No Flesh-Meat on Sanitarium Tables	307
Lectures to be Given	308
To a Physician Dying from Overwork and a Meager Diet	309
Light Given in Love and Pity	311
For Further Study	312
Section 16—The Worker's Health	314
We Belong to God	314
Faithful Guardians of Their Powers	315
Breaking Under the Strain	316
The Physician to Conserve Strength	316
Spiritual Loss Through Overfatigue	317
The Minister's Duty to Safeguard Health	317
Strengthening the Mental and Moral Powers	319
In Warm Climates	319
Gardening and Health	319
For Further Study	320
Section 17—Medical Missionary Work in the Great Cities	322
Christ's Labors in Cities and Towns	322
Medical Evangelism for the Cities	323
The Training of Workers	324
Difficulties Will Increase	324
No Time to Colonize	325
A Mission in Every City	326
A Mighty Movement	327
Cooperation	327
Move Forward	327
A Parable of What Should Be	328
Sanitariums and Hygienic Restaurants	329
Danger of Missing the Mark	329

A Sanitarium Near New York	331
Redeeming the Time	333
Seek Rural Homes	333
Rural Location for Institutions	334
Work for the Outcasts	334
Safeguard the Youth	336
Difficulties Overcome	336
For Further Study	336
Section 18—Extent of the Work	**338**
Co-workers With Christ	338
Truth to Be Presented in Many Ways	341
How to Reveal Christ	342
A New Element	342
Opportunities for All	343
Will Revive the Churches	343
Be Practical Missionaries	343
Work for Children and Youth	344
In Time of Persecution	344
The Appeal of Unpromising Fields	344
Self-Supporting Effort	345
Medical Missions in Every City	345
Advantages of Small Schools	345
Many Training Schools	346
Sanitariums Connected With Schools	346
Many Small Sanitariums	346
Opportunities to Purchase Sanitarium Properties	347
Not as a Business Speculation	349
Move With Understanding	351
Fulfilling God's Plans	352
Securing Help From the Wealthy	352
Our Needs to Be Presented	352
Plants in Foreign Fields	353
Health Institutions in Many Lands	354
Go Forward	354
For Further Study	358

Section 1—Healing Power and Its Source [6]

Nature the Servant of God

The material world is under God's control. The laws that govern all nature are obeyed by nature. Everything speaks and acts the will of the Creator. The clouds, the rain, the dew, the sunshine, the showers, the wind, the storm, all are under the supervision of God, and yield implicit obedience to Him who employs them. The tiny spear of grass bursts its way through the earth, first the blade, then the ear, and then the full corn in the ear. The Lord uses these, His obedient servants, to do His will.—Letter 131, 1897.

Christ the Life and Light

Christ, who created the world and all things that are therein, is the life and light of every living thing.—Testimonies for the Church 6:182.

In Jesus is our life derived. In Him is life, that is original, unborrowed, underived life. In us there is a streamlet from the fountain of life. In Him is the fountain of life. Our life is something that we receive, something that the Giver takes back again to Himself. If our life is hid with Christ in God, we shall, when Christ shall appear, also appear with Him in glory. And while in this world we will give to God, in sanctified service, all the capabilities He has given us.—Letter 309, 1905.

Life by the Power of God

The parable of the seed reveals that God is at work in nature. The seed has in itself a germinating principle, a principle that God himself has implanted; yet if left to itself the seed would have no power to spring up. Man has his part to act in promoting the growth of the grain....

There is life in the seed, there is power in the soil; but unless an infinite power is exercised day and night, the seed will yield no returns. The showers of rain must be sent to give moisture to the thirsty fields, the sun must impart heat, electricity must be conveyed to the buried seed. The life which the Creator has implanted, He alone can call forth. Every seed grows, every plant develops, by the power of God.—Christ's Object Lessons, 63.

Life of God in Nature

The Lord has given His life to the trees and vines of His creation. His word can increase or decrease the fruit of the land.

If men would open their understanding to discern the relation between nature and nature's God, faithful acknowledgments of the Creator's power would be heard. Without the life of God, nature would die. His creative works are dependent on Him. He bestows life-giving properties on all that nature produces. We are to regard the trees laden with fruit as the gift of God, just as much as though He placed the fruit in our hands.—Manuscript 114, 1899.

God Feeding Earth's Millions

In feeding the five thousand, Jesus lifts the veil from the world of nature, and reveals the power that is constantly exercised for our good. In the production of earth's harvests, God is working a miracle every day. Through natural agencies the same work is accomplished that was wrought in the feeding of the multitude. Men prepare the soil and sow the seed, but it is the life from God that causes the seed to germinate. It is God's rain and air and sunshine that cause it to put forth "first the blade, then the ear, after that the full corn in the ear." It is God who is every day feeding millions from earth's harvest fields.—D.A. 367.

Kept in Activity

The beating heart, the throbbing pulse, every nerve and muscle in the living organism, are kept in order and activity by the power of an infinite God. "Consider the lilies how they grow: they toil not, they spin not; and yet I say unto you, that Solomon in all his glory was not arrayed like one of these. If then God so clothe the grass, which is today in the field, and tomorrow is cast into the oven; how much more will He clothe you, O ye of little faith? And seek not ye what ye shall eat, or what ye shall drink, neither be ye of doubtful mind. For all these things do the nations of the world seek after: and your Father knoweth that ye have need of these things. But rather seek ye the kingdom of God; and all these things shall be added unto you."

[9]

Here Christ leads the mind abroad to contemplate the open fields of nature, and His power touches the eye and the senses, to discern the wonderful works of divine power. He directs attention first to nature, then up through nature to nature's God, who upholds the worlds by His power.—Manuscript 73, 1893.

Through Natural Laws

It is not to be supposed that a law is set in motion for the seed to work itself, that the leaf appears because it must do so of itself. God has laws that He has instituted, but they are only the servants through which He effects results. It is through the immediate agency of God that every tiny seed breaks through the earth and springs into life. Every leaf grows, every flower blooms, by the power of God.

The physical organism of man is under the supervision of God, but it is not like a clock, which is set in operation, and must go of itself. The heart beats, pulse succeeds pulse, breath succeeds breath, but the entire being is under the supervision of God. "Ye are God's husbandry; ye are God's building." In God we live, and move, and have our being. Each heartbeat, each breath, is the inspiration of Him who breathed into the nostrils of Adam the breath of life—the inspiration of the ever-present God, the great I AM.—The Review and Herald, November 8, 1898.

God in Nature

Upon all created things is seen the impress of the Deity. Nature testifies of God. The susceptible mind, brought in contact with the miracle and mystery of the universe, cannot but recognize the working of infinite power. Not by its own inherent energy does the earth produce its bounties, and year by year continue its motion around the sun. An unseen hand guides the planets in their circuit of the heavens. A mysterious life pervades all nature—a life that sustains the unnumbered worlds throughout immensity, that lives in the insect atom which floats in the summer breeze, that wings the flight of the swallow and feeds the young ravens which cry, that brings the bud to blossom and the flower to fruit.

[10]
Laws of Physical Life

The same power that upholds nature is working also in man. The same great laws that guide alike the star and the atom control human life. The laws that govern the heart's action, regulating the flow of the current of life to the body, are the laws of the mighty Intelligence that has the jurisdiction of the soul. From Him all life proceeds. Only in harmony with Him can be found its true sphere of action. For all the objects of His creation the condition is the same—a life sustained by receiving the life of God, a life exercised in harmony with the Creator's will. To transgress His law, physical, mental, or moral, is to place oneself out of harmony with the universe, to introduce discord, anarchy, ruin.

To him who learns thus to interpret its teachings, all nature becomes illuminated; the world is a lesson book, life a school. The unity of man with nature and with God, the universal dominion of law, the results of transgression, cannot fail of impressing the mind and molding the character....

The heart not yet hardened by contact with evil is quick to recognize the Presence that pervades all created things. The ear as yet undulled by the world's clamor is attentive to the Voice that speaks through nature's utterances....

The unseen is illustrated by the seen. On everything upon the earth ... they may behold the image and superscription of God.—Education, 99, 100.

Nature's Message

All nature is alive. Through its varied forms of life it speaks to those who have ears to hear and hearts to understand of Him who is the source of all life. Nature reveals the wonderful working of the Master Artist.—Letter 164, 1900.

The Message of Love

In the beginning, God was revealed in all the works of creation.... And upon all things in earth, and air, and sky, He wrote the message of the Father's love.

Now sin has marred God's perfect work, yet that handwriting remains. Even now all created things declare the glory of His excellence.... Every tree and shrub and leaf pours forth that element of life without which neither man nor animal could live; and man and animal, in turn, minister to the life of tree and shrub and leaf.—D.A. 20, 21.

Nature Is Not God

God's handiwork in nature is not God Himself in nature. The things of nature are an expression of God's character; by them we may understand His love, His power, and His glory; but we are not to regard nature as God. The artistic skill of human beings produces very beautiful workmanship, things that delight the eye, and these things give us something of the idea of the designer; but the thing made is not the man. It is not the work, but the workman, that is counted worthy of honor. So, while nature is an expression of God's thought, it is not nature but the God of nature that is to be exalted.—Testimonies for the Church 8:263.

The Source of Healing

Sickness, suffering, and death are work of an antagonistic power. Satan is the destroyer; God is the Restorer.

The words spoken to Israel are true today of those who recover health of body or health of soul: "I am the Lord that healeth thee."

The desire of God for every human being is expressed in the words, "Beloved, I wish above all things that thou mayest prosper and be in health, even as thy soul prospereth."

He it is who "forgiveth all thine iniquities; who healeth all thy diseases; who redeemeth thy life from destruction; who crowneth thee with loving-kindness and tender mercies."—Counsels on Health, 168.

The Great Healer

God's healing power runs all through nature. If a human being cuts his flesh or breaks a bone, nature at once begins to heal the injury, and thus preserve the man's life. But man can place himself in a position where nature is trammeled so that she cannot do her work.... If tobacco is used, ... the healing power of nature is weakened to a greater or less extent.... When intoxicating liquor is used, the system is not able to resist disease in its original God-given power as a healer. It is God who has made the provision that nature shall work to restore the exhausted powers. The power is of God. He is the Great Healer.—Letter 77, 1899.

A Combined Work

The sick are to be healed through the combined efforts of the human and the divine. Every gift, every power, that Christ promised to His disciples, He bestows upon those who will serve Him faithfully.—Letter 205, 1899.

The Holy Spirit Renews the Body

Sin brings physical and spiritual disease and weakness. Christ has made it possible for us to free ourselves from this curse. The Lord promises, by the medium of truth, to renovate the soul. The Holy Spirit will make all who are willing to be educated able to communicate the truth with power. It will renew every organ of the body, that God's servants may work acceptably and successfully. Vitality increases under the influence of the Spirit's action. Let us, then, by this power lift ourselves into a higher, holier atmosphere, that we may do well our appointed work.—The Review and Herald, January 14, 1902.

The Best Medicine

The religion of the Bible is not detrimental to the health of the body or of the mind. The influence of the Spirit of God is the very best medicine that can be received by a sick man or woman. Heaven is all health; and the more deeply the heavenly influences are realized, the more sure will be the recovery of the believing invalid.—Testimonies for the Church 3:172.

What the Physician Attempts, Christ Accomplishes

None but a Christian physician can discharge to God's acceptance the duties of his profession. In a work so sacred, no place should be given to selfish plans and interests. Every ambition, every motive, should be subordinate to the interest of that life which measures with the life of God. In all your business, let the claim of Jesus, the world's Redeemer, be recognized; let His example be copied. What the physician attempts to do, Christ can accomplish. They strive to prolong life; He is the Life-giver. Jesus, the Mighty Healer, is Physician in chief. All physicians are under one Master, and blessed indeed is every physician who has learned from his Lord to watch for souls while with all his professional skill he works to heal the bodies of the suffering sick.—Letter 26a, 1889.

Education Better Than Miraculous Healing

Some have asked me, "Why should we have sanitariums? Why should we not, like Christ, pray for the sick, that they may be healed miraculously?" I have answered, "Suppose we were able to do this in all cases; how many would appreciate the healing? Would those who were healed become health reformers, or continue to be health destroyers?"

Jesus Christ is the Great Healer, but He desires that by living in conformity with His laws we may cooperate with Him in the recovery and the maintenance of health. Combined with the work of healing there must be an imparting of knowledge of how to resist temptations. Those who come to our sanitariums should be aroused to a sense of their own responsibility to work in harmony with the God of truth.

We cannot heal. We cannot change the diseased conditions of the body. But it is our part, as medical missionaries, as workers together with God, to use the means that He has provided. Then we should pray that God will bless these agencies. We do believe in a God; we believe in a God who hears and answers prayer. He has said, "Ask, and ye shall receive; seek, and ye shall find; knock, and it shall be opened unto you."—The Review and Herald, December 5, 1907.

When Prayer for Healing Is Presumption

Many have expected that God would keep them from sickness merely because they have asked Him to do so. But God did not regard their prayers, because their faith was not made perfect by works. God will not work a miracle to keep those from sickness who have no care for themselves, but are continually violating the laws of health and make no efforts to prevent disease. When we do all we can on our part to have health, then may we expect that the blessed results will follow, and we can ask God in faith to bless our efforts for the preservation of health. He will then answer our prayer, if His name can be glorified thereby. But let all understand that they have a work to do. God will not work in a miraculous manner to preserve the health of persons who are taking a sure course to make themselves sick, by their careless inattention to the laws of health.

Those who will gratify their appetite, and then suffer because of their intemperance, and take drugs to relieve them, may be assured that God will not interpose to save health and life which are so recklessly periled. The cause has produced the effect. Many, as their last resort, follow the directions in the word of God, and request the prayers of the elders of the church for their restoration to health. God does not see fit to answer prayers offered in behalf of such, for He knows that if they should be restored to health, they would again sacrifice it upon the altar of unhealthy appetite.—4SG 144, 145.

Provision for Gospel Medical Missionary Work

The way in which Christ worked was to preach the word, and to relieve suffering by miraculous works of healing. But I am instructed that we cannot now work in this way; for Satan will exercise his power by working miracles. God's servants today could not work by means of miracles, because spurious works of healing, claiming to be divine, will be wrought.

For this reason the Lord has marked out a way in which His people are to carry forward a work of physical healing combined with the teaching of the word. Sanitariums are to be established, and with these institutions are to be connected workers who will carry forward genuine medical missionary work. Thus a guarding influence is thrown around those who come to the sanitariums for treatment.

This is the provision the Lord has made whereby gospel medical missionary work is to be done for many souls. These institutions are to be established out of the cities, and in them educational work is to be intelligently carried forward.—Letter 53, 1904.

Miracles Not a Sure Evidence of God's Favor

The time is at hand when Satan will work miracles to confirm minds in the belief that he is God. All the people of God are now to stand on the platform of truth as it has been given in the third angel's message. All the pleasant pictures, all the miracles wrought, will be presented in order that, if possible, the very elect shall be deceived. The only hope for anyone is to hold fast the evidences that have confirmed the truth in righteousness. Let these be proclaimed over and over again, until the close of this earth's history.—The Review and Herald, August 9, 1906.

When Christ Refused to Work Miracles

The scene of Christ's temptation was to be a lesson for all His followers. When the enemies of Christ, by the instigation of Satan, request them to show some miracle, they should answer them as meekly as the Son of God answered Satan, "It is written, Thou shalt not tempt the Lord thy God." If they will not be convinced by inspired testimony, a manifestation of God's power would not benefit them. God's wondrous works are not manifested to gratify the curiosity of any. Christ, the Son of God, refused to give Satan any proof of His power. He made no effort to remove Satan's "if" by showing a miracle.

The disciples of Christ will be brought into similar positions. Unbelievers will require them to do some miracle, if they believe God's special power is in the church and that they are the chosen people of God. Unbelievers who are afflicted with infirmities will require them to work a miracle upon them, if God is with them. Christ's followers should imitate the example of their Lord. Jesus, with His divine power, did not do any mighty works for Satan's diversion. Neither can the servants of Christ. They should refer the unbelieving to the written, inspired testimony for evidence of their being the loyal people of God and heirs of salvation.—4SG 150, 151.

Reformation to Precede Miracle Working

I am so thankful for the medical missionary work, carried in gospel lines. It is to be taught, it is to be carried forward; for it is the very work that Christ did when on this earth. He was the greatest Missionary the world ever saw.

You may say, "Why not, then, take hold of the work, and heal the sick as Christ did?" I answer, You are not ready. Some have believed; some have been healed; but there are many who make themselves sick by intemperate eating or by indulging in other wrong habits. When they get sick, shall we pray for them to be raised up, that they may carry on the very same work again? There must be a reformation throughout our ranks; the people must reach a higher standard before we can expect the power of God to be manifested in a marked manner for the healing of the sick....

If we will take hold of the Master, take hold of all the power He has given us, the salvation of God will be revealed. Let me tell you that the sick will be healed when you have faith to come to God in the right way. We thank God that we have the medical missionary work. Wherever we carry the gospel, we can teach the people how to take care of themselves.—G.C.B., April 3, 1901.

Prayer for the Sick

As to praying for the sick, it is too important a matter to be handled carelessly. I believe we should take everything to the Lord, and make known to God all our weaknesses and specify all our perplexities. When in sorrow, when uncertain as to what course to pursue, two or three who are accustomed to pray should unite together in asking the Lord to let His light shine upon them and to impart His special grace; and He will respect their petitions, He will answer their prayers. If we are under infirmities of body, it is certainly consistent to trust in the Lord, making supplications to our God in our own case, and if we feel inclined to ask others in whom we have confidence to unite with us in prayer to Jesus who is the Mighty Healer, help will surely come if we ask in faith. I think we are altogether too faithless, too cold and lukewarm.

I understand the text in James is to be carried out when a person is sick upon his bed, if he calls for the elders of the church, and they carry out the directions in James, anointing the sick with oil in the name of the Lord, praying over him the prayer of faith. We read, "The prayer of faith shall save the sick, and the Lord shall raise him up; and if he have committed sins, they shall be forgiven him."

It cannot be our duty to call for the elders of the church for every little ailment we have, for this would be putting a task upon the elders. If all should do this, their time would be fully employed, they could do nothing else; but the Lord gives us the privilege of seeking Him individually in earnest prayer, or unburdening our souls to Him, keeping nothing from Him who has invited us, "Come unto Me, all ye that labor and are heavy-laden, and I will give you rest." Oh, how grateful we should be that Jesus is willing and able to bear all our infirmities and strengthen and heal all our diseases if it will be for our good and for His glory.

Some died in the days of Christ and in the days of the apostles because the Lord knew just what was best for them.—Letter 35, 1890.

[17]

For Further Study

God, not Man, the Source of Healing:
Counsels on Health, 346 (The Ministry of Healing, 243).

The Church Empowered to Heal:
Counsels on Health, 30, 529.

Christ's Servants, Channels of Life-Giving Energy:
Counsels on Health, 30, 31 (The Desire of Ages, 823, 824).

The Love of Christ a Vitalizing Power:
Counsels on Health, 29 (The Ministry of Healing, 115).

When Education Is Better Than Miraculous Healing:
Counsels on Health, 469.

Prayer for the Sick:
Counsels on Health, 373-382;
The Ministry of Healing, 225-2;
Testimonies for the Church 2:145-150;
Testimonies for the Church 4:565-570.

Health of Willfully Ignorant Not Miraculously Preserved:
Counsels on Health, 504.

Incident: A Degenerate Seeks Healing:
Counsels on Health, 618-621.

Obedience to Follow Healing:
Counsels on Health, 138, 139 (Testimonies for the Church 9:164, 165).

Right Living and Prayer:
Counsels on Health, 247 (Testimonies For The Church 1:561).

Miracles of Healing to Be Counterfeited by Satan:
Counsels on Health, 460, 461 (The Great Controversy, 589, 590);
Testimonies For The Church 1:302.

Warning Against Spiritualist Physicians:
Counsels on Health, 454-460.

Section 2—The Divine Plan in the Medical Missionary Work

The Majesty of Heaven as a Medical Missionary

This world has been visited by the Majesty of heaven, the Son of God. "God so loved the world, that He gave His only-begotten Son, that whosoever believeth in Him should not perish, but have everlasting life." Christ came to this world as the expression of the very heart and mind and nature and character of God. He was the brightness of the Father's glory, the express image of His person. But He laid aside His royal robe and kingly crown, and stepped down from His high command to take the place of a servant. He was rich, but for our sake, that we might have eternal riches, He became poor. He made the world, but so completely did He empty Himself that during His ministry He declared, "Foxes have holes, and the birds of the air have nests; but the Son of man hath not where to lay His head."

He came to this world and stood among the beings He had created as a Man of Sorrows and acquainted with grief. "He was wounded for our transgressions, He was bruised for our iniquities: the chastisement of our peace was upon Him; and with His stripes we are healed." He was tempted in all points like as we are, yet without sin.

A Servant of All

Christ stood at the head of humanity in the garb of humanity. So full of sympathy and love was His attitude that the poorest was not afraid to come to Him. He was kind to all, easily approached by the most lowly. He went from house to house, healing the sick, feeding the hungry, comforting the mourners, soothing the afflicted, speaking peace to the distressed. He took the little children in His arms and blessed them, and spoke words of hope and comfort to the weary mothers. With unfailing tenderness and gentleness He met every form of human woe and affliction. Not for Himself, but for others, did He labor. He was willing to humble Himself, to deny Himself. He did not seek to distinguish Himself. He was the servant of all. It was His meat and drink to be a comfort and a consolation to others, to gladden the sad and heavy-laden ones with whom He daily came in contact.

An Expression of God's Love

Christ stands before us as the pattern Man, the great Medical Missionary—an example for all who should come after. His love, pure and holy, blessed all who came within the sphere of its influence. His character was absolutely perfect, free from the slightest stain of sin. He came as an expression of the perfect love of God, not to crush, not to judge and condemn, but to heal every weak, defective character, to save men and woman from Satan's power.

He is the Creator, Redeemer, and Sustainer of the human race. He gives to all the invitation, "Come unto Me, all ye that labor and are heavy-laden, and I will give you rest. Take My yoke upon you, and learn of Me; for I am meek and lowly in heart: and ye shall find rest unto your souls. For My yoke is easy, and My burden is light."

Following in His Footsteps

What, then, is the example that we are to set to the world? We are to do the same work that the great Medical Missionary undertook in our behalf. We are to follow the path of self-sacrifice trodden by Christ.

As I see so many claiming to be medical missionaries, the representation of what Christ was on this earth flashes before me. As I think of how far short the workers today fall when compared with the divine Example, my heart is bowed down with a sorrow that words cannot express. Will men and women ever do a work that bears the features and character of the great Medical Missionary? ...

Is there not woe enough in this sin-stricken, sin-cursed earth to lead us to consecrate ourselves to the work of proclaiming the message that "God so loved the world, that He gave His only-begotten Son, that whosoever believeth in Him should not perish, but have everlasting life"? This earth has been trodden by the Son of God. He came to bring men light and life, to set them free from the bondage of sin. He is coming again in power and great glory, to receive to Himself those who during this life have followed in His footsteps.

His Name to be Honored

Oh, how I long to see those who claim to be medical missionaries honoring the Great Exemplar, whose life declares what is comprehended in the claim to be a medical missionary! I would that they were learning the Saviour's meekness and lowliness. My heart aches to think that Christ is so greatly disappointed in His followers. They bear a name that their daily life does not give them the right to bear.

We must be sanctified, soul and body, through the truth; then we shall honor the name, medical missionary. Oh, this name means so much! It calls for a representation altogether different from the representation given by many who bear it. Soon these will understand how far they have departed from the principles of heaven, and how greatly they have grieved the heart of Christ.—Letter 117, 1903.

Understood Through Practice

When all our medical missionaries shall live the renewed life in Christ Jesus, and shall take His words as meaning all that they are designed to mean, there will be a much clearer and more comprehensive understanding of what constitutes genuine medical missionary work. And yet this line of work can best be understood by practicing it in simplicity. The unfolding of this work will have a deeper meaning to them after they obey the holy law engraven on tables of stone by the finger of God, including the Sabbath commandment, concerning which Christ Himself spoke through Moses to the children of Israel....

Follow the Master

God's servants who are doing genuine medical missionary work have a most solemn, sacred responsibility resting upon them to keep in view Christ's life of unselfish service. They should turn their eyes from everything else, and look unto Jesus, the Author and the

Finisher of their faith. He is the Source of all light, the Fountain of all heaven's blessings. To every medical missionary worker I am instructed to say, Follow your Leader. His is the way, the truth, the light, the life. He is the One whose example we as true medical missionaries must follow.

In this age of diseased piety and perverted principle, those who are converted in life and practice will reveal a healthy and influential spirituality. Those who have a knowledge of the truth as it is revealed in God's word must now come to the front. My brethren, God requires this of you. Every jot of your influence is now to be used on the right side. All are now to learn how to stand in defense of truth that is worthy of acceptance. Those who are endeavoring to live the Christ life must call things by the right name, and stand in defense of the truth as it is in Jesus.

Time to Advance

It behooves every soul whose life is hid with Christ in God to come to the front now. Something is to be done. We are to contend most earnestly for the faith once delivered to the saints. The spirit in which truth is defended and the kingdom of God advanced must be as it would be if Christ were on this earth in person. If He were here, He would be drawn out to render a solemn rebuke to many who claim to be medical missionaries, but who have not chosen to heed the injunction He has urged upon them, to learn of Him His meekness and lowliness of heart. In the lives of some of those who occupy the highest positions, self has been exalted. Until such ones rid themselves of every desire to uplift self, they cannot clearly discern the character and glory of the great Medical Missionary....

We are now to unify, and by true medical missionary work prepare the way for our coming King. Let us increase in a knowledge of the truth, and render all excellence and glory due to Him who is one with the Father. Let us seek most earnestly for the heavenly anointing, the Holy Spirit.—Manuscript 83, 1903.

The Purpose of Christ's Humility

There is too much of self and too little of Jesus in the ministry of all denominations. The Lord uses humble men to proclaim His messages. Had Christ come in the majesty of a king, with the pomp which attends the great men of earth, many would have accepted Him. But Jesus of Nazareth did not dazzle the senses with a display of outward glory, and make this the foundation of their reverence. He came as a humble Man, to be the Teacher and Exemplar as well as the Redeemer of the race. Had He encouraged pomp, had He come followed by a retinue of the great men of earth, how could He have taught humility? how could He have presented such burning truths as in His sermon upon the mount? His example was such as He wished all His followers to imitate. Where would have been the hope of the lowly in life, had He come in exaltation and dwelt as a king upon the earth? Jesus knew the needs of the world better than they themselves knew. He did not come as an angel, clothed with the panoply of heaven, but as a Man. Yet combined with His humility was an inherent power and grandeur that awed men while they loved Him. Although possessing such loveliness, such an unassuming appearance, He moved among them with the dignity and power of a heaven-born King.—Testimonies for the Church 5:253.

Disciples of Christ to Represent His Character

The Saviour lived on this earth a life that love for God will constrain every true believer in Christ to live. Following His example, in our medical missionary work we shall reveal to the world that our credentials are from above, that as representatives of the kingdom of heaven we are fulfilling the words of the Lord's Prayer, "Thy kingdom come." United with Christ in God, we shall reveal to the world that as God chose His Son to be His representative on the earth, even so has Christ chosen us to represent His character. Everyone who has genuine faith in Christ Jesus will represent Him in character....

To Heights of Faith

Our medical missionary workers must rise to heights that can be reached only by a living, working faith. At this time in our history the men at the head of the work are to allow no confusion of sentiment to prevail in regard to what should really be expected of medical missionaries sent of God. There should be a more clear, definite understanding of what medical missionary work comprehends. It must be defined as standing on an altogether higher plane, and as accomplishing results of a much more sanctified order, before God can endorse it as genuine. Those who desire to honor God will not mingle worldly policy plans with His plans in attempting to accomplish the results that this work is ordained of God to accomplish....

Our work is clearly defined. As the Father sent His only-begotten Son into our world, even so Christ sends us, His disciples, as His medical missionary workers. In fulfilling this high and holy mission, we are to do the will of God. No one man's mind or judgment is to be our criterion of what constitutes genuine medical missionary work....

True medical missionary work is of heavenly origin. It was not originated by any person who lives. But in connection with this work we see so much which dishonors God that I am instructed to say, The medical missionary work is of divine origin, and has a most glorious mission to fulfill. In all its bearings it is to be in conformity with Christ's work. Those who are workers together with God will just as surely represent the character of Christ as Christ represented the character of His Father while in this world.

Cleansed from Earthliness

I am instructed to say that God will have the medical missionary work cleansed from the tarnish of earthliness, and elevated to stand in its true position before the world. When schemes that imperil souls are brought into connection with this work, its influence is destroyed. This is why there have arisen in the carrying forward of medical missionary work many perplexities that demand our careful consideration....

Nothing will help us more at this stage of our work than to understand and to fulfill the mission of the greatest Medical Missionary that ever trod the earth; nothing will help us more than to realize how sacred is this kind of work and how perfectly it corresponds with the lifework of the Great Missionary. The object of our mission is the same as the object of Christ's mission. Why did God send His Son to the fallen world? To make known and to demonstrate to mankind

His love for them. Christ came as a Redeemer. Throughout His ministry He was to keep prominent His mission to save sinners....

God's purpose in committing to men and women the mission that He committed to Christ is to disentangle His followers from all worldly policy and to give them a work identical with the work that Christ did.—Manuscript 130, 1902.

The Source of Success

The Lord has instructed us that all our sanitariums are to be conducted, not as if the success of the work done were due to the skill of the physicians, but because of the divine power connected with the physician. The Great Healer is to be magnified. It is to be represented that the favor of God is on the institution because the principles of health reform are respected and because Christ is acknowledged as the Chief Physician. Our sanitariums have been in the past, and will continue to be, if rightly conducted, a means of blessing and uplifting to humanity. If the truth is rightly represented, those who patronize our sanitariums will learn much regarding its principles, and many will be converted. These institutions have been represented to me as beacon lights showing forth the truth as it is in Jesus. The Lord Jesus is the great minister of healing, and His presence in our institutions has been a savor of life unto life. Christ came to the world as the Great Physician of mankind. Our sanitariums, wherever they are established, should be made educational forces. The Lord would be pleased to have you with chosen helpers build up your work to do a more special work in religious lines.

Wonderful has been the working out of God's plan in the establishment of so many health institutions. Intemperance of every kind is taking the world captive, and those who are true educators at this time, those who instruct along the lines of self-denial and self-sacrifice, will have their reward. Now is our time, now is our opportunity, to do a blessed work.—Letter 50, 1909.

Types of God's Saving Power

In our medical institutions the people are to be brought in contact with the special truths for this time. God says there shall be institutions established under the supervision of men who have been healed through a belief in God's word, and who have overcome their defects of character. In the world all kinds of provision have been made for the relief of suffering humanity, but the truth in its simplicity is to be brought to these suffering ones through the agency of men and women who are loyal to the commandments of God. Sanitariums are to be established all through our world, and managed by a people who are in harmony with God's laws, a people who will cooperate with God in advocating the truth that determines the case of every soul for whom Christ died....

All the light of the past, which shines unto the present and reaches forth into the future, as revealed in the word of God, is for every soul who comes to our health institutions. The Lord designs that the sanitariums established among Seventh-day Adventists shall be symbols of what can be done for the world, types of the saving power of the truths of the gospel. They are to be agencies in the fulfillment of God's great purposes for the human race.

To God's people and His institutions in this generation as well as to ancient Israel belong the words written by Moses through the Spirit of Inspiration:

"Thou art an holy people unto the Lord thy God: the Lord thy God hath chosen thee to be a special people unto Himself, above all people that are upon the face of the earth."

"Behold, I have taught you statutes and judgments, even as the Lord my God commanded me.... Keep therefore and do them; for this is your wisdom and your understanding in the sight of the nations, which shall hear all these statutes, and say, Surely this great nation is a wise and understanding people. For what nation is there so great, who hath God so nigh unto them, as the Lord our God is in all things that we call upon Him for? And what nation is there so great, that hath statutes and judgments so righteous as all this law, which I set before you this day?"

Even these words fail of reaching the greatness and the glory of God's purpose to be accomplished through His people.—Manuscript 166, 1899.

The Highest Aim

Sanitariums are needed, in which successful medical and surgical work can be done. Those institutions, conducted in accordance with the will of God, would remove prejudice and call our work into favorable notice. The highest aim of the workers in these institutions is to be the spiritual health to the patients. Successful evangelistic work can be done in connection with medical missionary work. It is as these lines of work are united that we may expect to gather the most precious fruit for the Lord.—Letter 202, 1903.

Memorials for God

Our sanitariums in all their departments should be memorials for God, His instrumentalities for sowing the seeds of truth in human hearts. This they will be if rightly conducted.—Testimonies for the Church 6:225.

To Reform Medical Practices

As to drugs' being used in our institutions, it is contrary to the light which the Lord has been pleased to give. The drugging business has done more harm to our world and killed more than it has helped or cured. The light was first given to me why institutions should be established, that is, sanitariums were to reform the medical practices of physicians.—Letter 69, 1898.

An Honor to God

The God of heaven is honored by an institution managed in this way. The ---- Sanitarium was established in the order of God, that men and women might better understand the virtues of the tree of life. In His mercy God has made the sanitarium such a power in the relief of physical suffering that thousands are drawn to it to be cured of their maladies, and very often they are not only cured physically, but from the Saviour they receive the forgiveness of their sins, and they identify themselves completely with Christ, with His interests, His honor. Their sins are taken away and are placed at Christ's account. His righteousness is imputed to them. The healing balm is applied to the soul. They receive the grace of Christ and go forth to impart to others the light of truth. The Lord makes them His witnesses. Their testimony is, He was made "to be sin for us, who knew no sin; that we might be made the righteousness of God in Him." They never forget the prayers, the songs of praise and thanksgiving, that they heard while at the sanitarium. Can we realize how much God is glorified by this work?—Letter 38, 1899.

To Lift Up Christ

The purpose of our health institutions is not first and foremost to be that of hospitals. The health institutions connected with the closing work of the gospel in the earth stand for the great principles of the gospel in all its fullness. Christ is the one to be revealed in all the institutions connected with the closing work, but none of them can do it so fully as the health institution where the sick and suffering come for relief and deliverance from both physical and spiritual ailment. Many of these need, like the paralytic of old, the forgiveness of sin the first thing, and they need to learn how to "go, and sin no more."

If a sanitarium connected with this closing message fails to lift up Christ and the principles of the gospel as developed in the third angel's message, it fails in its most important feature, and contradicts the very object of its existence.—The Review and Herald, October 29, 1914.

Christ to Bring Relief and Healing

I have been instructed that we should lead the sick in our institutions to expect large things because of the faith of the physician in the Great Healer who, in the years of His earthly ministry, went through the towns and villages of the land, and healed all who came to Him. None were turned empty away; He healed them all. Let the sick realize that, although unseen, Christ is present to bring relief and healing.—Letter 82, 1908.

To Awaken Faith in the Great Healer

As Christ's followers, we are to work with all rational methods to preach the gospel of present truth. Not only by words but by deeds we are to give evidence that Christ is willing to unite with His devoted ministers today in healing the sick and suffering. The Lord would revive in the minds of His workers a living faith in His power. When we increase in the faith of the gospel of Christ, and encourage that faith as it is presented in the word of God, there will be in our sanitariums not only a practical knowledge of how to treat the sick upon right principles but the manifestation of a living faith in God that will lead the workers to call upon the Great Physician for divine assistance. And the Lord will come to the help of such in response to their faith in His power.

Because we have sanitariums for the healing of the sick we are not to cease to call upon the Great Healer. When we are urged to establish sanitariums, it is not that we may depend alone upon the simple remedies used, but that we may point the afflicted ones to the Mighty Healer of disease. We are to plead for His power to work in harmony with our medical ministrations. The work of our sanitariums would be far more successful if the physicians would read the word more earnestly and put its precepts into practice, if they would preach the kingdom of God and pray for the healing grace of Christ to come upon the afflicted.

Let us present the gospel to the sick, connecting Jesus, the Great Healer, with the simple remedies used; and our living faith will be answered. But those who come to the Great Healer must be willing to do His will, to humble their souls, and confess their sins. As we lay hold of divine power with a faith that will not be denied, we shall see the salvation of God.

Christ declared that He came to recover men's lives. This work is to be done by Christ's followers, and it is to be done by the most simple means. Families are to be taught how to care for the sick. The hope of the gospel is to be revived in the hearts of men and women. We must seek to draw them to the Great Healer. In the work of healing let the physicians work intelligently, not with drugs, but by following rational methods. Then let them by the prayer of faith draw upon the power of God to stay the progress of disease. This will inspire in the suffering ones belief in Christ and the power of prayer, and it will give them confidence in our simple methods of treating disease. Such work will be a means of directing minds to the truth, and will be of great efficiency in the work of the gospel ministry.—Letter 126, 1909.

* * * * *

For Further Study

Christ's Methods of Ministry:
Counsels on Health, 30, 31, 34, 316-318, 497-499, 526-528;
The Ministry of Healing, 17-50, 73-94, 143.

Christ Our Example in Simplicity:
Counsels on Health, 319, 320.

Objects and Aims of Sanitariums:
Counsels on Health, 203-254 (Testimonies for the Church 6:219-228);
Counsels on Health, 271-27 (Testimonies for the Church 7:95-97);
Testimonies for the Church 8:181-191.

Sanitariums and Gospel Work:
Counsels on Health, 212-214.

Greatest Danger in Sanitarium Work:
Testimonies For The Church 1:560.

Section 3—The Christian Physician and His Work

Responsibility for Soul and Body

Every medical practitioner, whether he acknowledges it or not, is responsible for the souls as well as the bodies of his patients. The Lord expects of us much more than we often do for Him. Every physician should be a devoted, intelligent gospel medical missionary, familiar with Heaven's remedy for the sin-sick soul as well as with the science of healing bodily disease.

Coming as he does in daily contact with disease and death, his mind should be filled with a knowledge of the Scriptures, that from this treasure-house he may draw words of consolation and hope and drop them as good seed into hearts ready to receive them. He should encourage the dying to trust in Christ as the sin-pardoning Saviour, and should prepare them to meet their Lord in peace.

Physicians need a double portion of religion. Of men in any calling, physicians are most in need of clearness of mind, purity of spirit, and that faith which works by love and purifies the soul, that they may make the right impression upon all who come within the sphere of their influence. The physician should not only give as much physical relief as possible to those who are soon to lie in the grave, but he should also relieve their burdened souls. Present before them the uplifted Saviour. Let them behold the Lamb of God, who taketh away the sin of the world....

Those who understand the science of Christianity have a personal religious experience. He who acts as a guardian of the health of the body should have tact to work for the salvation of the soul. Until the Saviour is indeed the Saviour of his own soul, the physician will not know how to respond to the question, "What shall I do to be saved?" ...

A Sad Mistake

What an opportunity the consecrated physician has to show a Christlike interest in the patients under his care! It is his privilege to speak encouragingly to them, and bow at their bedside to offer a few words of prayer. To stand by the sickbed and have nothing to say, is a sad mistake. Let the physician make his mind a storehouse, full of fresh thoughts. Let him learn to repeat the comforting words that Christ spoke during His earthly ministry when giving His lessons and healing the sick. Let him speak words of hope and confidence in God. A genuine interest will be manifested. The precious words of Scripture that the Holy Spirit fixes in the memory will win hearts to Jesus, their Saviour.—Letter 20, 1902.

Faithfulness and Perseverance

Physicians are to reveal the attributes of Christ, steadfastly persevering in the work God has given them to do. To those who do this work in faithfulness, angels are commissioned to give enlarged views of the character and work of Christ, and His power and grace and love. Thus they become partakers of His image, and day by day grow up to the full stature of men and women in Christ. It is the privilege of the children of God to have a constantly enlarging comprehension of the truth, that they may bring love for God and heaven into the work and draw from others praise and thanksgiving to God because of the richness of His grace....

Physicians must stand firmly under the banner of the third angel's message, fighting the good fight of faith perseveringly and successfully, relying not on their own wisdom, but on the wisdom of God, putting on the heavenly armor, the equipment of God's word, never forgetting that they have a Leader who never has been, and never can be, overcome by evil.—Manuscript 24, 1900.

Bringing the Lord's Work Into Disrepute

Never is a physician to do his work in a coarse, careless, or haphazard way. The physician is constantly to study refinement. In every sense of the word, he is to be one that ministers—a servant entrusted by an absent Lord with the care of his fellow beings. The lax, loose way that some of our physicians have of working brings into disrepute the work that should be kept on an elevated platform before the world. When a physician does a weak, inefficient work, his fellow physicians are injured.—Manuscript 105, 1902

Give Heed to Character Building

If ever there were those who need to give their character building careful examination, it is our physicians. There has been on the part of many of them a gradual relaxation of piety, of self-control, of purity, of holiness, of watchfulness. An entire change of mind and spirit is needed before they can claim to be acceptable workers....

That man only who daily and hourly lives a Christian life can perform aright the duties of a physician. Let our physicians seek to understand the solemn responsibilities of their profession, and to realize how much is involved in dealing with those who are sick in body and mind. Often the life of the patient is in the hands of the physician. One false movement of the instrument in an operation, and the life would be sacrificed. How solemn the thought!

How important that the physician shall be ever under the control of the divine Physician! Let the one who is trying to prolong life look to Him to direct his every movement. If the physician knows that by his side is One who is life itself, One who can accomplish that which human beings cannot attempt, what confidence this knowledge will inspire! And what a blessing the physician can be in a sickroom if he has learned to trust constantly in Him to whom belong the souls of those to whom he ministers. The Saviour will give him tact and skill in dealing with difficult cases.—Letter 61, 1904.

The Physician's Influence

Physicians who cultivate a sense of the presence of God will impress their patients with the influence of truth. As they show that they truly believe the words, "I know that my Redeemer liveth, to make intercession for me, and that because He lives, I shall live also," the influence of this is felt. Physicians little know the power they will have in the sickroom if they recognize the presence of God.

Their words will be of such a character that impressions for good will be made upon minds....

Open every window heavenward, welcoming the bright, heavenly rays of the Sun of Righteousness. "The fear of the Lord is the beginning of wisdom." Living and working under the constant impression, "Lo, God is here," brings a hallowed influence, which the Spirit is ever impressing on heart and mind.—Manuscript 33, 1901.

A Pattern of Good Judgment

The Lord wants you to be cheerful, and to have cheerful words for the sick. Let the Sun of Righteousness shine forth in your features. Be very decided in your religious service. Make the Lord Jesus your confidant. Make your aim a high one, and let your attainments be higher and higher still in the knowledge of your Lord and Saviour Jesus Christ.—Letter 128, 1905.

Heavenly Assistants

The time that has been spent in communing with God, in seeking His help before undertaking to relieve those who were in a critical condition, has brought angels to the side of the doctor and his assistants. You have succeeded according as you have trusted in God. He has been by your side just as verily as Christ was by the side of those who were suffering when He walked among them on earth."—Health, Philanthropic, and Medical Missionary Work, page 40.

Give God the Glory

God will work with every Christian physician. And to Him the physician is to give the honor and glory for the success that attends his work. The only safety for physicians is in walking and working in humility and faith....

You are wholly dependent upon the Great Physician for the ability and power to do good work. Cling to Jesus. He will give you sharpness of intellect to discern with readiness, and steadiness of nerve to execute with precision.—Letter 3, 1901.

God the Physician's Efficiency

The Lord is to be the efficiency of every physician. If in the operating room the physician feels that he is working only as the Lord's visible helping hand, the Great Physician is present to hold with His invisible hand the hand of the human agent and to guide in the movements made. The Lord knows with what trembling and terror many patients come to the point of undergoing an operation as the only chance for saving life. He knows that they are in greater peril than they ever have been in before. They feel as if their life were in the hands of one whom they believe to be a skillful physician. But when they see their physician on his knees, asking God to make the critical operations a success, the prayer inspires them, as well as the physician, with strong hope and confidence. This confidence, even in the most critical cases, is a means of making operations successful. Impressions are made upon minds that God designed should be made....

Although such a prayer may be offered before unbelievers and even infidels, yet it sweeps away the shadow by which Satan has darkened the mind, and when the sufferer is brought through the crisis, truth takes the place of doubt and unbelief. The mist of skepticism that beclouded the mind is dispelled.—Manuscript 26, 1902.

The Peril of Popularity

Dr. ----- has not been satisfied with a superficial education, but has made the most of his opportunities to obtain a thorough knowledge of the human system and the best methods of treating disease. This has given him an influence. He has earned the respect of the community as a man of sound judgment and nice discrimination, one who reasons carefully from cause to effect; and he is highly esteemed for his courtesy of deportment and his Christian integrity. But there are others also who can become men of influence, trust, and power in that institution....

November 23, 1879, some things were shown me in reference to the institutions among us, and the duties and dangers of those who occupy a leading position in connection with them. I saw that Dr.

----- had been raised up to do a special work as God's instrument, to be led, guided, and controlled by His Spirit. He is to answer the claims of God, and never to feel that he is his own property and that he can employ his powers as he shall deem most profitable to himself. Although it is his purpose to be and to do right, yet he will most surely err unless he is a constant learner in the school of Christ. His only safety is in humbly walking with God.

Safety Only by a Miracle

Dangers beset his path, and if he comes off conqueror he will indeed have a triumphant song to sing in the City of God. He has strong traits of character that will need to be constantly repressed. If kept under the control of the Spirit of God, these traits will be a blessing; but if not, they will prove a curse. If Dr. -----, who is now riding upon the wave of popularity, does not become giddy, it will be a miracle of mercy. If he leans to his own wisdom, as so many thus situated have done, his wisdom will prove to be foolishness. While he shall give himself unselfishly to the work of God, never swerving in the least from principle, the Lord will throw about him the everlasting arms and will prove to him a mighty Helper. "Them that honor Me, I will honor." ...

Evil Traits Strengthened by Indulgence

While he makes God his strength, and loves and fears Him, he will be rightly balanced; but as surely as he loses his connection with God and attempts to go in his own strength, this same will that has proved a blessing will prove an injury to himself and to others. He will become overbearing, tyrannical, exacting, and dictatorial. These traits must not be allowed to gain the ascendancy under any circumstances; for they will strengthen by indulgence and will soon become a controlling power. His character will thus become ill-balanced, and this will disqualify him for the work of God....

God calls for complete and entire consecration, and anything short of this He will not accept. The more difficult your position, the more you need Jesus. The love and fear of God kept Joseph pure and untarnished in the king's court. He was exalted to great wealth, to the high honor of being next to the king; and this elevation was as sudden as it was great.

Examples of Success in Humility

It is impossible to stand upon a lofty height without danger. The tempest leaves unharmed the modest flower of the valley, while it wrestles with the lofty tree upon the mountaintop. There are many men whom God could have used with wonderful success when pressed with poverty,—He could have made them useful here, and crowned them with glory hereafter,—but prosperity ruined them; they were dragged down to the pit because they forgot to be humble, forgot that God was their strength, and became independent and self-sufficient. These dangers are yours.

[37]

Joseph bore the test of character in adversity, and the gold was undimmed by prosperity. He showed the same lofty regard for God's will when he stood next the throne as when in a prisoner's cell. Joseph carried his religion everywhere, and this was the secret of his unwavering fidelity. As representative men, you must have the all-pervading power of true godliness. I tell you, in the fear of God, your path is beset by dangers which you do not see and do not sense. You must hide in Jesus. You are unsafe unless you hold the hand of Christ. You must guard against everything like presumption, and cherish that spirit that would suffer rather than sin. No victory you can gain will be half so precious as that gained over self.—Special Testimonies to Physicians and Helpers, pages 7-27.

The Physician's First Work

The Redeemer expects our physicians to make the saving of souls their first work. If they will walk and work with God, in His love and fear, they will receive leaves from the tree of life to give to the suffering. His peace will go with them, making them messengers of peace.

It is not enough for us to read the Scriptures merely. We are to ask the Lord to fill our wayward hearts with His Spirit, that we may understand the meaning of His words. In order to be benefited by the reading of the words of Christ, we must make a right application of them to our individual cases.

We have been given a message exceeding in importance any other message ever entrusted to mortals. This message Christ came in person to the Isle of Patmos to present to John. He told him to write down what he saw and heard during his vision, that the churches might know what was to come upon the earth. Do our medical workers realize the importance of the message of Revelation? ...

[38] The word, "Nevertheless I have somewhat against thee, because thou hast left thy first love," is applicable to many living in this time. God calls for immediate repentance and reformation. It is time for a great change to take place among the people who are looking for the second appearing of their Lord. Soon strange things will take place. God will hold us responsible for the way in which we treat the truth. Our purity of faith and action will decide our future.

God is in earnest with us. To every man He has given his work. Everyone is to do his part. A clear, decided testimony is to be borne, for a people is to be prepared to meet a time of trouble such as never was since there was a nation.—Manuscript 136, 1902

To Prepare Souls for Death

The question has been asked many times, Should the physician feel it his duty to open the truth to his patients? That depends on circumstances. In many cases all that should be done is to point to Christ as a personal Saviour. There are those who would only be injured should any new doctrine not in accordance with their previous views be brought before them. God must guide in this work. He can prepare minds to receive the word of truth. It is just as much a physician's duty to prepare the souls before him for what is to take place as to minister to their physical needs. Let them know their danger. Be a faithful steward for God. Do not let anyone be launched into eternity without a word of warning or caution. You cannot neglect this and be a faithful steward. God requires you to be true to Him wherever you are. There is a great work to be done. Take hold of it, and do it intelligently. God will help everyone who does this.—Manuscript 62, 1900.

The Duty of Truthfulness

Never, never should the physician feel that he may prevaricate. It is not always safe and best to lay before the invalid the full extent of his danger. The truth may not all be spoken on all occasions, but never speak a lie. If it is important for the good of the invalid not to alarm him lest such a course might prove fatal, do not lie to him....

Religious faith and principles have become deteriorated, mingled with worldly customs and practices, and for this reason pure and undefiled religion is rare. The soul, the precious soul, is of value, and it must be made white in the blood of the Lamb. The strength and grace of God was provided at an infinite sacrifice that you might be victorious over Satan's suggestions and temptations and come forth unsullied and unpolluted as did Joseph and Daniel. Let the life, the character, be the strongest argument for Christianity, for by this will all men be compelled to take knowledge of you that you have been with Jesus and learned of Him. The life, the words, and the deportment are the most forcible argument, the most solemn appeal, to the careless, irreverent, and skeptical....

You all need a living religion, that you may stand as God's witnesses, proclaiming to the sick that sin is always followed with suffering; and while combating pain and disease, you should plainly lay before them that which you know to be the real cause, and the remedy—"Cease to sin;" and point them to the sin-pardoning Saviour.—Manuscript 4a, 1885.

Leading Souls to the Mighty Healer

In no other line of the work is the truth to shine more brightly than in the medical missionary work. Every true medical missionary has a remedy for the sin-sick soul as well as for the diseased body. By faith in Christ he is to act as an evangelist, a messenger of mercy. As he uses the simple remedies which God has provided for the cure of physical suffering, he is to speak of Christ's power to heal the maladies of the soul.

Through the efforts of the Christian physician, the accumulated light of the past and the present is to produce its effect. Not only is the physician to give instruction from the word of God, line upon line, precept upon precept; he is to moisten this instruction with his tears and make it strong with his prayers, that souls may be saved from death....

In their work of dealing with disease and death, physicians are in danger of losing the solemn reality of the future of the soul. In their earnest, feverish anxiety to avert the peril of the body, there is danger that they will neglect the peril of the soul. I would say to you, Be on your guard; for you must meet your dying ones before the judgment seat of Christ.—Letter 120, 1901.

Evangelistic Duties

Our physicians need a deeper insight into the evangelistic work that God expects them to do. Let them remember that if they do not work for the healing of the soul as well as for the healing of the body, they are not following the example of the great Medical Missionary. Let them study the word of God diligently, that they may be familiar with its promises and may be able, in tenderness and love, to point sinners to the Great Healer. It was to bring spiritual as well as physical healing to the sick that our sanitariums were established.

The physician is to be a constant receiver of the grace of Christ. He is to remember that the God-fearing physician is authorized to regard himself as a laborer together with God. The Saviour is willing to help all who call upon Him for wisdom and clearness of thought. And who needs wisdom and clearness of thought more than the physician, upon whose decision so much depends?

The Lord would have our physicians cooperate with Him in their treatment of the sick, showing more faith and using fewer drugs. Let us rely upon God. Our faith is feeble, and our hearts remain unchanged. God would have a change take place. He says, "A new heart also will I give you." When this promise is fulfilled to the people of God, the condition of things will be very different from what it now is.—Manuscript 14, 1904.

A Deeper Yearning for Souls

Into the medical missionary work there must be brought more of a yearning for souls. It was this yearning that filled the hearts of those who established our first medical institution. Christ is to be present in the sickroom, filling the heart of the physician with the fragrance of His love. When his life is such that Christ can go with him to the bedside of the sick, there will come to them the conviction that He, the compassionate Saviour, is present, and this conviction will do much to restore them to health.

In word and deed the physicians and nurses in our medical institutions are to say, so plainly that it cannot be misunderstood, "God is in this place," to save, not to destroy. Christ invites our physicians to become acquainted with Him. When they respond to His invitation, they will know that they receive the things they ask for. Their minds will be enlightened by wisdom from above. Constantly beholding the Saviour, they will become more and more like Him, till at last it can be said of them in the heavenly courts, "Ye are complete in Him." Christ has pledged Himself to give His disciples what they ask for in His name. As they labor in harmony with Him, they can ask Him to aid them in every time of need.—Manuscript 14, 1904.

Take Time to Commune With God

The physician who is truly converted will not gather to himself responsibilities which interfere with his work for souls. It is a mistake to lay upon the Christian physician, whom God has appointed to represent Him in His own way, so many responsibilities that he has no time to commune with God by reading His word and by prayer. Christ declares, "Without Me ye can do nothing." How, then, can a medical missionary engage successfully in his important work without earnestly seeking the Lord in prayer? Prayer and a study of the word bring life and health to the believing worker.—Manuscript 159, 1899.

To a Young Physician Under Discouragement

My heart is drawn out toward you. The Lord has not left you. He is a God of tender compassion and wonderful loving-kindness, and He does not desire you to walk in darkness. You need not cast yourself away; for the Lord says, "His life need not be a failure. I will make him Mine. I will show him that I prize his soul. I will strive with him, and lift him up. He must not perish. I have a special work for him to do. If he will unite with Me, believe in Me, and work for Me, his weakest points of character, notwithstanding his past failures, will become his strongest points."

Do not keep your mind fixed on the defective example of professing Christians. You will, of course, see in their lives things that are not right. But if you keep looking at their faults, you will become like them. Instead of looking at the lives of your fellowmen, look to Jesus. There you will see no imperfection, but perfection, righteousness, goodness, mercy, and truth. Take the Saviour as your example in all things. It is in looking to men instead of beholding Christ that you have made your great mistake.

Without Excuse

You are not excusable for living an un-Christlike life. Christ came to this world, subject to His Father's will, for one great purpose—to show men and women what God desires them to be and what, through His grace, they may be. He came to develop for man a character after the similitude of heaven.

But I did not begin to write this letter to condemn you, but to encourage you to look away from sinful examples to the perfect Example, to point you to the path of peace and holiness. The Lord's merciful love is still for you. But He would have you follow a better way than you have followed in the past. This you are to do, not by keeping your eyes fixed on the defective lives of professing Christians, but by beholding Christ, the Sent of God, who in this world and in human nature lived a pure, noble, perfect life, setting an example that all may safely follow.

The Lord is reaching out His hand to save you. I long to see you responding to His invitation, "Let him take hold of My strength, that he may make peace with Me; and he shall make peace with Me." ...

There have been many things to tempt you to swerve from your allegiance to the truth, but the Saviour has been willing to lead you at every step. It is young men whom the Lord claims as His helping hand. Samuel was a mere child when the Lord used him to do a good and gracious work....

Building a Character for Eternity

Because some serve on the enemy's side, all need not forsake the Lord. Gather to your soul the light of the word of God. Remember that day by day you are building character for time and for eternity.

The teaching of the Bible in regard to character building is very explicit. "Whatsoever ye do in word or deed, do all in the name of the Lord Jesus." Place yourself under His control, and then ask for His protecting power. He gave His life for you. Do not cause Him sorrow. Be guarded in all that you say and do. Christ wants you to be to other young men His representative, His delegated gospel medical missionary.

[43]

Remember that in your life religion is not to be merely one influence among others. It is to be an influence dominating all others. Be strictly temperate. Resist every temptation. Make no concessions to the wily foe. Listen not to the suggestions that he puts into the mouths of men and women. You have a victory to win. You have nobility of character to gain; but this you cannot gain while you are depressed and discouraged by failure. Break the bands with which Satan has bound you. There is no need for you to be his slave. "Ye are My friends," Christ said, "if ye do whatsoever I command you."

Jesus loves you, and He has given me a message for you. His great heart of infinite tenderness yearns over you. He sends you the message that you may recover yourself from the snare of the enemy. You may regain your self-respect. You may stand where you regard yourself, not as a failure, but as a conqueror, in and through the uplifting influence of the Spirit of God. Take hold of the hand of Christ, and do not let it go.

You may be a great blessing to others if you will give yourself unreservedly to the Lord's service. Power from on high will be given you if you will take your position on the Lord's side. Through Christ you can escape the corruption that is in the world through lust, and be a noble example of what Christ can do for those who cooperate with Him.

Choice of Associates

Do not choose the society of those who are the servants of sin, and thus place yourself in temptation. Nobility of character is not gained by placing oneself in objectionable society. Do not put on one side the grand requirements of the word of God. Your only hope is in placing yourself in right relation to God. You have supposed that you could so harden your heart that you would be regardless of truth and righteousness. But this you have not been able to do. You have longed to clasp the hand of One who could be a stay, a strength, a support.

God's purpose for us is that we shall ever move upward. Even in the smaller duties of common life we are to make continual growth in grace, supplied with high and holy motives, powerful because they proceed from One who gave His life to furnish us with the incentive to be wholly successful in the formation of Christian character.

Christ has made an atonement for you. You are not to go through life with a half-formed character. You are to be strong in the strength of God, grounded in the hope of the gospel. You are acquainted with God's requirements, and I beg of you not to remain a weakling....

I am very hopeful that you will become all that the Lord desires you to be—a gospel medical missionary. You are to be not only an increasingly skillful physician, but one of the Lord's appointed missionaries, in all your work placing His service first.

Give Christ the Best

Let nothing mar your peace. Give your heart's best and holiest affections to Him who gave His life that you might be among the redeemed family in the heavenly courts. Striving for the crown of life will not make you dissatisfied or less useful. The Great Teacher desires to acknowledge you as His helping hand. He calls for your cooperation. Will you not now give Him all that you have and are? Will you not consecrate your talents to His service?

This life is your sowing time. Will you not pledge yourself to God that your seed sowing shall be that which will produce, not tares, but a harvest of wheat? God will work with you; He will increase your usefulness. He has entrusted to you talents that in His strength you may use to produce a precious harvest.—Letter 228, 1903.

To a Physician in Perplexity

I have wished so much that I might have an opportunity to talk with you. Could I see you, I should say to you what I have been saying to you recently in the visions of the night. You were apparently undecided as to what you would do in the future. I asked, "Why are you perplexed?" You replied, "I am perplexed in regard to what is the best course for me to pursue." Then One who has authority stepped up to you and said: "You are not your own. You have been bought with a price. Your time, your talents, every jot of your influence, is the Lord's. You are His servant. Your part is to do His bidding, and learn daily of Him. You are not to set up in business for yourself. This is not the Lord's plan. You are not to unite with unbelievers in medical work. Neither is this the Lord's plan. His word to you is, "Be ye not unequally yoked together with unbelievers: for what fellowship hath righteousness with unrighteousness? and what communion hath light with darkness? And what concord hath Christ with Belial? or what part hath he that believeth with an infidel? And what agreement hath the temple of God with idols? for ye are the temple of the living God; as God hath said, I will dwell in them, and walk in them, and I will be their God, and they shall be My people." ...

[45]

You are to receive the grace of Christ, the great Medical Missionary. His divine wisdom will be given to you if you will refuse to yield to the inclination to link up with the world. God desires you to place yourself where you can work in connection with other physicians. You and the one with whom you are associated may not be of the same temperament. It is better if you are not. That which one needs the other may supply, if each will learn to wear the yoke of Christ....

My brother, choose to obey Christ. In His meekness and lowliness, receive His counsel. Stand shoulder to shoulder with your brethren, and this will encourage them to stand shoulder to shoulder with you. Hide self in Christ, and the Saviour will be to you a present help in every time of need.

To Impart God's Love

God's people have many lessons to learn. They will have perfect peace if they will keep the mind stayed on Him who is too wise to err and too good to do them harm. They are to catch the reflection of the smile of God, and reflect it to others. They are to see how much sunshine they can bring into the lives of those around them. They are to keep near to Christ, so close that they sit together with Him as His little children, in sweet, sacred unity. They are never to forget that as they receive the affection and love of God, they are under the most solemn obligation to impart it to others. Thus they may exert an influence of rejoicing, which blesses all who come within its reach, irradiating their pathway.

[46]

This is where the people of God make so many mistakes. They do not express thankfulness for the great gift of God's love and grace. Selfishness must be expelled from the soul. The heart must be purified from all envy, all evil surmising. Believers must constantly receive and impart the love of God. Then unbelievers will say of them, "They have been with Jesus, and learned of Him. They are living in intimate companionship with Christ, who is love." The world has keenness of perception, and will take knowledge to some purpose of those who sit together in heavenly places in Christ Jesus. The character of God's human agencies must be a transcript of the character of their Saviour....

To Link Up with Brethren

I write this to you, my dear brother, in the hope of helping you. You are in an unsettled state of mind, and are tempted to do a strange work which God has not appointed you to do. None of us are to strike out alone; we are to link up with our brethren, and pull together, and God will give us influence and self-control. We are to draw near to God, that He may draw near to us.

No one can gain completeness in Christ, who, having the means of gaining a deeper experience in the things of God, fails to realize that every ray of heavenly light, every jot of blessing, is given to him to give to all who come within the sphere of his influence. If we are qualifying ourselves to live in heaven, we are daily drawing nearer and nearer to our Redeemer. We are to represent Christ in every phase of character.

What is the Bible test of character? "If a man love Me, he will keep My words: and My Father will love him, and We will come unto him, and make Our abode with him." No one need perish in spiritual blindness. A plain "Thus saith the Lord" has been given for the guidance of all.—Letter 40, 1903.

Counsel with Your Brethren

Do not refuse to unite with your brethren, fearing that if you put yourself on an equality with them you will not be able to do all that your own judgment might suggest. God's workers are to counsel together. Ministers, physicians, or directors are walking in false paths when they regard themselves as a complete whole; when they feel no need of counsel from men of experience, who have been led by the Lord, who, as they have moved forward in self-denial to advance the work, have given evidence that they were led and controlled by the Holy Spirit and were thus enabled to speak and plan and act wisely and understandingly.

The Lord calls for men who are willing to yoke up with Christ and with their brethren; men who are willing to strive to be altogether that which they must be in order to carry forward the work of God intelligently; men who look to Jesus, complying with the invitation, "Come unto Me, ... and I will give you rest. Take My yoke upon you, and learn of Me; for I am meek and lowly in heart: and ye shall find rest unto your souls."—Letter 13, 1902.

Shall Self Rule?

There is need for every physician closely and critically to examine himself. What is his religious experience? Does he allow self to rule? Does he make his own wishes and desires supreme? Does he keep the glory of God ever before him? Is he learning daily of Jesus? If this is your experience, those with whom you are connected will be led nearer to the Saviour. Why? Because you are constantly beholding Him who is the way, the truth, and the life....

Temptation to Feel Self-sufficient

I wish to say that there is danger of our physicians' taking themselves into their own hands, thinking that they understand best what they should do. They think that those who offer them counsel do not understand their capabilities or appreciate their value. This is the stumbling stone over which some at least have fallen. You are not beyond the temptation of thinking that you can do better work alone than when linked up with your brethren. The very ones who think this are the ones who need the companionship and help of a fellow laborer.

My brother, the Lord needs your help in His work. Will you not be His helping hand? It would be a serious mistake for you to accept a worldly position, where it would not be possible for you to do the medical missionary work that God desires you to do. Do not make this mistake. Place yourself under the guidance of the greatest Medical Missionary the world has ever known. Under His direction you will gain increased capabilities for doing His work.

The Lord's people are to testify, by Christlike lives, that God has a people on the earth who represent the pure and holy company that will meet round the throne of God when the redeemed are gathered into the Holy City. Those who on this earth love and obey God will be accounted true and pure and loyal, worthy to dwell with Him in the heavenly courts.—Letter 41, 1903.

A Plea for Brotherly Union

To fear God and to walk with Him is the privilege and duty of every physician. I have been shown that Satan presses in his temptations with greater force upon physicians who are among our people than upon those outside of our faith. It is Satan's work to excite pride and ambition, selfishness, and love for supremacy, that he may prevent that strong, brotherly union which should exist among our physicians, which would give vigor to their purposes and would go far to ensure success in all their undertakings. In all our institutions the physicians who believe the truth should strive for harmony.

There should be no rivalry. Variance and rivalry are even more offensive to God when manifest among physicians than among those who claim to be called to the ministry; for the godly physician is Christ's ambassador to hold forth the word of life to suffering ones who are letting go their hold of this life. If he has wisdom to speak a word in season, leading the sufferer to rely upon Jesus, he may be the instrument in the hands of God of the saving of the soul. How firmly garrisoned should be the soul of the physician, that impure, sensual thoughts may not find a lodgment there.

I have been shown that much is lost when the physicians of our faith draw apart because of their different methods of practice. Physicians' meetings should be held, where all might counsel together, exchanging ideas and laying plans whereby they could work unitedly. The Lord formed man for companionship, and He designs that we shall be imbued with the kind, loving nature of Christ, and shall, through association, be bound together in close relationship as children of God, doing work for time and for eternity....

Physicians to Counsel Together

In the love and fear of God, let the physicians have meetings for counsel, and talk up the best ways and means of serving the Lord in their branch of His great work. Let them bring together all their intelligence and skill, that they may be a help to one another. I know that there are ways by which they can come into harmony so that no one shall follow his own independent judgment.—Letter 26a, 1889.

A Student of Cause and Effect

The intelligent Christian physician has an increasing knowledge of the connection between sin and disease. He is constantly striving to perfect his knowledge of the relation between cause and effect. He sees the necessity of educating those who are taking the nurse's course to be strictly temperate in all things, because carelessness in regard to the laws of health, a neglect to properly care for the body, is the cause of much of the disease on our world. A failure to care for the living machinery is an insult to the Creator. There are divinely appointed rules which, if observed, will keep human beings from disease and premature death....

When a physician sees that the ailment which has taken hold of the body is the result of improper eating and drinking, yet neglects to tell the patient that his suffering is caused by a wrong course of action, he is doing the human brotherhood an injury. Present the matter tenderly, but never keep silent as to the cause of the affliction.—Letter 120, 1901.

The Physician as a Sabbath Observer

Christ was a Seventh-day Adventist, to all intents and purposes. It was He who called Moses into the mount and gave him instruction for His people.... In awful grandeur Christ made known the law of Jehovah, giving, among other charges, this charge: "Remember the Sabbath day, to keep it holy." My brother, you have not placed upon the Sabbath the sanctity that is required by God. Irreverence has come in, and an example has been set that the Lord does not approve. He is not honored and glorified.

There will always be duties which have to be performed on the Sabbath for the relief of suffering humanity. This is right, and in accordance with the law of Him who says, "I will have mercy, and not sacrifice." But there is danger of falling into carelessness on this point, and of doing that which it is not positively essential to do on the Sabbath.

Unnecessary traveling is done on the Sabbath, with many other things which might be left undone. "Take heed," saith the Lord, "to all thy ways, lest I remove My Holy Spirit because of the lax regard given to My precepts." "Remember the Sabbath day, to keep it holy." Bear in mind the charge to remember. Do not carelessly forget, "Six days shalt thou labor, and do all thy work." In this time all the duties necessary to prepare for the Sabbath are to be done.—Letter 51, 1901.

Rest for the Overweary

The temptations that come to a physician are great, for he is often pressed beyond measure, overworked, overwearied. But if he will commit the keeping of his soul to God as unto a faithful Creator, he will find rest and peace. A soothing influence from Jesus will come to him.

Infidel physicians abound. They refuse to be illuminated by the light which irradiates others. They exalt self, and they lose spiritual and eternal advantages. But medical practitioners who have the influence of the truth upon the mind and heart are skilled in the use of remedies for the sin-sick soul as well as the body. They can with the wisdom of heaven speak words that will cause melody in the soul because of spiritual growth.

You are a shepherd of the soul as well as a physician of the body. You need divine aid, and you may have it if you will come to the Lord as a little child. You may have a rich experience. But you must not wear yourself out by overworry and overtaxation. If you are balanced by the Holy Spirit, you will seek first the kingdom of God and His righteousness. You will place yourself in a position where the truth for this time can come in clear, distinct rays of light to you. You will see the truth as it bears upon the present time, and your experience will be in complete harmony with the message of the third angel....

Behold the Eternal and the Unseen

We cannot keep our eyes fixed upon the things that are seen, and yet appreciate eternal realities. We need, and especially you who are so bound up with the afflictions and necessities of humanity, to keep the eye of faith beholding the eternal and unseen, that you may become more and more intelligent in regard to the great plan of God to bring these suffering ones to discern the value of the human soul. You are to esteem the reproach of Christ greater riches than the treasures of Egypt.

Discouragements come to you, I know, and trials press upon your soul, and you almost forget that Jesus is your Helper, and that His eye is upon you every moment. In the working out of your plans for the blessing and relief of humanity ever bear in mind that it is not you who are doing the work. Christ requires you to wear His yoke, and lift His burdens. The great and sympathetic heart of Christ is ever identifying itself with suffering humanity. You cannot of your own self do anything. Regard yourself as an instrument in God's hands, and let His mind, His peace, His grace, rule in heart and life.

Be God's thread to work out His design. You can never handle yourself. You can never place yourself in position with any success. You must work as an agent cooperating with God. "Work out your own salvation with fear and trembling. For it is God which worketh in you both to will and to do of His good pleasure." Here are the combined elements, God and the human agent, both working harmoniously.—Letter 97, 1894.

Hiding Self in Christ

Dr. John Cheyne, while he rose to a high point in his profession, did not forget his obligations to God. He once wrote to a friend, "You may wish to know the condition of my mind. I am humbled in the dust by the thought that there is not one action of my busy life which will bear the eye of a holy God. But when I reflect on the invitation of the Redeemer, 'Come unto Me,' and that I have accepted this invitation; and, moreover, that my conscience testifies that I earnestly desire to have my will in all things conformed to the will of God, I have peace; I have the promised rest promised by Him in whom was found no guile."

Before his death this eminent physician ordered a column to be erected near the spot where his body was to lie, on which were to be inscribed these texts, as voices from eternity: "God so loved the world, that He gave His only-begotten Son, that whosoever believeth in Him should not perish, but have everlasting life." "Come unto Me, all ye that labor and are heavy-laden, and I will give you rest." "Follow peace with all men, and holiness, without which no man shall see the Lord."

And while Dr. Cheyne thus strove, even from the tomb, to beckon sinners to the Saviour and to glory, he concealed his own name, withholding it from the column entirely. He was not less careful to say, as speaking to the passerby, "The name and profession and age of him whose body lies beneath are of little consequence, but it may be of great importance to you to know that by the grace of God he was brought to look to the Lord Jesus as the only Saviour of sinners, and that this looking unto Jesus gave peace to his soul." "Pray to God, pray to God," it says, "that you may be instructed in the gospel; and be assured that God will give the Holy Spirit, the only Teacher of true wisdom, to them that ask Him." This memorial was designed to turn the attention of all to God and cause them to lose sight of the man.

This man brought no reproach upon the cause of Christ. I tell you, dear brother, in Christ we may do all things. It is an encouragement to remember that there have been physicians who were consecrated to God, who were led and taught by God; and there may be such in this age—physicians who do not exalt self, but who walk and work with the eye single to the glory of God, men who are true to principle, true to duty, ever looking unto Jesus for His light....

As we examine the records of the past, physician after physician rises up before us qualified to minister to the soul as well as to the body, and some of them actually doing so. Driven by the perils of their profession, they sought the wisdom of God, and were guided by His Spirit in the path whose end is glory....

The God-fearing, God-loving physician longs to reveal Jesus to the sin-sick soul and tell him how free, how complete, is the provision made by the sin-pardoning Redeemer. "His tender mercies are over all His works;" but for humanity more ample provision is made, and the promise is full which points to Jesus as the Fountain opened for sin and uncleanness. What can make a heart so light, what can spread so much sunshine through the soul, as the sense of sins forgiven? The peace of Christ is life and health.

[53]

Then let the physician realize his accountability and improve his opportunities to reveal Christ as a forgiving Saviour. Let him have a high regard for souls and do all in his power to win them to Christ and the truth. May the Lord put His Spirit upon our physicians, and help them to work intelligently for the Master because they love Jesus and the souls for whom Christ died.—Manuscript 17, 1890.

*****

For Further Study

The Christian Physician:
Counsels on Health, 321-386
(Testimonies for the Church 6:229-234;
Testimonies for the Church 4:566-569);

The Ministry of Healing, 111-124;
Testimonies for the Church 6:243-253.

Better Qualified Than Minister Who Merely Preaches:
Counsels on Health, 503, 504.

A Messenger of Mercy:
Counsels on Health, 351-354
(Testimonies for the Church 7:72-75).

Practical Results of Communion With God:
The Ministry of Healing, 511, 512.

Neglect of Religious Duties:
Counsels on Health, 362;
403, 404.

Moral and Intellectual Culture:
Counsels on Health, 257-260
(Testimonies for the Church 4:545-549).

Value of Trial, Danger of Self-Sufficiency:
Testimonies for the Church 8:123-132.

Habits of Temperance:
Counsels on Health, 321-32;
Testimonies for the Church 5:439-442).

Patience and Sympathy for the Undeserving:
Counsels on Health, 347-354
(Testimonies for the Church 3:178-184;
Testimonies for the Church 7:72-75).

To Be Firm, Yet Courteous and Tender:
Testimonies for the Church 3:170.

Duty of Truthfulness:
The Ministry of Healing, 245.

To Teach Causes of Disease:
Counsels on Health, 366.

Appropriate Promises for the Dying:
The Ministry of Healing, 121-124.

Divinely Helped in Operations:
Testimonies for the Church 8:187, 188.

Praising God for Recovery:
Counsels on Health, 334, 335;
The Ministry of Healing, 119.

No Place for Graduation:

Counsels on Health, 405 (Testimonies for the Church 4:554-562).

[54]
[55]

Section 4—Our Medical College

In the Providence of God

Sunday, April 15, the beautiful buildings and grounds of the Loma Linda Sanitarium were solemnly dedicated to the service of God....

During the exercises, the people were told of the remarkable providences that had attended every step taken to secure the property. The purpose we have in view in the establishment of many sanitariums was also dwelt upon. I was present at the meeting only a portion of the time, and spoke with freedom for nearly half an hour on the advantages of outdoor life in the treatment of disease.

I tried to make it plain that sanitarium physicians and helpers were to cooperate with God in combating disease not only through the use of the natural remedial agencies He has placed within our reach, but also by encouraging their patients to lay hold on divine strength through obedience to the commandments of God....

One of the chief advantages of situation at Loma Linda is the pleasing variety of charming scenery on every side. But more important than magnificent scenery and beautiful buildings and spacious grounds is the close proximity of this institution to a densely populated district, and the opportunity thus afforded of communicating to many, many people a knowledge of the third angel's message. We are to have clear spiritual discernment, else we shall fail of understanding the opening providences of God that are preparing the way for us to enlighten the world.

The great crisis is just before us. Now is the time for us to sound the warning message, by the agencies that God has given us for this purpose. Let us remember that one most important agency is our medical missionary work. Never are we to lose sight of the great object for which our sanitariums are established—the advancement of God's closing work in the earth.

To Be An Educational Center

Loma Linda is to be not only a sanitarium, but an educational center. With the possession of this place comes the weighty responsibility of making the work of the institution educational in character. A school is to be established here for the training of gospel medical missionary evangelists.

Much is involved in this work, and it is very essential that a right beginning be made.—The Review and Herald, June 21, 1906.

A Place to Be Appreciated

In Loma Linda we have an advantageous center for the carrying on of various missionary enterprises. We can see that it was in the providence of God that this sanitarium was placed in the possession of our people. We should appreciate Loma Linda as a place which the Lord foresaw we should need, and which He gave.—Manuscript 3, 1908.

A Practical Training

We have a work to do in securing the best talent, and in placing these workers in positions where they can educate other workers. Then when our sanitariums and mission fields call for physicians, we shall have young men who, through their experience gained by practical work, have become fitted to bear responsibilities.—Counsels to Parents, Teachers, and Students, 473

An Appeal in Behalf of Our Medical College

The proper development of the work at Loma Linda calls for prayerful thought and planning, that the instruction which the Lord has given concerning the work there may be fulfilled.... The work of the medical college at Loma Linda must not be crippled for lack of room. There must be some way devised to enlarge quickly the buildings for the rooming of students, so that those who seek a training at Loma Linda may not be turned away.

The students at Loma Linda are seeking for an education that is after the Lord's order, an education that will help them to develop into successful teachers and laborers for others. When their education at Loma Linda is completed, they should be able to go forth and join the intelligent workers in the world's great harvest fields who are carrying forward the work of reform that is to prepare a people to stand in the day of Christ's coming. Everywhere workers are needed to know how to combat disease and give skillful care to the sick and suffering. We should do all in our power to enable those who desire to be thus fitted for service to gain the necessary training....

Our people should become intelligent in the treatment of sickness without the aid of poisonous drugs. Many should seek to obtain the education that will enable them to combat disease in its various forms by the most simple methods. Thousands have gone down to the grave because of the use of poisonous drugs, who might have been restored to health by simple methods of treatment. Water treatments, wisely and skillfully given, may be the means of saving many lives. Let diligent study be united with careful treatments. Let prayers of faith be offered by the bedside of the sick. Let the sick be encouraged to claim the promises of God for themselves.—Manuscript 15, 1911.

To Provide What Is Essential

The light given me is, We must provide that which is essential to qualify our youth who desire to be physicians, so that they may intelligently fit themselves to be able to stand the examinations required to prove their efficiency as physicians. They should be taught to treat understandingly the cases of those who are diseased, so that the door will be closed for any sensible physician to imagine that we are not giving in our school the instruction necessary for properly qualifying young men and young women to do the work of a physician. Continually the students who are graduated are to advance in knowledge; for practice makes perfect.

The medical school at Loma Linda is to be of the highest order, because those who are in that school have the privilege of maintaining a living connection with the wisest of all physicians, from whom there is communicated knowledge of a superior order. And for the special preparation of those of our youth who have clear convictions of their duty to obtain a medical education that will enable them to pass the examinations required by law of all who practice as regularly qualified physicians, we are to supply whatever may be required, so that these youth need not be compelled to go to medical schools conducted by men not of our faith. Thus we shall close a door that the enemy would be pleased to have left open; and our young men and young women, whose spiritual interests the Lord desires us to safeguard, will not feel compelled to connect with unbelievers in order to obtain a thorough training along medical lines.—Pacific Union Recorder, February 3, 1910.

The Wisest Talent Called For

Loma Linda has been specified to me as a very important place, and one which demands the best Bible teacher we can supply. There are promising youth here who are to be qualified to fill important positions in the work. They should have the best class of instructors, and capable Bible teachers who understand the truths of the word. The truth and righteousness revealed in the word of God is to be the stronghold of our workers.

There has been given to me an outline of the work that must be done at Loma Linda, and I know that we must give to that place our best labors. The Lord wants the wisest talent there, for by means of our very best educational talent we are to train our ministerial laborers. The work is to be carried after the Lord's order, and not according to the suppositions of men.

The Lord has given us a wonderful advantage in enabling us to secure Loma Linda for the establishment of the work in progress there. A school is to be built up at Loma Linda that will train Bible workers and missionary nurses for efficient service.—Letter 196, 1908.

The Classes of Workers to Be Trained

The cause of God today would have been far in advance of what it is, had we in former years been more active in the training of nurses who, in addition to their acquirement of more than ordinary skill in the care of the sick, had also learned to labor as evangelists in soul-winning service.

It is for the training of such workers, as well as for the training of physicians, that the school at Loma Linda has been founded. In this school many workers are to be qualified with the ability of physicians, to labor, not in professional lines as physicians, but as medical missionary evangelists. This training is to be in harmony with the principles underlying true higher education. The cause is in need of hundreds of workers who have received a practical and thorough education in medical lines, and who are also prepared to labor from house to house as teachers, Bible workers, and colporteurs. Such students should come out of the school without having sacrificed the principles of health reform or their love for God and righteousness.

Those who take advanced training in nursing and go forth into all parts of the world as medical missionary evangelists, cannot expect to receive from the world the honor and the rewards that often come to fully accredited physicians. Yet as they go about their work of teaching and of healing, and link up closely with God's servants who have been called to the ministry of His word, His blessing will rest upon their labors, and marvelous transformations will be wrought. In a special sense they will be His helping hand.—Counsels to Parents, Teachers, and Students, 471

To Prepare for Many Lines of Work

There is a very precious work to be done in connection with the interests of the sanitarium and school at Loma Linda; and this will be done when all work to that end. The word of God is to be our lesson book. In the unity that is coming in among our people we can see that God is working in our midst....

In our school at Loma Linda many can be educated to work as missionaries in the cause of health and temperance. The best teachers are to be employed in this educational work—not men who esteem highly their own capabilities, but men who will walk circumspectly, depending wholly upon the Lord....

If the teachers in medical lines will stand in their lot and place, we shall see a good work done. My soul is drawn out in earnest prayer to God that He will preserve the honest in heart from being led astray by those who are themselves in confusion and darkness.

Teachers are to be prepared for many lines of work. Schools are to be established in places where no efforts have been made.... Truth, Bible truth, is to be presented in many places. Christ is represented as identifying Himself with all the needy upon earth when He says, "Inasmuch as ye have done it unto one of the least of these My brethren, ye have done it unto Me."

All should put forth efforts to enlarge their experience. We are in a most critical situation; but Christ identifies Himself with our necessities. Christians are to learn daily of Christ. Spiritual sinew and muscle are now needed to work out right principles in every city and town and village. Varied talents are to be appreciated and cultivated, and withal we need true wisdom. We may not see our need of counseling with God; but the true Christian in every place will inquire what is the will of the Lord concerning His individual work....

The work of promulgating the principles of health reform which the Lord has outlined to us must be accomplished. When we study the self-denial of Christ, and make His life our example, truth and righteousness will prevail among us. We will esteem as of highest value the ornament of a meek and quiet spirit, which is in the sight of God of great price.—Letter 132, 1908.

Women to Be Especially Trained

I have words of instruction for you and your co-workers who are ministers and physicians and counselors at Loma Linda....

In a remarkable way God has brought into our possession some of the institutions through whose agency we are to accomplish the work of reformation to which as a people we are called. At this time every talent of every worker should be regarded as a sacred trust to be used in extending the work of reform. The Lord instructed me that our sisters who have received a training that has fitted them for positions of responsibility are to serve with faithfulness and discernment in their calling, using their influence wisely and, with their brethren in the faith, obtaining an experience that will fit them for still greater usefulness....

In ancient times the Lord worked in a wonderful way through consecrated women who united in His work with men whom He had chosen to stand as His representatives. He used women to gain great and decisive victories. More than once in times of emergency He brought them to the front and worked through them for the salvation of many lives....

[61] There are many who have ability to stand with their husbands in sanitarium work, to give treatments to the sick, and to speak words of counsel and encouragement to others. There are those who should seek an education that will fit them to act the part of physicians.

In this line of service a positive work needs to be done. Women as well as men are to receive a thorough medical training. They should make a special study of the diseases common to women, that they may understand how to treat them. It is considered most essential that men desiring to practice medicine shall receive the broad training necessary for the following of such a profession. It is just as essential that women receive such training, and obtain their diplomas certifying their right to act as physicians.

Our institutions should be especially thorough in giving to women a training that will fit them to act as midwives. There should be in our sanitariums lady physicians who understand well their profession, and who can attend women at the time of childbirth. Light has been given me that women instead of men should take the responsibility in such cases. I was directed to the Bible plan, in which at such times women acted the part of the physician. This plan should be carried out by us; for it is the Lord's plan.

Again and again light has been given me that women should be chosen and educated for this line of work. Now the time has come when we should face the matter clearly. More women should be educated for this work, and thus a door of temptation may be closed. We should allow no unnecessary temptation to be placed in the way of physicians and nurses, or the people for whom they minister.—Letter 22, 1911.

No Compromise

I am instructed to say that in our educational work there is to be no compromise in order to meet the world's standards. God's commandment-keeping people are not to unite with the world to carry various lines of work according to worldly plans and worldly wisdom.

Our people are now being tested as to whether they will obtain their wisdom from the greatest Teacher the world ever knew, or seek to the God of Ekron. Let us determine that we shall not be tied by so much as a thread to the educational policies of those who do not discern the voice of God and who will not hearken to His commandments.

We are to take heed to the warning: "Enter ye in at the strait gate." Matthew 7:13, 14. Those who walk in the narrow way are following in the footprints of Jesus. The light from heaven illuminates their path.

Shall we represent before the world that our physicians must follow the pattern of the world before they can be qualified to act as successful physicians? This is the question that is now testing the faith of some of our brethren. Let not any of our brethren displease the Lord by advocating in their assemblies the idea that we need to obtain from unbelievers a higher education than that specified by the Lord.

The representation of the Great Teacher is to be considered an all-sufficient revelation. Those in our ranks who qualify as physicians are to receive only such education as is in harmony with these divine truths. Some have advised that students should, after taking some work at Loma Linda, complete their medical education in worldly colleges. But this is not in harmony with the Lord's plan. God is our wisdom, our sanctification, and our righteousness. Facilities should be provided at Loma Linda that the necessary instruction in medical lines may be given by instructors who fear the Lord and who are in harmony with His plans for the treatment of the sick.

I have not a word to say in favor of the world's ideas of higher education in any school that we shall organize for the training of physicians. There is danger in their attaching themselves to worldly institutions and working under the ministrations of worldly physicians. Satan is giving his orders to those whom he has led to depart from the faith. I would now advise that none of our young people attach themselves to worldly medical institutions in the hope of gaining better success or stronger influence as physicians.—Letter 132, 1909.

Christ's Part and Ours

The Saviour's work of ministering to suffering humanity was always combined with His ministry of the word. He preached the gospel and He healed infirmities both by the same mighty power. He will do the same today; but we must do our part by bringing the sick in touch with the Mighty Healer. The Saviour left the courts of glory and came to our world to bear temptation and resist evil that man might have power to take hold of His strength. The soul that comes to Christ by living faith receives His power and is healed of his disease.

Today we are combining the work of ministry and of healing as we have never done before. We are working to educate our people how to treat the body in sickness, how to regain health, and how to keep well when health is restored.—Manuscript 95, 1908.

Genuine Missionaries as Pioneers

One night I was awakened and instructed to write a straight testimony regarding the work of our school at Loma Linda. By that school a solemn and sacred work was to be done. The teachings of health reform were to stand out clearly and brightly, that all the youth in attendance might learn to practice then. All our educators should be strict health reformers. The Lord desires that genuine missionaries shall go out as pioneers from our schools. They are to be fully consecrated to the work as laborers together with God, daily enlarging their sphere of usefulness and becoming more fully sanctified through the truth. The influence of a consecrated medical missionary teacher in our schools is invaluable.—Manuscript 31, 1908.

The Medical Student

While seeking a preparation for his lifework, the medical student should be encouraged to attain the highest possible development of all his powers. His studies, taxing though they are, need not necessarily undermine his physical health or lessen his enjoyment of spiritual things. Throughout his course of study he may continually grow in grace and in a knowledge of truth, while at the same time he may be constantly adding to the store of knowledge that will make him a wise practitioner.

To medical students I would say, Enter upon your course of study with a determination to do right and to maintain Christian principles. Flee temptation, and avoid every influence for evil. Preserve your integrity of soul. Maintain a conscientious regard for truth and righteousness. Be faithful in the smaller responsibilities, and show yourselves to be close, critical thinkers, having soundness of heart and uprightness, being loyal to God and true to mankind.

[64]

Opportunities

Opportunities are before you; if studious and upright, you may obtain an education of the highest value. Make the most of your privileges. Be not satisfied with ordinary attainments; seek to qualify yourselves to fill positions of trust in connection with the Lord's work in the earth. United with the God of wisdom and power, you may become intellectually strong, and increasingly capable as soul winners. You may become men and women of responsibility and influence, if, by the power of your will coupled with divine strength, you earnestly engage in the work of securing a proper training.

Exercise the mental powers, and in no case neglect the physical. Let not intellectual slothfulness close up your path to greater knowledge. Learn to reflect as well as to study, that your minds may expand, strengthen, and develop. Never think that you have learned enough and that you may now relax your efforts. The cultivated mind is the measure of the man. Your education should continue during your lifetime; every day you should be learning, and putting to practical use the knowledge gained.

In order for you to become men and women that can be depended upon, there must be a growth of the powers, the exercise of every faculty, even in little things; then greater power is acquired to bear larger responsibilities. Individual responsibility and accountability are essential. In putting into practice that which you are learning during your student days, do not shrink from bearing your share of responsibility because there are risks to take, because something must be ventured. Do not leave others to be brains for you. You must train your powers to be strong and vigorous; then the entrusted talents will grow, as a steady, uniform, unyielding energy is exercised in bearing individual responsibility. God would have you add, day by day, little by little, to your stock of ideas, acting as if the moments were jewels to be carefully gathered and discreetly cherished. You will thus acquire breadth of thought and strength of intellect.

No Wasted Hours

God will not require of man a more strict account of anything than of the way in which he has occupied his time. Have its hours been wasted and abused? God has granted to us the precious boon of life, not to be devoted to selfish gratification. Our work is too solemn, our time to serve God and our fellowmen too short, to be spent in seeking for fame. Oh, if men would stop in their aspirations where God has set the bounds, what different service would the Lord receive!

Thoroughness

There are many who are in such haste to climb to distinction that they skip some of the rounds of the ladder and in so doing lose experience which they must have in order to become intelligent workers. In their zeal, the knowledge of many things looks unimportant to them. They skim over the surface, and do not go deep into the mine of truth, thus by a slow and painstaking process gaining an experience that will enable them to be of special help to others. We want our medical students to be men and women who are most thorough, and who feel it their duty to improve every talent lent them, that they may finally double their entrusted capital.

The light that God has given in medical missionary lines will not cause His people to be regarded as inferior in scientific medical knowledge, but will fit them to stand upon the highest eminence. God would have them stand as a wise and understanding people because of His presence with them. In the strength of Him who is the source of all wisdom, all grace, defects and ignorance may be overcome.

A High Aim

Let every medical student aim to reach a high standard. Under the discipline of the greatest of all teachers our course must ever tend upward to perfection. All who are connected with the medical missionary work must be learners. Let no one stop to say, "I cannot do this." Let him say instead, "God requires me to be perfect. He expects me to work away from all commonness and cheapness, and to strive after that which is of the highest order."

There is only one power that can make medical students what they ought to be, and keep them steadfast—the grace of God and the power of the truth exerting a saving influence upon life and character. These students, who intend to minister to suffering humanity, will find no graduating place this side of heaven. That knowledge which is termed science should be acquired, while the seeker daily acknowledges that the fear of God is the beginning of wisdom. Everything that will strengthen the mind should be cultivated to the utmost of their power, while at the same time they should seek God for wisdom; for unless they are guided by the wisdom from above, they will become an easy prey to the deceptive power of Satan. They will become large in their own eyes, pompous, and self-sufficient.

Integrity of Students

The teachers in our medical college should encourage the students to gain all the knowledge they can in every department. If they find any students deficient in care-taking, in a comprehension of their responsibilities, they should lay the matter frankly before such ones, giving them an opportunity to correct their habits and to reach a higher standard.

The teachers should not become discouraged because some are slow to learn. Neither should they discourage the students when mistakes are made. As errors and defects are kindly pointed out, the students in turn should feel grateful for any instruction given. A haughty spirit on the part of the students should not be encouraged. All should be willing to learn, and the teachers should be willing to instruct, training the students to be self-reliant, competent, careful, painstaking. As the students study under wise instructors, and unite with them in sharing responsibilities, they may by the aid of the teachers climb to the topmost round of the ladder.

Students should be willing to work under those of experience, to heed their suggestions, to follow their advice, and to go as far as possible in thought, training, and intelligent enterprise; but they should never infringe upon a rule, never disregard one principle, that has been interwoven with the upbuilding of the institution. The dropping down is easy enough; the disregard of regulations is natural to the heart inclined to selfish ease and gratification. It is much easier to tear down than to build up. One student with careless ideas may do more to let down the standard than ten men with all their effort can do to counteract the demoralizing influence....

Without Boasting

God-fearing physicians speak modestly of their work; but novices with limited experience in dealing with the bodies and souls of men will often speak boastingly of their knowledge and attainments. These need a better understanding of themselves; then they would become more intelligent in regard to their duties and would realize that in every department where they have to labor they must possess a willing mind, an earnest spirit, and a hearty, unselfish zeal in trying to do others good. They will not study how best to preserve their dignity, but by thoughtfulness and care-taking will earn a reputation for thoroughness and exactitude, and by sympathetic ministry will gain the hearts of those whom they serve.

In the medical profession there are many skeptics and atheists who exalt the works of God above the God of science. Comparatively few of those who enter worldly medical colleges come out from them pure and unspotted. They have failed to become elevated, ennobled, sanctified. Material things eclipse the heavenly and eternal. With many, religious faith and principles are mingled with worldly customs and practices, and pure and undefiled religion is rare. But it is the privilege of every student to enter college with the same fixed, determined principle that Daniel had when he entered the court of Babylon, and throughout his course to keep his integrity untarnished.

Victory

The strength and grace of God have been provided at an infinite sacrifice, that men might be victorious over Satan's suggestions and temptations and come forth unsullied. The life, the words, and the deportment are the most forcible argument, the most solemn appeal, to the careless, irreverent, and skeptical. Let the life and character be the strong argument for Christianity; then men will be compelled to take knowledge of you that you have been with Jesus and have learned of Him.

Let not medical students be deceived by the wiles of the devil or by any of his cunning pretexts which so many adopt to beguile and ensnare. Stand firm to principle. At every step inquire, "What saith the Lord?" Say firmly, "I will follow the light. I will respect and honor the Majesty of truth."

Especially should those who are studying medicine in the schools of the world guard against contamination from the evil influences with which they are constantly surrounded. When their instructors are worldly wisemen, and their fellow students infidels who have no serious thought of God, even Christians of experience are in danger of being influenced by these irreligious associations. Nevertheless, some have gone through the medical course and have remained true to principle. They would not continue their studies on the Sabbath; and they have proved that men may become qualified for the duties of a physician, and not disappoint the expectations of those who have encouraged them to obtain an education.

Welfare of Patients

In training workers to care for the sick, let the student be impressed with the thought that his highest aim should always be to look after the spiritual welfare of his patients. He should learn to repeat the promises of God's word and to offer fervent prayers daily, while preparing for service. Help him to realize that he is always to keep the sweetening, sanctifying influence of the great Medical Missionary before his patients. If those who are suffering can be impressed with the fact that Christ is their sympathizing, compassionate Saviour, they will have rest of mind, which is so essential to recovery of health.

Preparatory Education

It is because of these peculiar temptations which our youth must meet in worldly medical schools that provision should be made for preparatory and advanced medical training in our own schools, under Christian teachers. Our larger union conference training schools in various parts of the field should be placed in the most favorable position for qualifying our youth to meet the entrance requirements specified by state laws regarding medical students. The very best teaching talent should be secured, that our schools may be brought up to the proper standard. The youth, and those more advanced in years, who feel it their duty to fit themselves for work requiring the passing of certain legal tests, should be able to secure at our union conference training schools all that is essential for entrance into a medical college.

Prayer will accomplish wonders for those who give themselves to prayer, watching thereunto. God desires us all to be in a waiting, hopeful position. What He has promised, He will do; and inasmuch as there are legal requirements making it necessary that medical students shall take a certain preparatory course of study, our colleges should arrange to carry their students to the point of literary and scientific training that is necessary.

And not only should our larger training schools give this preparatory instruction to those who contemplate taking a medical course, but we must also do all that is essential for the perfecting of the courses of study offered by our Loma Linda College of Medical Evangelists. As pointed out about the time this school was founded, we must provide that which is essential to qualify our youth who desire to be physicians, so that they may intelligently fit themselves to stand the examinations required to prove their efficiency a physicians. They should be taught to treat understandingly the cases of those who are diseased, so that the door will be closed for any sensible physician to imagine that we are not giving in our school the instruction necessary for properly qualifying young men and women to do the work of a physician. Continually the students who are graduated are to advance in knowledge, for practice makes perfect....

Importance of Bible Study

If medical students will study the word of God diligently, they will be far better prepared to understand their other studies; for enlightenment always comes from an earnest study of the word of God. Nothing else will so help to give them a retentive memory as a study of the Scriptures. Let our medical missionary workers understand that the more they become acquainted with God and with Christ, and the more they become acquainted with Bible history, the better prepared will they be to do their work.

Bible Classes [70]

Faithful teachers should be placed in charge of the Bible classes, teachers who will strive to make the students understand their lessons, not by explaining everything to them, but by requiring them to explain clearly every passage they read. Let these teachers remember that little good is accomplished by skimming over the surface of the word. Thoughtful investigation and earnest, taxing study are necessary to an understanding of this word.

Christ, the great Medical Missionary, came to this world at infinite sacrifice, to teach men and women the lessons that would enable them to know God aright. He lived a perfect life, setting an example that all may safely follow. Let our medical students study the lessons that Christ has given. It is essential that they have a clear understanding of these lessons. It would be a fearful mistake for them to neglect the study of God's word for study of theories which are misleading, which divert minds from the words of Christ to the fallacies of human production. God would have all who profess to be gospel medical missionaries learn diligently the lessons of the Great Teacher. This they must do if they would find rest and peace. Learning of Christ, their hearts will be filled with the peace that He alone can give.

Make the Bible the man of your counsel. Your acquaintance with it will grow rapidly if you keep your minds free from the rubbish of the world. The more the Bible is studied, the deeper will be your knowledge of God. The truths of His word will be written in your soul, making an ineffaceable impression.

These things God has been opening before me for many years. In our medical missionary training schools we need men who have a deep knowledge of the Scriptures, men who can teach these lessons to others clearly and simply just as Christ taught His disciples that which He deemed most essential.

And the needed knowledge will be given to all who come to Christ, receiving and practicing His teachings, making His word a part of their lives. The Holy Spirit teaches the student of the Scriptures to judge all things by the standard of righteousness and truth and justice. The divine revelation supplies him with the knowledge that he needs. Those who place themselves under the instruction of the great Medical Missionary, to be workers together with Him, will have a knowledge that the world, with all its traditionary lore, cannot supply.—Counsels to Parents, Teachers, and Students, 474-484

Development of Experience

Spiritual Growth

To every student who is seeking a medical education I would say, Look beyond the present. Turn away from the transitory things of this life, from selfish pursuits and gratifications. For what purpose are you seeking an education? Is it not that you may relieve suffering humanity? As the mind is enlarged by true knowledge, the heart is warmed by a sense of the goodness, compassion, and love of God. The soul is filled with an earnest longing to tell others how they may cooperate with the great Master Worker. You will do much for yourselves as you impart the knowledge you receive. Thus you will gain more knowledge to impart, and your ability to work for God will increase

There are those who will suggest to you that in order to be successful in your profession you must be a policy man; you *must* at times depart from strict rectitude. These temptations find a ready welcome in the heart of man; but I speak that which I know. Do not be deceived or deluded. Do not pamper self. Do not throw open a door through which the enemy may enter to take possession of the soul. There is danger in the first and slightest departure from the strictest rectitude. Be true to yourself. Preserve your God-given dignity in the fear of God. There is great need that every medical worker get hold and keep hold of the arm of Infinite Power.

Be True

The policy principle is one that will assuredly lead into difficulties. He who regards the favor of men as more desirable than the favor of God will fall under the temptation to sacrifice principle for worldly gain or recognition. Thus fidelity to God is constantly being sacrificed. Truth, God's truth, must be cherished in the soul and held in the strength of heaven, or the power of Satan will wrest it from you. Never entertain the thought that an honest, truthful physician cannot succeed. Such a sentiment dishonors the God of truth and righteousness. He *can* succeed; for he has God and heaven on his side. Let every bribe to dissimulate be sternly refused. Hold fast your integrity in the strength of the grace of Christ, and He will fulfill His word to you.

The medical student, however young, has access to the God of Daniel. Through divine grace and power he may become as efficient in his calling as Daniel was in his exalted position. But it is a mistake to make a scientific preparation the all-important thing, while religious principles which lie at the very foundation of a successful practice are neglected. Many are lauded as skillful men in their profession who scorn the thought that they need to rely upon Christ for wisdom in their work. But if these men who trust in their knowledge of science were illuminated by the light of heaven, to how much greater excellence might they attain! How much stronger would be their powers, with how much greater confidence could they undertake difficult cases! The man who is closely connected with the Great Physician has the resources of heaven and earth at his command, and he can work with a wisdom, an unerring precision, that the godless man cannot possess.

Like Enoch, the physician should be a man who walks with God. This will be to him a safeguard against all the delusive, pernicious sentiments which make so many infidels and skeptics. The truth of God, practiced in the life and constantly guiding in all that concerns the interests of others, will barricade the soul with heavenly principles. God will not be unmindful of our struggles to maintain the truth. When we place every word that proceeds out of the mouth of God above worldly policy, above all the assertions of erring, failing men, we shall be guided into every good and holy way.

The Christian physician, in his acceptance of the truth by his baptismal vows, has pledged himself to represent Christ, the Physician in chief. But if he does not keep strict guard over himself, if he allows the barriers against sin to be broken down, Satan will overcome him with specious temptations. There will be a blemish in his character that by its evil influence will mold other minds. The moral palsy of sin will not only destroy the soul of the one who departs from strict principles, but will have the power to reproduce in others the same evil.

Be Steadfast

It is not safe to be occasional Christians. We must be Christlike in our actions all the time. Then, through grace, we are safe for time and for eternity. The experimental knowledge of the power of grace received in times of trial is of more value than gold or silver. It confirms the faith of the trusting, believing one. The assurance that Jesus is to him an ever-present Helper gives him a boldness that enables him to take God at His word, and trust Him with unwavering faith under the most trying circumstances.

Our only security against falling into sin is to keep ourselves constantly under the molding influence of the Holy Spirit, at the same time engaging actively in the cause of truth and righteousness, discharging every God-given duty, but taking no burden that God has not laid upon us. Physicians and medical students must stand firm under the banner of the third angel's message, fighting the good fight of faith perseveringly and successfully, relying not on their own wisdom, but on the wisdom of God, putting on the heavenly armor, the equipment of God's word, never forgetting that they have a Leader who never has been and never can be overcome by evil.

Study Your Leader

To every medical student who desires to be an honor to the cause of God during the closing scenes of this earth's history, I would say: Behold Christ, the Sent of God, who in this world and in human nature lived a pure, noble, perfect life, setting an example that all may safely follow. The Lord is reaching out His hand to save. Respond to His invitation, "Let him take hold of My strength, that he may make peace with Me; and he shall make peace with Me." Isaiah 27:5.... How eagerly the Saviour will take the trembling hand in His own, holding it with a warm, firm grasp, until the feet are placed on vantage ground! ...

Trust in Him who understands your weakness. Keep close to the side of Christ; for the enemy stands ready to take captive everyone who is off his guard....

It is young men whom the Lord claims as His helping hand. Samuel was a mere child when the Lord used him to do a good and gracious work....

To those who with steadfast perseverance strive to reveal the attributes of Christ, angels are commissioned to give enlarged views of His character and work, His power and grace and love. Thus they become partakers of His nature, and day by day grow up to the full stature of men and women in Christ. The sanctification of the Spirit is seen in thought, word, and deed. Their ministry is life and salvation to all with whom they associate. Of such ones it is declared, "Ye are complete in Him." Colossians 2:10.—Counsels to Parents, Teachers, and Students, 485-491

Caution Needed in Encouraging Students

Many, knowing how trying are the duties of the physician and how few opportunities physicians have for release from care, even upon the Sabbath, will not choose this for their lifework. But the great enemy is constantly seeking to destroy the workmanship of God's hands, and men of culture and intelligence are called for to combat his cruel power. More of the right kind of men are needed to devote themselves to this profession. Painstaking effort should be made to induce suitable men to qualify themselves for this work. They should be men whose characters are based upon the broad principles of the word of God—men who possess a natural energy, force, and perseverance that will enable them to reach a high standard of excellence.

It is not everyone who can make a successful physician. Many have entered upon the duties of this profession in every way unprepared. They have not the requisite knowledge, neither have they the skill and tact, the carefulness and intelligence, necessary to ensure success. A physician can do much better if he has physical strength. If he is feeble, he cannot endure the wearing labor incident to his calling. A man who has a weak constitution, who is a dyspeptic, or who is lacking in self-control, cannot become qualified to deal with all classes of disease. Great care should be taken not to encourage persons who might be useful in some less responsible position, to study medicine at a great outlay of time and means, when there is no reasonable hope that they will succeed.

[75] I have been instructed that in view of the trying nature of medical missionary work, those who desire to take up this line should first be thoroughly examined by competent physicians to ascertain whether or not they have the strength necessary to endure the course of study through which they must pass in the training school.—Counsels to Parents, Teachers, and Students, 472-473

A Call for the Best Talent

The Lord calls for the best talents to be united at this center [Loma Linda] for the carrying on of the work as He has directed—not the talent that will demand the largest salary, but the talent that will place itself on the side of Christ to work in His lines. We must have medical instructors who will teach the science of healing without the use of drugs.... We are to prepare a company of workers who will follow Christ's methods.—Letter 196, 1908.

The High Order of the Loma Linda School

Here we have ideal advantages for a school and for a sanitarium. Here are advantages for the students, and great advantages for the patients. I have been instructed that here we should have a school conducted on the principles of the ancient schools of the prophets. It may not be carried on in every respect as are the schools of the world, but it is to be especially adapted for those who desire to devote their lives, not to commercial pursuits, but to unselfish service for the Master.

We want a school of the highest order—a school where the word of God will be regarded as essential and where obedience to its teachings will be taught. For the carrying forward of such a school, we must have carefully selected educators. Our young people are not to be wholly dependent on the schools where they are told, "If you wish to complete your course of instruction, you must take this study, or some other study"—studies that perhaps would be of no practical benefit to those whose only desire is to give to the world God's message of health and peace. In the education that many receive, there are not only subjects that are nonessential, but much that is decidedly objectionable. We should endeavor to give instruction that will prepare students quickly for service to their fellowmen.

We are to seek for students who will plow deep into the word of God, and who will conform the life practice to the truths of the word. Let the education given be such as will qualify consecrated young men and young women to go forth in harmony with the great commission....

Physicians are to receive their education here. Here they are to receive such a mold that when they go out to labor, they will not seek to grasp the very highest wages or else do nothing.—Talk given by E. G. W., Oct. 30, 1907. Manuscript 151, 1907.

Who Should Apply

Only those whose hearts are filled with the love of God and who reveal that Christ has given them His grace to adorn their office work as missionaries for Him, should make application to engage in medical missionary work. Those who take up this line of missionary effort should look upon their work as a high and holy calling. This work is committed to them as a sacred trust; and wherever they may be, the Lord expects them to reveal the excellency of their mission.—Letter 186, 1903.

Students Should Have Moral Strength

In almost every church there are young men and women who might receive education either as nurses or physicians.... I would urge that this subject be considered prayerfully, that special effort be made to select those youth who give promise of usefulness and moral strength.—Counsels on Health, 506-507

Strength of Character Essential

Many of the young men who present themselves as being desirous of being educated as physicians have not those traits of character which will enable them to withstand the temptations so common to the work of a physician. Only those should be accepted who give promise of becoming qualified for the great work of imparting the principles of true health reform.—Letters from Ellen G. White to Sanitarium Workers, No. 15, 21.

Amenable to Authority

The first appearance of irregularity in conduct should be repressed, and the young should be taught to be frank, yet modest and dignified in all their associations. They should be taught to respect just rules of authority. If they refuse to do this, let them be dismissed, whatever position they occupy, or they will demoralize others.—Selections from the Testimonies for Students and Workers of our Sanitariums, No. 16, 3.

Mental and Physical Effort Proportionate

Youth who are kept in school, and confined to close study, cannot have sound health. Mental effort without corresponding physical exercise calls an undue proportion of blood to the brain, and thus the circulation is unbalanced. The brain has too much blood, while the extremities have too little. The hours of study and recreation should be carefully regulated, and a portion of the time should be spent in physical labor. When the habits of students in eating and drinking, dressing and sleeping, are in accordance with physical law, they can obtain an education without sacrificing health. The lesson must be often repeated, and pressed home to the conscience, that education will be of little value if there is no physical strength to use it after it is gained.

Students should not be permitted to take so many studies that they will have no time for physical training. The health cannot be preserved unless some portion of each day is given to muscular exertion in the open air. Stated hours should be devoted to manual labor of some kind, anything which will call into action all parts of the body. Equalize the taxation of the mental and physical powers, and the mind of the student will be refreshed. If he is diseased, physical exercise will often help the system to recover its normal condition. When students leave college they should have better health and a better understanding of the laws of life than when they entered it. The health should be as sacredly guarded as the character.

Dull Minds and Dietetic Errors

Many students are deplorably ignorant of the fact that diet exerts a powerful influence upon the health. Some have never made a determined effort to control the appetite or to observe proper rules in regard to diet. They eat too much, even at their meals, and some eat between meals whenever the temptation is presented. If those who profess to be Christians desire to solve the questions so perplexing to them, why their minds are so dull, why their religious aspirations are so feeble, they need not, in many instances, go farther than the table; here is cause enough, if there were no other.

The Teacher's Health Habits

Many separate themselves from God by their indulgence of appetite. He who notices the fall of a sparrow, who numbers the very hairs of the head, marks the sin of those who indulge perverted appetite at the expense of weakening the physical powers, benumbing the intellect, and deadening the moral perceptions.

The teachers themselves should give proper attention to the laws of health, that they may preserve their own powers in the best possible condition, and by example as well as by precept may exert a right influence upon their pupils. The teacher whose physical powers are already enfeebled by disease or overwork should pay special attention to the laws of life. He should take time for recreation. He should not take upon himself responsibility outside of his schoolwork which will so tax him, physically or mentally, that his nervous system will be unbalanced; for in this case he will be unfitted to deal with minds and cannot do justice to himself or to his pupils.

Our institutions of learning should be provided with every facility for instruction regarding the mechanism of the human system. Students should be taught how to breathe, how to read and speak so that the strain will not come on the throat and lungs, but on the abdominal muscles. Teachers need to educate themselves in this direction. Our students should have a thorough training, that they may enter upon active life with an intelligent knowledge of the habitation which God has given them. Teach them that they must be learners as long as they live. And while you are teaching them, remember that they will teach others. Your lessons will be repeated for the benefit of many more than sit before you day by day.—F.E. 146-148.

Educate in the Simplicity of Christ

The Lord has instructed us that in our institutions of education we should ever be striving for the perfection of character to be found in the life of Christ and in His instruction to His disciples. Having received our commission from the highest authority, we are to educate, educate, educate, in the simplicity of Christ. Our aim must be to reach the highest standard in every feature of our work. He who healed thousands with a touch and a word is our Physician. The precious truths contained in His teachings are to be our front guard and our rereward.

The standard set for our sanitariums and schools is a high one, and a great responsibility rests upon the physicians and teachers connected with these institutions. Efforts should be made to secure teachers who will instruct after Christ's manner of teaching, regarding this of more value than any human methods. Let them honor the educational standards established by Christ, and following His instruction give their students lessons in faith and in holiness.

Christ was sent of the Father to represent His character and will. Let us follow His example in laboring to reach the people where they are. Teachers who are not particular to harmonize with the teachings of Christ, and who follow the customs and practices of worldly physicians, are out of line with the charge that the Saviour has given us.—Letter 61, 1910.

Count the Cost

I have had presented before me the fact that in your class of medical missionary students are those whose first work should be to understand themselves, to count the cost and know when they begin to build whether they are able to finish. Let not God be dishonored by breaking down the man in the process of educating him; for a broken-down, discouraged man is a burden to himself. To think that in any work that he may plan to do God will sustain him, while he piles upon himself studies and subjects himself to exposures that imperil health and life and violate the laws of nature, is contrary to the light that God has given. Nature will not be imposed upon. She will not forgive the injuries done to the wonderful, delicate machinery.

The pale, weak student is a continual reproach to health reform. Far better would it be for students to go outdoors and work in the soil. Exercise is good. God designs that all parts of the human machinery shall be worked. There should be regular hours for working, regular hours for eating, without studying the exact cost of every article of food and providing the cheapest kind. Procure those articles of food that are the best for making steam to run the living machinery. There is no extravagance in providing those articles of food that the system can best take in and digest and send to every part of the living organization that all may be nourished.

He Must Know Himself

This is the first duty of every student. No one is to measure out what he supposes his fellow student is capable of doing. Let every student reason soundly regarding what he can endure. Each has an individuality that no one can handle as successfully as himself. No one can submerge his identity in another's. He must know himself, and give himself a favorable chance to come forth with an unbroken constitution, with a clear mind, with well-balanced nerves, and a good digestion. With these, he will be fitted to do the work he has qualified himself to do. If he disqualifies himself by imprudence, by eating hurriedly because he has little time to spend, he is unfitting himself for ever doing sound, wholesome work....

Accountability to God

The first and highest and most acceptable missionary work that the student can do is to obey God in all he undertakes, in every action of the wonderful machinery God devised in the formation of man. He is not to treat himself indifferently; he is to know himself, and work with an intelligent knowledge of what he can do, and do safely, and what he should avoid in eating and in working.... A disordered stomach means a disordered mind.

I would say to each student, You need to take yourself in hand, and let no one whip up your tired nerves and muscles to meet his individual measurement. You are God's workmanship, and under a full sense of your accountability to God you are to treat yourself aright. Give yourself proper time to sleep. They who sleep give nature time to build up and repair the weary waste of the organism....

Overtaxing the Body

You can do the very best home missionary work by taking care of God's temple.... Do not presume to overtax this wonderful machinery, lest some part give way and bring your work to a standstill.

I am pained as I have presented to me students who are being educated to work for the salvation of the souls and bodies of those perishing around them, but who will themselves perish before they can accomplish that for which they are striving so earnestly. Will all teachers and students learn before they go any further how to treat themselves, that they may intelligently cooperate with God, to bear His message, to do His work, and not be cut off at the very time when they are most needed?

Manual Labor in the Schools

In all our educational institutions physical and mental work should have been combined. In vigorous physical exercise, the animal passions find a healthy outlet and are kept in proper bounds.

Healthful exercise in the open air will strengthen the muscles, encourage a proper circulation of blood, help to preserve the body from disease, and will be a great help in spirituality. For many years it has been presented to me that teachers and students should unite in this work. This was done anciently in the schools of the prophets.—Letter 116, 1898.

Study Practical Matters

Too great devotion to study, even of true science, creates an abnormal appetite, which increases as it is fed. This creates a desire to secure more knowledge than is essential to do the work of the Lord. The pursuit of knowledge merely for its own sake diverts the mind from devotion to God and checks advance along the path of practical holiness.... The Lord Jesus imparted only such a measure of instruction as could be utilized.... The minds of the disciples were often excited by curiosity; but instead of gratifying their desire to know things which were not necessary for the proper conduct of their work, He opened new channels of thought to their minds. He gave them much needed instruction upon practical godliness....

Intemperance in Study

Intemperance in study is a species of intoxication, and those who indulge in it, like the drunkard, wander from safe paths and stumble and fall in the darkness. The Lord would have every student bear in mind that the eye must be kept single to the glory of God. He is not to exhaust and waste his physical and mental powers in seeking to acquire all possible knowledge of the sciences, but is to preserve the freshness and vigor of all his powers to engage in the work which the Lord has appointed him in helping souls to find the path of righteousness.—Counsels to Parents, Teachers, and Students, 405-406

Not Amusements, but Consecrated Work

There are some who feel that if there is prosperity here [Loma Linda], it will be necessary to get up some amusement. Let us not cherish such thoughts as this. Rather let the people see that you have a mind for usefulness and duty, and that to the saving of the soul. The amusements that consume time, just to gratify self, do not pay....

Some will think that by having amusements here we will gain more influence. But what we want is to go steadily forward, with our hands firmly holding the divine promise, believing that Christ will lead and guide and bless and place a heavenly stamp upon our work. Do not feel that there is not enough in all that we have to do in this place for Christ and heaven, and that you must reach out for some amusement outside of your God-given work. Do not do it; for this will not harmonize with Christ's example. Stand solidly for God. Tell the students, Here we have Riverside and other places. If you want to do a good work, take our publications and carry them to these places. Hold meetings, and let the people see that you have a living connection with heaven.—Manuscript 9, 1911.

Missionary Labor

Encourage the students to greater activity in missionary labor while taking their course of study.—Manuscript 53, 1909.

Let Not Truth Be Supplanted

Students are authorized to go to school for a certain length of time, in order to acquire scientific knowledge; but in doing this they should ever consider their physical necessities, and seek their education in such a way as not to injure in the least the temple of the body. Let them be sure not to indulge in any sinful practice, not to burden themselves with too many studies, not to become so absorbed in devotion to their studies that the truth will be supplanted, the knowledge of God expelled from the soul, by the inventions of men.

Let every moment that is devoted to study be a moment in which the soul is conscious of its God-given responsibilities. There will be no need then of enjoining the students to be true and just and to preserve their soul's integrity. They will breathe a heavenly atmosphere, and every transaction will be inspired by the Holy Spirit, and equity and righteousness will be revealed.

But if the body is neglected, if unsuitable hours are consumed in study, if the mind is overtaxed, if the physical powers are left unemployed and become enfeebled, then the human machinery is trammeled, and matters that are essential for our future welfare and eternal peace are neglected. Book knowledge is made all-important, and God is dishonored....

Many are ruining themselves physically, mentally, and morally by overdevotion to study. They are defrauding themselves for time and eternity through practicing habits of intemperance in seeking to gain an education. They are losing their desire to learn, in the school of Christ, lessons of meekness and lowliness of heart. Every moment that passes is fraught with eternal results. Integrity will be the sure result of following in the way of righteousness.—Special Testimonies On Education, 126, 127.

Advice to Those Having Limited Powers of Endurance

I have been instructed that in view of the trying nature of medical missionary work, those who desire to take up this line should first be thoroughly examined by competent physicians, to ascertain whether or not they have the strength necessary to endure the course of study through which they must pass in the training school.

If they are not able to carry a line of mental work covering a period of two, three, or five years, as the case may be, they should be told this, and counseled to spend their summer vacations in working in the open air; or, if unable to stand the strain of constant schoolwork, they should be counseled to spend much of their time in outdoor work, and to study books by themselves. If they are careful to exercise sufficiently, the brain will be clear to grasp the subjects that they study alone, and their progress will be rapid. Let them endeavor to treat the sick, as they have opportunity, putting into practice the theory that they gain from the study of books. I have been instructed that in many instances more practical knowledge can be obtained in this way than by a long course of study in a medical school.—Manuscript 123, 1902.

Our Relation to Legal Requirements

Some questions have been asked me regarding our relation to the laws governing medical practitioners. We need to move understandingly, for the enemy would be pleased to hedge up our work so that our physicians would have only a limited influence. Some men do not act in the fear of God, and they may seek to bring us into trouble by placing on our necks yokes that we could not consent to bear. We cannot submit to regulations if the sacrifice of principles is involved; for this would imperil the soul's salvation.

But whenever we can comply with the law of the land without putting ourselves in a false position, we should do so. Wise laws have been framed in order to safeguard the people against the imposition of unqualified physicians. These laws we should respect, for we are ourselves by them protected from presumptuous pretenders. Should we manifest opposition to these requirements, it would tend to restrict the influence of our medical missionaries.

We must carefully consider what is involved in these matters. If there are conditions to which we could not subscribe, we should endeavor to have these matters adjusted, so that there would not be strong opposition against our physicians. The Saviour bids us be wise as serpents, and harmless as doves.

The Lord is our Leader and Teacher. He charges us not to connect with those who do not acknowledge God. "Verily My Sabbaths ye shall keep: for it is a sign between Me and you throughout your generations." Connect with those who honor God by keeping His commandments. If the recommendation goes forth from our people that our workers are to seek for success by acknowledging as essential the education which the world gives, we are virtually saying that the influence the world gives is superior to that which God gives. God will be dishonored by such a course. God has full knowledge of the faith and trust and confidence that His professed people have in His providence.

Our workers are to become intelligent in regard to Christ's life and manner of working. The Lord will help those who desire to cooperate with Him as physicians, if they will become learners of Him how to work for the suffering. He will exercise His power through them for the healing of the sick.

Cooperation with the Great Physician

Intemperance and ungodliness are increasing everywhere. The work of temperance must begin in our own hearts. And the work of the physician must begin in an understanding of the works and teachings of the Great Physician. Christ left the courts of heaven that He might minister to the sick and suffering of earth. We must cooperate with the Chief of physicians, walking in all humility of mind before Him. Then the Lord will bless our earnest efforts to relieve suffering humanity. It is not by the use of poisonous drugs that this will be done, but by the use of simple remedies. We should seek to correct false habits and practices, and teach the lessons of self-denial. The indulgence of appetite is the greatest evil with which we have to contend.

The truth brought to light by Christ teaches that humanity, through obedience to the truth as it is in Jesus, may realize power to overcome the corruptions that are in the world through lust. Through living faith in the merits of Christ the soul may be converted and transformed into Christlikeness. Angels of God will be by the side of those who in humbleness of mind learn daily the lessons taught by Christ—Letter 140, 1909.

* * * * *

For Further Study

Loma Linda College of Evangelists:
Testimonies for the Church 9:173-178.
The Workers to Be Trained at Loma Linda:
Counsels to Parents, Teachers, and Students, 465-471.
Students to Cooperate With Church and Ministry:
Counsels on Health, 516, 517 (Testimonies for the Church 6:291).
Importance of Bible Study by Medical Students:
Counsels on Health, 369-37;
Testimonies for the Church 8:156, 157.
Integrity Among Medical Students:
Counsels on Health, 328, 329.

The Peril of Novices as Physicians or Teachers of Health Reform:
Testimonies for the Church 2:375, 385-387.

Section 5—Warning Against Spiritistic Sophistry

Building on the Rock

Christ illustrated character building by a house built on a rock, against which storm and tempest were powerless, and the house built on the sand, which was swept away. We are living in perilous times. Amidst the changing scenes, with heresy and false doctrines coming in that will test the faith of all, the house built on the solid rock cannot be shaken. But when storm and tempest come, the house built on the sand will fall, and great will be the fall of it.

Let us take heed, then, how we build. Let no one build unwisely. The word of God is our only foundation. Every semblance of error will come upon us. Some of these errors will be very specious and attractive, but if received, they would remove the pillars of the foundation that Christ has established and set up a structure of man's building. There are those who seeing, see not, and hearing, hear not, and under Satan's guidance they prepare false foundations for human minds.

Christ's lessons should be studied by everyone. The truth is solid, substantial. This truth is to be presented to all; for Satan will come in with his pleasing sentiments, which make nothingness of God's word and turn aside minds from the truth to fables.—Letter 223, 1905.

Spurious Scientific Theories

Spurious scientific theories are coming in as a thief in the night, stealing away the landmarks and undermining the pillars of our faith. God has shown me that the medical students are not to be educated in such theories, because God will not endorse these theories. The most specious temptations of the enemy are coming in, and they are coming in on the highest, most elevated plane. These spiritualize the doctrines of present truth until there is no distinction between the substance and the shadow.

You know that Satan will come in to deceive if possible the very elect. He claims to be Christ, and he is coming in, pretending to be the great medical missionary. He will cause fire to come down from heaven in the sight of men to prove that he is God. We must stand barricaded by the truths of the Bible. The canopy of truth is the only canopy under which we can stand safely.—Testimonies to the Church Regarding our Youth Going to Battle Creek Obtain An Education, 32-33.

The True Higher Education

Human fallacies are abundant and specious. Unseen agencies are at work to make falsehood appear as truth; errors are clothed with a deceptive garb that men may be led to accept them as essential to a higher education. And these fallacies will deceive many of our students unless they are thoroughly guarded, and unless they are led by the Spirit of God to take the grand and holy truths of the word into their hearts and minds, accepting these as the principles underlying the higher education. No instruction can exceed in value the pure instruction of God, which comes for the enlightenment of all who will be enlightened.

Our students must be educated to understand that there can be no education higher than that which was given by the Great Teacher to the world. We must guard our students from temptation by making the sacred truths of the word of God the basis of their education. This higher knowledge, the knowledge of the glory of God, is to shine into their hearts, that the excellency of the power may be of God and not of men....

Warn every student that he must be wide-awake. Let this truth be firmly fixed upon the mind by our ministers and by all who in faith are acting a part to rid the human mind of error, that there can be no higher education than that which came forth from Him who gave His life that humanity might grasp divinity, and fallen man become one with God. The teacher who is so foolish as to think that he can give to the students a more perfect knowledge than that given by the Great Teacher, Christ Jesus, is ignorant of what constitutes the higher education.—Letter 98, 1909.

Truth Strengthens the Understanding

The word of God, regarded and studied as it should be, will give light and knowledge. Its perusal will strengthen the understanding. By contact with the purest, most lofty truths, the mind will be enlarged, the taste refined.

We are dependent on the Bible for a knowledge of the early history of our world, of the creation of man, and of his fall. Remove the word of God, and what can we expect than to be left to fables and conjectures, and to that enfeebling of the intellect which is the sure result of entertaining error. We need the authentic history of the origin of the earth, of the fall of the covering cherub, and of the introduction of sin into our world. Without the Bible, we should be bewildered by false theories. The mind would be subjected to the tyranny of superstition and falsehood. But having in our possession an authentic history of the beginning of our world, we need not hamper ourselves with human conjectures and unreliable theories.

Wherever Christians are, they may hold communion with God. And they may enjoy the intelligence of sanctified science. Their minds may be strengthened even as Daniel's was. God gave him "knowledge and skill in all learning and wisdom."

Mental Effect of Receiving Error

The mind in which error has once taken possession can never expand freely to truth, even after investigation. The old theories will claim recognition. The understanding of things that are true and elevated and sanctifying will be confused. Superstitious ideas will enter the mind, to mingle with the true, and these ideas are always debasing in their influence. Christian knowledge bears its own stamp of unmeasured superiority in all that concerns the preparation for the future, immortal life. It distinguishes the Bible reader and believer, who has been receiving the precious treasures of truth, from the skeptic and the believer in pagan philosophy.

Cleave to the word, "It is written." Cast out of the mind the dangerous, obtrusive theories which, if entertained, will hold the mind in bondage so that the man shall not become a new creature in Christ. The mind must be constantly restrained and guarded. It must be given as food that only which will strengthen the religious experience.—Manuscript 42, 1904.

The Church is Christ's Fortress

The church is Christ's fortress in a revolted world, and it must be strictly guarded against the enemy's wily arts. In it no laws are to be acknowledged but the laws of God. Those whom God has set as watchmen are not to look on quietly while efforts are being made to lead men and women away from the truth into false paths. Careful watch is to be kept against seducing spirits and doctrines of devils. God calls upon ministers and medical missionaries to take a firm stand for the right. The severe denunciations that Christ uttered against the Pharisees for teaching for doctrine the commandments of men show the necessity for guarding against all theories that are not in harmony with the truth of God's word.—Manuscript 78, 1904.

Exalting Nature Above Nature's God

The general method of educating the youth does not meet the standard of true education. Infidel sentiments are interwoven in the matter placed in schoolbooks, and the oracles of God are placed in a questionable or even an objectionable light. Thus the minds of the youth become familiar with Satan's suggestions, and the doubts once entertained become to those who entertain them assured facts, and scientific research is made misleading on account of the way its discoveries are interpreted and perverted.

Men take it upon themselves to rein up the word of God before a finite tribunal, and sentence is pronounced upon the inspiration of God according to finite measurement, and the truth of God is made to appear as a thing uncertain before the records of science.

Work of False Educators

These false educators exalt nature above nature's God and above the Author of all true science. At the very time when teachers should have been firm and unwavering in their testimony, at the very time when it should have been made manifest that their souls were riveted to the eternal Rock, when they should have been able to inspire faith in those who were doubting, they made admission of their own uncertainty as to whether the word of God or the discoveries of science falsely so-called were true.

Those who were truly conscientious have been made to waver in their faith because of the hesitation of those who were professed expositors of the Bible when they dealt with the living oracles. Satan has taken advantage of the uncertainty of the mind, and through unseen agencies he has crowded in his sophistries and has caused men to become befogged in the mists of skepticism.

Learned men have given lectures in which have been mingled truth and error; but they have unbalanced the minds of those who leaned toward error instead of toward truth. The nicely woven sophistries of the so-called wise men have a charm for a certain class of students; but the impression that these lectures leave upon the mind is that the God of nature is restricted by His own laws.

The Theory of Nature's Immutability

The immutability of nature has been largely dwelt upon, and skeptical theories have been readily adopted by those whose minds chose the atmosphere of doubt because they were not in harmony with God's holy law, the foundation of His government in heaven and earth. Their natural tendency to evil made it easy for them to choose false paths and to doubt the reliability of both the Old and the New Testament's records and history.

Poisoned with error themselves, they have watched every opportunity to sow the seeds of doubt in other minds. Nature is exalted above the God of nature, and the simplicity of faith is destroyed; for the foundation of faith is made to appear uncertain. Befogged in skepticism, the minds of those who doubt are left to beat on the rocks of infidelity.—The Youth's Instructor, January 31, 1895

A Right Knowledge of God

I have a message to bear to those who feel sure that they are prepared to do medical missionary work. Do those engaged in this work realize that we are nearing the end of this earth's history, and that we should understand fully the work before us? The very first thing that medical missionaries need to do is to gain a right conception of God, not a conception based on their own human judgment, but a conception based on a constant study of God's word and of the character and life of Christ.

[92] God's word and His works contain the knowledge of Himself that He has seen fit to reveal to us. We may understand the revelation that He has thus given of Himself. But it is with fear and trembling, and with a sense of our own sinfulness, that we are to take up this study, not with a desire to try to explain God, but with a desire to gain that knowledge which will enable us to serve Him more acceptably.

Let no one venture to explain God. Human beings cannot explain themselves, and how, then, dare they venture to explain the Omniscient One? Satan stands ready to give such ones false conceptions of God.

To the curious I bear the message that God has instructed me not to frame answers to the questions of those who inquire in regard to the things that have not been revealed. The things that are revealed belong unto us and to our children. Beyond this, human beings are not to attempt to go. We are not to attempt to explain that which God has not revealed. We are to study the revelation that Christ, the Great Teacher, has given of the character of God, that in spirit and word and act we may represent Him to those who know Him not.

Where Silence is Eloquence

In regard to the personality and prerogatives of God, where He is, and what He is, this is a subject which we are not to dare to touch. On this theme silence is eloquence. It is those who have no experimental knowledge of God who venture to speculate in regard to Him. Did they know more of Him, they would have less to say about what He is. The one who in the daily life holds closest communion with God, and who has the deepest knowledge of Him, realizes most keenly the utter inability of human beings to explain the Creator....

God always has been. He is the great I AM. The psalmist declares, "Before the mountains were brought forth, or ever Thou hadst formed the earth and the world, even from everlasting to everlasting, Thou art God." He is the high and lofty One that inhabiteth eternity. "I am the Lord, I change not," He declares. With Him there is no variableness, neither shadow of turning. He is "the same yesterday, and today, and forever." He is infinite and omnipresent. No words of ours can describe His greatness and majesty.

The Simplicity of Christ's Teaching [93]

The Bible teaching of God is the only teaching that it is safe for human beings to follow. We are to regulate our faith by a plain "Thus saith the Lord." The knowledge of Himself that God desires us to gain from His word will, if brought into the daily life, make men and women strong to resist evil and fit them to represent Him.

We need to study the simplicity of Christ's teachings. He urges the need of prayer and humility. These are our safeguards against the erroneous reasoning by which Satan seeks to lead us to turn aside to other gods, and to accept misleading theories, clothed by him in garments of light.

A man who is spiritually blind is easily led by those who improve every favorable opportunity to advance theories and conjectures regarding God. The one deceived by Satan imparts to a fellow being the new light that he supposes he has received, as Eve placed the forbidden fruit in the hand of Adam. Unenlightened heathen are in no worse condition spiritually than is the man who has known the truth but has accepted error....

Resisting the Enemy

Satan presents his theories cautiously at first, and if he sees that his efforts are successful, he brings in theories that are still more misleading, seeking to lead men and women away from the foundation principles that God designs shall be the safeguards of His people.

Let not our medical missionary workers accept theories that God has not given to anyone. God will not excuse men for teaching theories that Christ has not taught. He calls upon His army of workers to fall into line, taking their stand under the banner of truth. He warns them to beware of occupying their time in the discussion of matters that God has not authorized any human being to discuss.

Let us put on every piece of the Christian armor, and steadfastly resist the enemy. We shall have to meet fallen angels and the prince of the powers of darkness. Satan is by no means asleep; he is wide-awake, and is playing the game of life for the souls of the people of God. He will come to them with flattery of all kinds, in the hope of leading them to swerve from their allegiance. He desires to call their attention from the real issues to false theories.

A Call to Awake

Ministers and physicians, sound an alarm. Call upon the people of God to be true and faithful. Be on your guard. Remember that as you cooperate with God you have as your helpers angels that excel in strength. Accept not the theories advanced by those who are not standing on the true foundation, those who are charmed with that of which they do not know the true meaning.

Wake up, my brethren, wake up, and lift the danger signal. Sound the warning. Let no man persuade you to accept theories that are opposed to the truths of God's word. The servants of God have a solemn message to bear to this fallen, sin-cursed world. They are to hold aloft the banner on which is inscribed the words, "The commandments of God, and the faith of Jesus."—Manuscript 132, 1903.

God Revealed in His Word and His Works

Let no one teach things that the Redeemer, He who owns man, body, soul, and spirit, has not taught. We need not any fanciful teaching regarding the personality of God. What God desires us to know of Him is revealed in His word and His works. The beautiful things of nature reveal His character and His power as Creator. They are His gift to the race, to show His power and to show that He is a God of love. But no one is authorized to say that God Himself in person is in flower or leaf or tree. These things are God's handiwork, revealing His love for mankind.

But to take the works of God, and represent them as being God, is a fearful misrepresentation of Him. This representation I was called upon to meet at the beginning of my work, when in my youth the Lord commissioned me to go forth and proclaim what He should command me to proclaim. And as the Lord shall direct me, I must now do what I can to counteract all such teaching, and the theories which lead to such views. Those who hold these theories do not know whither their feet are tending.

What we most need is an experimental knowledge of God as He is revealed in His word. Such knowledge would enable us to see our imperfection of character and our ignorance of our Lord and Saviour Jesus Christ....

Conjectures Regarding God

Human talents and human conjecture have tried by searching to find out God. Many have trodden this pathway. The highest intellect may tax itself until it is wearied out, in conjectures regarding God, but the effort will be fruitless, and the fact will remain that man by searching cannot find out God. This problem has not been given us to solve. All that man needs to know and can know of God has been revealed in the life and character of His Son, the Great Teacher. As we learn more and more of what man is, of what we ourselves are, in God's sight, we shall fear and tremble before Him.

Is Man Born a King?

To those who would represent every man as born a king, to those who would make no distinction between the converted and the unconverted, to those who are losing their appreciation of their need of Christ as their Saviour, I would say, Think of yourselves as you have been during the period of your existence! Would it be pleasant or agreeable for you to contemplate feature after feature of your lifework, in the sight of Him who knows every thought of man and before whose eyes all man's doings are as an open book?

Peril in Vanity

I call upon all who are engaged in the service of God to place themselves fully on Christ's side. There are dangers on the right hand and on the left. Our greatest danger will come from men who have lifted up their souls unto vanity, who have not heeded the words of warning and reproof sent them by God. As such men choose their own will and way, the tempter, clothed in angel robes, is close beside them ready to unite his influence with theirs, He opens to them delusions of a most attractive character, which they present to the people of God. Some of those who listen to them will be deceived and will work in dangerous lines.

The Lord calls. Will men and women hear His voice? He gives the warning. Will they heed it? Will they listen to the last message of mercy to a fallen world? Will they accept Christ's yoke and learn from Him His meekness and lowliness?—Letter 240, 1903.

Speculation Regarding God's Personality

Your knowledge of God and of His attributes has been lessened since you have begun to theorize regarding His nature and prerogatives.

The church is now engaged in a warfare that will increase in intensity on the very point on which you have been misled. Not one pillar of our faith is to be moved. Not one line of revealed truth is to be replaced by new and fanciful theories.

In clear lines truth has been given us. Under the guidance of God, books have been prepared which state clearly the truth for this time. If you will not believe these evidences, neither would you believe if one rose from the dead.

You must make thorough work for repentance. Come before God in humiliation and contrition. There must be harmonious working among God's people. We must know who is going to follow the light. "If the Lord be God, follow Him: but if Baal, then follow him."—Letter 247, 1903.

Subtle Theories Regarding God

Let no one beguile you into the belief that God is an essence pervading nature. Such an idea is a specious delusion. Let all be on guard against such suppositions. These subtle theories clothed in beautiful garments prepare the way for greater errors which, if accepted, will lead even conscientious believers in the truth away from their steadfastness, to false doctrines.

From time to time we need unitedly to examine the reasons of our faith. It is essential that we study carefully the truths of God's word; for we read that "some shall depart from the faith, giving heed to seducing spirits, and doctrines of devils [demons]." We are in grave danger when we lightly regard any truth; for then the mind is opened to error. We must take heed how and what we hear. We need not seek to understand the arguments that men offer in support of their theories, when it may be readily discerned that these theories are not in harmony with the Scriptures. Some who think that they have scientific knowledge are by their interpretations giving wrong ideas both of science and of the Bible. Let the Bible decide every question that is essential to man's salvation.—Letter 25, 1904.

Restraint and Moral Control Destroyed

We are not called upon to enter into controversy with those who hold false theories. Controversy is unprofitable. Christ never entered into it. "It is written," is the weapon used by the world's Redeemer. Let us keep close to the word. Let us allow the Lord Jesus and His messengers to testify. We know that their testimony is true.

Christ is over all the works of His creation. In the pillar of fire He guided the children of Israel, His eyes seeing past, present, and future. He is to be recognized and honored by all who love God. His commandments are to be reverenced and cherished and obeyed. They are to be the controlling power in the lives of His people.

The tempter comes with the supposition that Christ has removed His seat of honor and power into some unknown region, and that men need no longer to be inconvenienced by exalting His character and obeying His law. Human beings are to be a law unto themselves, he declares. The sophistries he brings in discount and make nothing of God. Restraint and moral control in the human family are destroyed. Restraint upon vice grows more and more feeble. The world loves not, fears not, God. And those who do not love or fear God soon lose all sense of obligation to one another. They are without God and without hope in the world.—Manuscript 92, 1904.

Not a Thread of Pantheism

From Christ all truth radiates. Apart from Christ, science is misleading and philosophy is foolishness. Those who are separated from the Saviour will advance theories which originate with the wily foe. Christ's life stands out as the contrast of all false science, all erroneous theories, all misleading methods.

Pretenders will arise with theories that have no foundation in the word of God. We are to hold aloft the banner bearing the inscription, "The commandments of God, and the faith of Jesus." We are to hold the beginning of our confidence firm unto the end. Let no one attempt to dilute truth with a mixture of sophistry. Let no one attempt to tear down the foundation of our faith, or to spoil the pattern by bringing into the web threads of human devising. Not one thread of pantheism is to be drawn into the web. Sensuality, ruinous to soul and body, is always the result of drawing these threads into the web.—Letter 249, 1903.

The Issue Foreseen

I have been warned [1890] that henceforth we shall have a constant contest. Science, so called, and religion will be placed in opposition to each other, because finite men do not comprehend the power and greatness of God. These words of Holy Writ were presented to me, "Of your own selves shall men arise, speaking perverse things, to draw away disciples after them."

This will surely be seen among the people of God, and there will be those who are unable to perceive the most wonderful and important truths for this time, truths which are essential for their own safety and salvation, while matters that are in comparison as the merest atoms, matters in which there is scarcely a grain of truth, are dwelt upon and are magnified by the power of Satan so that they appear of the utmost importance. The moral sight of these men is diseased; they do not feel their need of the heavenly anointing that they may discern spiritual things. They think themselves too wise to err.

Men who have not a daily experience in the things of God will not move wisely in dealing with sacred responsibilities; they will mistake light for error, and specious error they will pronounce light, mistaking phantoms for realities and realities for phantoms, calling a world an atom and an atom a world. They will fall into deceptions and delusions that Satan has prepared as concealed nets to entangle the feet of those who think they can walk in their human wisdom without the special grace of Christ. Jesus wants men to see not men as trees walking, but all things clearly. There is only one remedy for the sinful soul, and unless it is received, men will accept one delusion after another until their senses are perverted....

Morality Inseparable from Religion [99]

Morality cannot be separated from religion. Conservative tradition received from educated men and from the writings of great men of the past are not all a safe guide for us in these last days; for the great struggle before us is such as the world has never seen. The brethren who have not acted a part in this work in the past need to move with far greater caution in regard to that which they accept and that which they refuse; they need to penetrate much deeper than their limited spiritual knowledge or their present habits or opinions would lead them to do. All these may need reforming.

We are not one of us safe, even with past experience in the work, and certainly are not safe if we have not had that experience, unless we live as seeing Him who is invisible. Daily, hourly, we must be actuated by the principles of Bible truth—righteousness, mercy, and the love of God. He who would have moral and intellectual power must draw from the divine Source. At every point and decision inquire, Is this the way of the Lord?

With your Bibles open before you consult sanctified reason and a good conscience. Your heart must be moved, your soul touched, your reason and intellect awakened, by the Spirit of God; the holy principles laid down in His word will give light to the soul. I tell you, my brethren, our true source of wisdom and virtue and power is in the cross of Calvary. Christ is the Author and Finisher of our faith. He says, "Without Me ye can do nothing." Jesus is the only sure guarantee for intellectual success and advancement.—Manuscript 16, 1890.

Speculation Regarding the Future Life

There are men today who express their belief that there will be marriages and births in the new earth, but those who believe the Scriptures cannot accept such doctrines. The doctrine that children will be born in the new earth is not a part of the "sure word of prophecy." The words of Christ are too plain to be misunderstood. They should forever settle the question of marriages and births in the new earth. Neither those who shall be raised from the dead, nor those who shall be translated without seeing death, will marry or be given in marriage. They will be as the angels of God, members of the royal family.

Preach the Word

I would say to those who hold views contrary to this plain declaration of Christ: Upon such matters silence is eloquence. It is presumption to indulge in suppositions and theories regarding matters that God has not made known to us in His word. We need not enter into speculation regarding our future state.

To my ministering brethren I would say, "Preach the word; be instant in season, out of season." Do not bring to the foundation wood, and hay, and stubble—your own surmisings and speculations, which can benefit no one.

Christ withheld no truths essential to our salvation. Those things that are revealed are for us and our children, but we are not to allow our imagination to frame doctrines concerning things not revealed.

The Lord has made every provision for our happiness in the future life. But He has made no revelations regarding these plans, and we are not to speculate concerning them. Neither are we to measure the conditions of the future life by the conditions of this life.—Manuscript 28, 1904

Deception Regarding Spiritual Affinity

You have been represented to me as being in great peril. Satan is on your track, and at times he has whispered to you pleasing fables and has shown you charming pictures of one whom he represents as a more suitable companion for you than the wife of your youth, the mother of your children.

Satan is working stealthily, untiringly, to effect your downfall through his specious temptations. He is determined to become your teacher, and you need now to place yourself where you can get strength to resist him. He hopes to lead you into the mazes of spiritualism. He hopes to wean your affections from your wife, and to fix them upon another woman. He desires that you shall allow your mind to dwell upon this woman, until through unholy affection she becomes your god.

The enemy of souls has gained much when he can lead the imagination of one of Jehovah's chosen watchmen to dwell upon the possibilities of association, in the world to come, with some woman whom he loves, and of there raising up a family. We need no such pleasing pictures. All such views originate in the mind of the tempter.

We have the plain assurance of Christ that in the world to come, the redeemed "neither marry, nor are given in marriage: neither can they die anymore: for they are equal unto the angels; and are the children of God, being the children of the resurrection."

It is presented to me that spiritual fables are taking many captive. Their minds are sensual, and, unless a change comes, this will prove their ruin. To all who are indulging these unholy fancies I would say, Stop; for Christ's sake, stop right where you are. You are on forbidden ground. Repent, I entreat of you, and be converted.—Letter 231, 1903.

A Counterfeit Heaven

How untiringly God has kept guard over His church! Shall we not act our part that He may give us the grace that will enable us to attain to perfection of Christian character? Do not allow yourself to be led to think that you will live in heaven while in this fallen world. Those who think this keep their minds on the strain for some wonderful experience that will waft their souls into a refined, spiritual atmosphere. But this is not the true science of Christian experience. When they suppose they have reached spiritual heights of refinement, Satan, in the garb of an angel of light, presents to them indulgences in which he makes it appear there is no sin.

I would warn you against these apparently refined doctrines, which say that sin is not sin, and teach the possibility of living a spiritualistic life above the grossness of sin. I write this because there are minds entering into temptation in regard to this refined science of spiritualistic attainments. You will meet this science, and you will hardly know how to handle it.

We have reached the perils of the last days, when some, yes, many, shall depart from the faith, giving heed to seducing spirits and doctrines of devils. Be cautious in regard to what you read and how you hear. Take not a particle of interest in spiritualistic theories. Satan is waiting to steal a march upon everyone who allows himself to be deceived by his hypnotism. He begins to exert his power over them just as soon as they begin to investigate his theories.—Letter 123, 1904.

Neglecting Fundamental Truths for Idle Speculation

In the word of God are grand truths that are worthy of intense study. Shall we neglect these great fundamental truths in order that we may enter into speculation over what has not been clearly revealed? I am frequently asked, regarding some theoretical doctrine, questions that I feel no liberty to answer. I sometimes reply to those who ask me such questions, "You have the word. If the Lord desired you to know in regard to this matter, you would find your knowledge in the word of God, and would not need to ask me. If we reach heaven, we may then understand the matters that are not clear to us now." Let us study the great truths of the Scriptures; they are sufficient to tax our minds to their utmost capacity.

"This is life eternal, that they might know Thee the only true God, and Jesus Christ, whom Thou hast sent." Oh, do we know God as we should? What comfort, what joy, we should have if we were to learn daily the lessons He desires us to learn! We must know Him by an experimental knowledge. It will be profitable for us to spend more time in secret prayer, in becoming personally acquainted with our heavenly Father. In our weakness we may come to Him and ask Him to impart to us an understanding of what He will do for us in separating from us everything that is unlike His own character.—The Review and Herald, August 15, 1907.

Honoring Superstition and Falsehood

I pray that our people may not fall victims to the snares that Satan has laid to entrap unwary souls. But even now many are bewildered. All need to be independent Bible students. I am writing words of warning, that no one need be deceived by the enemy, to lead others into crooked paths.

I have carried a heavy burden because of the publication of -----. I think that the Lord has permitted this matter to develop in order to arouse our people to understand and value aright the fundamental truths that, as a people, we have received from the word of God. We must know that we have not followed cunningly devised fables. Our Father bids us call to mind the former days, after which, when we were illumined, we endured a great fight of affliction. I have received most precious assurances that our early experiences were of God. I wish that every one of our people might know, as I know, of the sure and certain way in which the Lord led us in times past....

It causes me great sorrow of heart to see that there are among our workers those who do not realize the dangerous character of the doctrines that some are entertaining regarding God. I know how dangerous these sentiments are. Before I was seventeen years old, I had to bear testimony against them before large companies....

Now, false interpretations are being given to the truths of the word, in order that deluded minds may be pleased. Error is made to appear as truth. I am instructed to bear a decided testimony against these misleading theories. I am charged with a message opposed to the heresies and sophistries that are being propagated by Satan. The life and teachings of our Lord give no place to these cunningly devised fables. The loss of eternal life is the price that must be paid for continuing to honor superstition and falsehood above the word of God, making His teaching of no effect.

The character and power of God are revealed by the works of His hands. In the natural world are to be seen evidences of God's love and goodness. These tokens are given to call attention from nature to nature's God, that His "eternal power and Godhead" may be understood.—Letter 262, 1903.

* * * * *

For Further Study

The Essential Knowledge:
The Ministry of Healing, 407-466;

Testimonies for the Church 8:255-335.
(These sections parallel one another, but there are adaptations and variations, because prepared for different classes of readers.)

Dangers in Speculative Study:
Patriarchs and Prophets, 111.

Philosophy and Vain Deceit:
Testimonies For The Church 1:290-302.

Professed Ministers Advocating Speculative Theories:
Testimonies to Ministers and Gospel Workers, 281.

False Theories Will Bring "Shaking":
Testimonies to Ministers and Gospel Workers, 112.

Section 6—True and False Systems of Mind Cure

Happiness and Health

The sympathy which exists between the mind and the body is very great. When one is affected, the other responds. The condition of the mind has much to do with the health of the physical system. If the mind is free and happy under a consciousness of rightdoing and a sense of satisfaction in causing happiness to others, it will create a cheerfulness that will react upon the whole system, causing a freer circulation of the blood and a toning up of the entire body. The blessing of God is a healer; and those who are abundant in benefiting others will realize that wondrous blessing in their hearts and lives.—Testimonies for the Church 4:60.

Thousands Needlessly Sick

Thousands are sick and dying around us who might get well and live if they would; but their imagination holds them. They fear that they will be made worse if they labor or exercise, when this is just the change they need to make them well. Without this they never can improve. They should exercise the power of the will, rise above their aches and debility, engage in useful employment, and forget that they have aching backs, sides, lungs, and heads. Neglecting to exercise the entire body, or a portion of it, will bring on morbid conditions. Inaction of any of the organs of the body will be followed by a decrease in size and strength of the muscles and will cause the blood to flow sluggishly through the blood vessels.—Testimonies for the Church 3:76.

Health Through Service for Others

Those who, so far as it is possible, engage in the work of doing good to others by giving practical demonstration of their interest in them, are not only relieving the ills of human life in helping them bear their burdens, but are at the same time contributing largely to their own health of soul and body. Doing good is a work that benefits both giver and receiver. If you forget self in your interest for others, you gain a victory over your infirmities. The satisfaction you will realize in doing good will aid you greatly in the recovery of the healthy tone of the imagination.

The pleasure of doing good animates the mind and vibrates through the whole body. While the faces of benevolent men are lighted up with cheerfulness, and their countenances express the moral elevation of the mind, those of selfish, stingy men are dejected, cast down, and gloomy. Their moral defects are seen in their countenances....

Invalids, I advise you to venture something. Arouse your willpower, and at least make a trial of this matter. Withdraw your thoughts and affections from yourselves. Walk out by faith. Are you inclined to center your thoughts upon yourselves, fearing to exercise, and fearing that if you expose yourself to the air you will lose your life; resist these thoughts and feelings. Do not yield to your diseased imagination.—Testimonies for the Church 2:534.

Drudgery Versus Healthful Activity

Manual labor quickens the circulation of the blood. The more active the circulation the more free will be the blood from obstructions and impurities. The blood nourishes the body. The health of the body depends upon the healthful circulation of the blood. If work is performed without the heart being in it, it is simply drudgery, and the benefit which should result from the exercise is not gained.—The Health Reformer, May, 1873.

Contentment and Cheerfulness

A contented mind, a cheerful spirit, is health to the body and strength to the soul. Nothing is so fruitful a cause of disease as depression, gloominess, and sadness. Mental depression is terrible.—Testimonies for the Church 1:702.

Enlisting the Willpower

In journeying I have met many who were really sufferers through their imaginations. They lacked willpower to rise above and combat disease of body and mind, and therefore they were held in suffering bondage. A large share of this class of invalids is found among the youth.

I sometimes meet with young women lying in bed sick. They complain of headache. Their pulse may be firm, and they be full in flesh; yet their sallow skins indicate that they are bilious. My thoughts have been that, if I were in their condition, I should know at once what course to pursue to obtain relief. Although I might feel indisposed, I should not expect to recover while lying in bed. I should bring willpower to my aid, and should leave my bed and engage in active physical exercise. I should strictly observe regular habits of rising early. I should eat sparingly, thus relieving my system of unnecessary burden, and should encourage cheerfulness, and give myself the benefits of proper exercise in the open air. I should bathe frequently, and drink freely of pure, soft water. If this course should be followed perseveringly, resisting the inclination to do otherwise, it would work wonders in the recovery of health.

Deceptive Ailments

I feel sad for those who are not only deceived themselves in thinking that they are sick, but who are kept deceived by their parents and friends, who pet their ailments and relieve them from labor. If these were so situated as to be compelled to labor, they would scarcely notice difficulties which, while indolent, keep them in bed. Physical exercise is a precious blessing for both mental and physical ailments. Exercise, with cheerfulness, would in many cases prove a most effective restorer to the complaining invalid. Useful employment would bring into exercise the enfeebled muscles, and would enliven the stagnant blood in the system, and would arouse the torpid liver to perform its work. The circulation of the blood would be equalized and the entire system invigorated to overcome bad conditions.

I frequently turn from the bedside of these self-made invalids, saying to myself, Dying by inches, dying of indolence, a disease which no one but themselves can cure. I sometimes see young men and women who might be a blessing to their parents, if they would share with them the cares and burdens of life. But they feel no disposition to do this, because it is not agreeable but is attended with some weariness. They devote much of their time in vain amusement, to the neglect of duties necessary for them to perform in order to obtain an experience which will be of great value to them in their future battles with the difficulties of real life. They live for the present only, and neglect the physical, mental, and moral qualifications which would fit them for the emergencies of life and give them self-reliance and self-respect in times of trial and of danger.—The Health Reformer, January, 1871, pages 132, 133.

The Holy Spirit as a Restorative

Dr. E. has made a great mistake in regard to exercise and amusements, and a still greater in his teaching concerning religious experience and religious excitement. The religion of the Bible is not detrimental to the health of body or mind. The exalting influence of the Spirit of God is the best restorative for the sick. Heaven is all health, and the more fully the heavenly influences are felt, the more sure the recovery of the believing invalid....

Let invalids do something, instead of occupying their minds with a simple play, which lowers them in their own estimation and leads them to think their lives useless. Keep the power of the will awake, for the will aroused and rightly directed is a potent soother of the nerves. Invalids are far happier to be employed, and their recovery is more easily effected.—Testimonies for the Church 1:556, 557.

Sanctified Mind Cure

The light given me is that if the sister you mention would brace up and cultivate her taste for wholesome food, all these sinking spells would pass away. She has cultivated her imagination; the enemy has taken advantage of her weakness of body, and her mind is not braced to bear up against the hardships of everyday life. It is good, sanctified mind cure she needs, an increase of faith, and active service for Christ. She needs also the exercise of her muscles in outside practical labor. Physical exercise will be to her one of the greatest blessings of her life. She need not be an invalid, but a wholesome-minded, healthy woman, prepared to act her part nobly and well.

All the treatment that may be given to this sister will be of little advantage unless she acts her part. She needs to strengthen muscle and nerve by physical labor. She need not be an invalid, but can do good, earnest labor. Like many others, she has a diseased imagination. But she can overcome and be a healthy woman. I have had this message to give to many, and with the best results.

Chronic Invalidism

Once I was called to see a young woman with whom I was well acquainted. She was sick, and was running down fast. Her mother wished me to pray for her. The mother stood there weeping and saying, "Poor child; she cannot live long." I felt her pulse. I prayed with her, and then addressed her, "My sister, if you get up and dress and go to your usual work in the office, all this invalidism will pass away." "Do you think this would pass away?" she said. "Certainly," I said. "You have nearly smothered the life forces by invalidism." I turned to the mother and told her that her daughter would have died of a diseased imagination if they had not been convinced of their error. She had been educating herself to invalidism. Now this is a very poor school. But I said to her, "Change this order; arise and dress." She was obedient, and is alive today.—Letter 231, 1905.

Indigestion Caused by Fear

Exercise will aid the work of digestion. To walk out after a meal, hold the head erect, put back the shoulders, and exercise moderately, will be a great benefit. The mind will be diverted from self to the beauties of nature. The less the attention is called to the stomach after a meal, the better. If you are in constant fear that your food will hurt you, it most assuredly will. Forget self, and think of something cheerful.—Testimonies for the Church 2:530.

Inspire the Despondent

Tell the suffering ones of a compassionate Saviour.... He looks with compassion upon those who regard their case as hopeless. While the soul is filled with fear and terror, the mind cannot see the tender compassion of Christ. Our sanitariums are to be an agency for bringing peace and rest to the troubled minds. If you can inspire the despondent with hopeful, saving faith, contentment and cheerfulness will take the place of discouragement and unrest. Wonderful changes can then be wrought in their physical condition. Christ will restore both body and soul, and, realizing His compassion and love, they will rest in Him. He is the bright and morning Star, shining amid the moral darkness of this sinful, corrupt world. He is the Light of the world, and all who give their hearts to Him will find peace, rest, and joy.—Letter 115, 1905.

Counterfeit Miracles

Satan is a diligent Bible student. He knows that his time is short, and he seeks at every point to counterwork the work of the Lord upon this earth. It is impossible to give any idea of the experience of the people of God who shall be alive upon the earth when celestial glory and a repetition of the persecutions of the past are blended. They will walk in the light proceeding from the throne of God. By means of the angels there will be constant communication between heaven and earth. And Satan, surrounded by evil angels and claiming to be God, will work miracles of all kinds, to deceive, if possible, the very elect.

God's people will not find their safety in working miracles; for Satan will counterfeit the miracles that will be wrought. God's tried and tested people will find their power in the sign spoken of in Exodus 31:12-18. They are to take their stand on the living word, "It is written." This is the only foundation upon which they can stand securely. Those who have broken their covenant with God will in that day be without God and without hope.—Testimonies for the Church 9:16.

Taking Hold of the Eternal

The mind cure must be free from all human enchantment. It must not grovel to humanity but soar aloft to the spiritual, taking hold of the eternal.—Letter 120, 1901.

Satan's Apparent Miracles

We are to be on guard against Satan's deceptive arts. He will take possession of human bodies, and make men and women sick. Then he will suddenly cease to exercise his evil power, and it will be proclaimed that a miracle has been wrought. We need now to have a true understanding of the power of Jesus Christ to save to the uttermost all who come unto Him....

Men and women are not to study the science of how to take captive the minds of those who associate with them. This is the science that Satan teaches. We are to resist everything of the kind. We are not to tamper with mesmerism and hypnotism— the science of the one who lost his first estate and was cast out of the heavenly courts.

The science of a pure, wholesome, consistent Christian life is obtained by studying the word of the Lord. This is the highest education that any earthly being can obtain. These are the lessons that the students in our schools are to be taught, that they may come forth with pure thoughts and clean minds and hearts, prepared to ascend the ladder of progress and to practice the Christian virtues.— Manuscript 86, 1905.

Efforts of Satan to Confuse Minds

For thousands of years Satan has been experimenting upon the properties of the human mind, and he has learned to know it well. By his subtle workings in these last days he is linking the human mind with his own, imbuing it with his thoughts; and he is doing this work in so deceptive a manner that those who accept his guidance know not that they are being led by him at his will. The great deceiver hopes so to confuse the minds of men and women that none but his voice will be heard.—Letter 244, 1907.

A Dangerous System of Mind Cure

I am so weighed down in your case that I must continue to write to you, lest in your blindness you will not see where you need to reform. I am instructed that you are entertaining ideas with which God has forbidden you to deal. I will name these as a species of mind cure. You suppose that you can use this mind cure in your professional work as a physician. In tones of earnest warning the words were spoken: Beware, beware where your feet are placed and your mind is carried. God has not appointed you this work. The theory of mind controlling mind is originated by Satan to introduce himself as the chief worker, to put human philosophy where divine philosophy should be.

No man or woman should exercise his or her will to control the senses or reason of another, so that the mind of the person is rendered passively subject to the will of the one who is exercising the control. This science may appear to be something beautiful, but it is a science which you are in no case to handle.... There is something better for you to engage in than the control of human nature over human nature.

I lift the danger signal. The only safe and true mind cure covers much. The physician must educate the people to look from the human to the divine. He who has made man's mind knows precisely what the mind needs.

In taking up the science you have begun to advocate, you are giving an education which is not safe for you or for those you teach. It is dangerous to tinge minds with the science of mind cure.

A Deceptive Fallacy

This science may appear to you to be very valuable; but to you and to others it is a fallacy prepared by Satan. It is the charm of the serpent which stings to spiritual death. It covers much that seems wonderful, but it is foreign to the nature and spirit of Christ. This science does not lead to Him who is life and salvation.

The poor, afflicted souls with whom you are brought in contact have needed more of your attention than they have received. You have it in your power to encourage them to look to Jesus, and, by beholding, be changed to His image.

The true knowledge of Jesus Christ will lead your mind ... in a safe direction. It gives the inspiration of true worship. It is the fellowship of the soul with Him who is its life. Coming in contact with Him, the mind is drawn to His heart of life and is inspired with the essence of His sanctification.

Be careful, my brother, ... in regard to where your faith is tending. Jesus lives to make intercession for you. Let your mind be one with the mind of Christ. Having His mind, you will not soar to heights which will at last bring you down to the lowest depths. Dabble not in those things which now appear to you so attractive, but which do not lead to Christ. Let your ambition ascend higher, to pure, true fellowship with Him in whom you may safely glory. Then your religion will be a power for good. You will not then communicate that which will prove a snare unto death.

A Call to Perfection

Our Saviour understood all about human nature, and He says to every human being, "Be ye therefore perfect, even as your Father which is in heaven is perfect." As God is perfect in His sphere, so man is to be perfect in his sphere. Those who receive Christ are among the number to whom the words so full of hope are spoken, "As many as received Him, to them gave He power to become the sons of God, even to them that believe on His name." These words declare to us that we should be content with nothing less than the best and highest character, a character formed after the divine similitude. When such a character is possessed, the life, the faith, the purity of the religion, is an instructive example to others. "Righteousness exalteth a nation: but sin is a reproach to any people." ...

[113]

"I fear, lest by any means, as the serpent beguiled Eve through his subtilty, so your minds should be corrupted from the simplicity that is in Christ." ...

"Put on the whole armor of God, that ye may be able to stand against the wiles of the devil. For we wrestle not against flesh and blood, but against principalities, against powers, against the rulers of the darkness of this world, against spiritual wickedness in high places. Wherefore take unto you the whole armor of God, that ye may be able to withstand in the evil day, and having done all, to stand. Stand therefore, having your loins girt about with truth, and having on the breastplate of righteousness; and your feet shod with the preparation of the gospel of peace; above all, taking the shield of faith, wherewith ye shall be able to quench all the fiery darts of the wicked. And take the helmet of salvation, and the sword of the Spirit, which is the word of God."

Personal Experience in Meeting False Science

At the beginning of my work I had the mind-cure science to contend with. I was sent from place to place to declare the falseness of this science, into which many were entering. The mind cure was entered upon very innocently—to relieve the tension upon the minds of nervous invalids. But, oh, how sad were the results! God sent me from place to place to rebuke everything pertaining to this science.

I wish to speak plainly to you. You have entered upon a work which has no place in the work of a Christian physician, and which must find no place in our health institutions. Innocent though it may appear, this mind cure, if exercised upon the patients, will in its development be for their destruction, not their restoration. The third chapter of Second Timothy describes persons who accept error, such as one mind exercising complete control over another mind. God forbids any such thing. The mind cure is one of Satan's greatest sciences, and it is important that our physicians see clearly the real character of this science; for through it great temptations will come to them. This science must not be allowed a particle of standing room in our sanitariums.

Through the Mind Satan May Control the Body

God has not given one ray of light or encouragement for our physicians to take up the work of having one mind completely control the mind of another, so that one acts out the will of another. Let us learn the ways and purposes of God. Let not the enemy gain the least advantage over you. Let him not lead you to dare to endeavor to control another mind until it becomes a machine in your hands. This is the science of Satan's working. Thus he works when he entices men to sell the soul for liquor. He takes possession of body, mind, and soul, and it is no longer the man, but Satan, who acts. And the cruelty of Satan is expressed as the drunkard lifts his hand to strike down the wife he has promised to love and cherish as long as life shall last. The deeds of the drunkard are an expression of Satan's violence.

A Positive Peril

Now, my brother, I consider you to be in positive peril. I present this because I know that you are in great danger of being seduced by Satan. We are living in a time when every phase of fanaticism will press its way in among believers and unbelievers. Satan will come in, speaking lies in hypocrisy. Everything that he can invent to deceive men and women will be brought forward.

Just in proportion as men lose their sense of the need of vital religion, so they become filled with common, earthly ideas, which they exalt as wonderful knowledge. Physicians who lose their hold on Christ become filled with ideas of their own, which they look upon as some wonderful science, to be brought into the medical profession as something new and strange.

I have been awakened at the early hour of twelve to write out these things. Let me tell you plainly that you are in an uncertain condition of mind, and that the efforts you put forth to rescue yourself are in vain. No man can serve two masters. If you try to serve the world and the Lord at the same time, the result will be that worldly policy and worldly schemes will become supreme in your life. Why? Because the word of God will become uncongenial; for the heart is not committed to the molding and fashioning of the Holy Spirit. The will is not given up to God, and therefore enmity to God is revealed. The natural impulses of the heart, ministering to the natural man, are chosen to control....

[115]

My brother, while you cherish your own suppositions as truth, God cannot enlighten you. With your present phase of character, you are not capable of understanding the best course to pursue in introducing principles which rest upon a solid basis. Your greatest consideration is, "Is my proper position recognized? Am I called upon as I should be to decide matters?" Your selfish ideas must never become the ruling power in any sanitarium. You are to blend with other men and women who have understanding....

Our physicians must not rest content with a half conversion. They need to place their whole trust in Christ. Then the healthy beats of a new heart will change the atmosphere surrounding the soul. Make sure that you are accepted by Christ because you rely on the merits of a crucified and risen Saviour. His righteousness must be your righteousness. He wrought it out for you, and when you receive it you stand justified in the presence of God.—Letter 121, 1901.

Directing the Mind to Christ

Christ, the Mighty Healer, is to be exalted—and not any human physician. Physicians, Jesus will hear your prayers. Nurses, if you have a living connection with God, you can in confidence present the sick before Him. He will comfort and bless the suffering ones, molding and fashioning the mind, inspiring it with faith and hope and courage. The Christ life, the Christ grace, is the only power that can safely be brought to bear upon the human mind. Every other influence is to be taken away.

No individual should be permitted to take control of another person's mind, thinking that in so doing he is causing him to receive great benefit. The mind cure is one of the most dangerous deceptions which can be practiced upon any individual. Temporary relief may be felt, but the mind of the one thus controlled is never again so strong and reliable. We may be as weak as was the woman who touched the hem of Christ's garment; but if we use our God-given opportunity to come to Him in faith, He will respond as quickly as He did to that touch of faith.

It is not God's design for any human being to yield his mind to another human being. The risen Christ, who is now set down on the throne at the right hand of the Father, is the Mighty Healer. Look to Him for healing power. Through Him alone can sinners come to God just as they are. Never can they come through any man's mind. The human agent must never interpose between the heavenly agencies and those who are suffering.

Everyone should be in a position to cooperate with God in directing the minds of others to Him. Tell them of the grace and power of Him who is the greatest Physician the world ever knew. He came to the world to restore in man the moral image of God. Seeing that Satan was exercising a controlling influence over the minds of men and women in order to further his evil designs, Christ came to combat the powers of darkness, to break the control which Satan had gained over human minds. Make the Saviour the center of attraction.

A minister once said that he could but think that Christ must have known something about science. Of what could this minister have been thinking? Science! Christ could have opened door after door of science. He could have revealed to men treasures of science on which they might have feasted to the present time. But knowing that this knowledge would have been appropriated to unholy uses, He did not open the door.

A Perilous Science

We do not ask you to place yourself under the control of any man's mind. The mind cure is the most awful science which has ever been advocated. Every wicked being can use it in carrying through his own evil designs. We have no business with any such science. We should be afraid of it. Never should the first principles of it be brought into any institution.

Christ can do nothing for those who are yoked up with the enemy. His invitation to us is, "Come unto Me, all ye that labor and are heavy-laden, and I will give you rest. Take My yoke upon you, and learn of Me; for I am meek and lowly in heart: and ye shall find rest unto your souls. For My yoke is easy, and My burden is light." When in our daily experience we learn His meekness and lowliness, we find rest. There is then no necessity to search for some mysterious science to soothe the sick. We already have the science which gives them real rest—the science of salvation, the science of restoration, the science of a living faith in a living Saviour.—Manuscript 105, 1901.

* * * * *

For Further Study

Mind Cure:
Counsels on Health, 344-346;

The Ministry of Healing, 241-260;
Testimonies for the Church 3:168, 169.

Relation of Mind to Body:
Counsels on Health, 28, 29.

Healing of Body Through the Mind:
Counsels on Health, 349, 350 (Testimonies for the Church 3:184).

Diseased Imagination, Instances of Effect of, on Various Disorders:
Testimonies For The Church 1:700;
Testimonies for the Church 2:523-536;

Caused by Exciting Reading:
Fundamentals of Christian Education, 163, 164.

Power of the Will in Healing:
Counsels on Health, 94, 439, 440;
The Desire of Ages, 202, 20;
Testimonies for the Church 2:325, 428, 533.

Illustrated by Healing of Paralytic:
Testimonies for the Church 3:168, 169;
The Desire of Ages, 267-269.

Control of Imagination:
Counsels on Health, 95-97 (Testimonies for the Church 2:522-525).

Dealing With Spiritual Maladies:
Counsels on Health, 323-325.

Effect of Godliness on Health:
Counsels on Health, 627-630;
Testimonies for the Church 4:552-554.

Faith Destroyed by False Systems:
Testimonies For The Church 1:291, 296, 297.

Counterfeit Miracles:
Early Writings, 59, 60.

Clairvoyant and Magnetic Healers:
Prophets and Kings, 210, 211.

Section 7—Fees and Wages

Exorbitant Fees

Traditions and customs have become so interwoven with the belief of the medical profession that physicians need to be taught the very first principles of the way of the Lord. The physician ministers to the body in healing, yet all the work is the Lord's. He must cooperate with the physicians, else there cannot be success.

Please read carefully the fifteenth chapter of Exodus. The Lord gave Moses a message of encouragement for the children of Israel. They did not deserve the good He had done and was doing for them, yet He made a covenant of mercy with them, saying, "If thou wilt diligently hearken to the voice of the Lord thy God, and wilt do that which is right in His sight, and wilt give ear to His commandments, and keep all His statutes, I will put none of these diseases upon thee, which I have brought upon the Egyptians: for I am the Lord that healeth thee." Read also the seventh, eighth, and twenty-eighth chapters of Deuteronomy.

God's Lesson For Israel

The Lord had a lesson to teach the children of Israel. The waters of Marah were an object lesson, representing the diseases brought upon human beings because of sin. It is no mystery that the inhabitants of the earth are suffering from disease of every stripe and type. It is because they transgress the law of God. Thus did the children of Israel. They broke down the barriers which God in His providence had erected to preserve them from disease, that they might live in health and holiness and so learn obedience in their journeying through the wilderness. They journeyed under the special direction of Christ, who had given Himself as a sacrifice to preserve a people who would ever keep God in their remembrance, notwithstanding Satan's masterly temptations. Enshrouded in the pillar of cloud, it was Christ's desire to keep under His sheltering wing of preservation all who would do His will.

[120] It was not by chance that in their journey the children of Israel came to Marah. Before they left Egypt the Lord began His lessons of instruction, that He might lead them to realize that He was their God, their Deliverer, their Protector. They murmured against Moses and against God, but still the Lord sought to show them that He would relieve all their perplexities if they would look to Him. The evils they met and passed through were part of God's great plan, whereby He desired to prove them.

"When they came to Marah, ... the people murmured against Moses, saying, What shall we drink? And he cried unto the Lord; and the Lord showed him a tree, which when he had cast into the waters, the waters were made sweet: there he made for them a statute and an ordinance, and there he proved them, and said, If thou wilt diligently hearken to the voice of the Lord thy God, and wilt do that which is right in His sight, and wilt give ear to His commandments, and keep all His statutes, I will put none of these diseases upon thee, which I have brought upon the Egyptians, for I am the Lord that healeth thee." Though invisible to human eyes, God was the leader of the Israelites, their mighty Healer. He it was who put into the tree the properties which sweetened the waters. Thus He desired to show them that by His power He could cure the evils of the human heart.

In Christ's Stead

Christ is the Great Physician, not only of the body, but of the soul. He restores man to his God. God permitted His only-begotten Son to be bruised, that healing properties might flow forth from Him to cure all our diseases. Physicians are to act in Christ's stead. Every physician who has planted his feet upon the Rock of Ages draws from the Great Physician his restoring power. Christ's plans are to be carried out more definitely by the Christian physician.

As Christ was about to leave His disciples, those who were to represent Him to the world, He gave them a new commandment. "A new commandment I give unto you," He said, "That ye love one another; as I have loved you, that ye also love one another. [121] By this shall all men know that ye are My disciples, if ye have love one for another." That love they knew not until they saw the suffering and death of Jesus Christ upon the cross of Calvary. The new commandment of love was given in behalf of the weak, the wretched, the helpless.

To the heart of Christ the very presence of trouble was a call for help. The poor, the sick, the desolate, the outcasts, the discouraged, the desponding, found in Him a compassionate Saviour, a Mighty Healer. "A bruised reed shall He not break, and smoking flax shall He not quench, till He send forth judgment unto victory." Christ identifies His interests with those of suffering humanity, and He tells us that whatever we do to relieve a sufferer, we do for Him....

There are great lessons to be learned by all who minister for Christ. The Sabbath mark must be placed upon God's commandment-keeping people. The Sabbath, if kept in the spirit of true obedience, will show that all God's commandments are to be practiced, "that ye may know that I am the Lord that doth sanctify you."

The Source of the Physician's Skill

The Lord has His eye upon every human being, and He has His plans concerning each one. He would have His commandment-keeping people a distinguished people, who practice the holy precepts specified in His word. He would have the members of the medical profession expel from their practice everything which has been brought in by selfishness, avariciousness, injustice. He has given wisdom and skill to physicians, and He designs that nothing savoring of robbery and injustice shall be practiced by those who make the law of Jehovah the rule of their life. By His own working agencies He has created material which will restore the sick to health. If men would use aright the wisdom God has given them, this world would be a place resembling heaven....

We all need a far higher, purer, holier trust in God. Every physician should be true and honest. He is not in any case to defraud his patients. If he performs a simple operation, he is to charge a simple price. The charges made by other practicing physicians are not to be his criterion. The diseased bodies over which he works are God's property. He has said, "Ye are not your own; for ye are bought with a price: therefore glorify God in your body, and in your spirit, which are God's."

The exorbitant price charged by physicians in this country [Australia], when called upon to attend suffering humanity is robbery, fraud. God gave physicians their wisdom and skill. It is not man who saves life; it is the Great Restorer. But poor men are often charged for services they never received....

Called To Righteous Judgment

God calls for physicians who will make reforms in the methods of treating the sick. He calls for physicians who will cooperate with Him. He calls for righteous judgment among medical practitioners, who are acting in His stead. The physician who loves his brother as he loves himself will not charge exorbitant prices. A change must take place. It is just as essential that there be reforms in medical lines as in other business lines. There is grave overreaching in the charges made by lawyers and doctors. The Lord views all these things. No tradition, custom, or practice condemned by God must be followed by the believing physician. He is God's servant, working in Christ's stead, as His representative, and his work, his weights and measures, pass in review before God. The commandments of God must be the physician's standard. He must measure his daily life by principles of the law.

The Cleansing of the Temple

Christ rebuked the Pharisees and doctors of the law because of the dishonest practices which they had brought into the temple courts. These men influenced the buyers and sellers to purchase cattle at the lowest prices, and then to sell them for a high price to those coming from a distance, who could not bring their offerings with them and were therefore compelled to buy them in Jerusalem. As these men sat at the table, counting the money they had gained by robbery and extortion, Christ stood before them. His eye flashed with indignation as He saw the fraudulent transactions which were carried on. Picking up a scourge of small cords which had been used to drive cattle to the temple, He drove out those who sold and bought, and overthrew the tables of the money changers and the seats of them that sold doves, saying, "It is written, My house shall be called the house of prayer; but ye have made it a den of thieves."

Then the Restorer practiced His medical missionary work. "The blind and the lame came to Him in the temple; and He healed them."

The marketplaces, the merchandise stores, need cleansing. Courts of justice, lawyers' offices, the medical fraternity, need purifying. Shall we say that the medical missionary work needs cleansing? Christ, who came to our world to reveal the Father's heart of tender compassion, has shown us the methods which Sabbath keepers are to follow in their work. These are plainly specified in the fifty-eighth chapter of Isaiah. God will not be a party to any dishonest transaction. The soul who keeps the Sabbath is stamped with the sign of God's government, and he must not dishonor this sign. By closely examining the word of God, we may know whether we have the King's mark, whether we have been chosen and set apart to honor God. Please read Deuteronomy 6:4-9 and Ezekiel 20:12-20....

God will never, never allow any man to pass through the pearly gates of the City of God who does not bear the signet of the faithful, His government mark. Every soul who is saved will cherish pure principles, which proceed from the very essence of truth. He must fasten himself by golden links to the everlasting power and love of the God of truth. He must be loyal to the principles of God's word, loyal to the everlasting covenant which is a sign between man and his Maker.

A Conscience Taught of God

Righteousness, high and elevated, is to control the conduct. Strength of mind, learning, power of influence, will not give man his eternal life insurance papers. God weighs the action. Each must form an individual character after the likeness of Christ. He must have a conscience taught of God. He must see behind every promise the All-powerful One, with whom he must work as an agent to do His will. If man will not take this position, he will make shipwreck of faith. God will never insure a man for everlasting life whose anchor is not securely fastened to heaven's unalterable law. He must reveal the Christ working in him, in his doctrinal precepts, in his practical obedience.

[124] The soul that converses with God through the Scriptures, who prays for light and opens the door of his heart to the Saviour, will not have evil imaginings, worldly scheming, or ambitious lust after honor or distinction in any line. He who seeks for the truth as for hidden treasure will find it in God's means of communication with man, His word. David says, "The entrance of Thy words giveth light; it giveth understanding unto the simple." This does not mean those who are weak in intellect, but those who, whatever their position, have a true sense of their need of conversing with God as did Enoch. The word of God will ennoble the mind and sanctify the human agent, enabling him to become a co-worker with divine agencies. The elevated standard of God's holy law will mean very much to him, as a standard of all his life practice. It will mean holiness, which is wholeness to God. As the human agent presses forward in the path cast up for the ransomed of the Lord to walk in, as he receives Jesus Christ as his personal Saviour, he will feed on the bread of life. The word is spirit and life, and if it is brought into the daily practice it will ennoble the whole nature of man. There will be opened to his soul such a view of the Saviour's love as portrayed by the pen of Inspiration that his heart will be melted into tenderness and contrition.

We are to see and understand the instruction given us by the great apostle, "As newborn babes, desire the sincere milk of the word, that ye may grow thereby," in perception, in likeness to the character of Christ. Development of character, growth in knowledge and wisdom, will be the sure result of feeding on the word.

What Would Jesus Do?

We present to all our workers, our ministers and physicians, the necessity of careful consideration in all their work, perfect and entire obedience to the precepts of the word of God. Carefully inquire at every step: How would my Saviour act in this line of work? What impression will I leave upon the people? I am to yoke up with Christ in the work as a restorer of health to the body, the mind, the heart, the soul. How careful should every physician be to represent the Master! ...

New Methods

It is time for the people of God, those who wear the sign of His kingdom, and whose authority is derived from "It is written," to work. The world is the field of our labor, and we are to strive to give the last message of mercy to the world. Our every action is being watched with jealous eyes. Be on guard as physicians. You can serve the Lord in your position by working with new methods and discarding drugs.

As reformers we are to reform the medical practice by educating toward the light. Our work is to be done in the full recognition of God. We are to practice the strict principles of mercy and justice. Our work is not to be as a garment put together with basting threads. We must imitate God's perfection. "Ye are God's husbandry, ye are God's building." We are to make the foundation of every building thorough and solid, as for eternity.—Manuscript 63, 1899.

Represent Upright Principles

Honesty, integrity, justice, mercy, love, compassion, and sympathy are embraced in medical missionary work. In all this work the religion of the Bible is to be practiced. The Lord does not want anyone to labor as His representative who follows the wrong customs and practices of worldly physicians in treating suffering humanity. Our physicians need to reform in the matter of making high charges for critical operations. And the reform should extend farther than this. Often an exorbitant sum is charged for even small services, because physicians are supposed to be governed in their charges by the practices of worldly physicians. Some follow worldly policy in order to accumulate means, as they say, for God's service. But God does not accept such offerings. He says, "I hate robbery for burnt offering." Isaiah 61:8. Those who deal unjustly with their fellowmen while professing to believe My word, I will judge for thus misrepresenting Me.

As these things were presented before me, my Teacher said: "The institutions that depend upon God and receive His cooperation must ever work according to the principles of His law. To charge a large sum for a few minutes' work, is not just. Physicians who are under the discipline of the greatest Physician the world ever knew must let the principles of the gospel regulate every fee. Let mercy and love of God be written on every dollar received."

When our sanitariums are conducted as they should be, a large medical missionary work will be done. Everyone will do his work in such a way and with such a spirit that he will shine as a light in the world.

God calls for practical Christlike work. The patients who come to our sanitariums are to see carried out the principles laid down in the fifty-eighth chapter of Isaiah. Those who have accepted the truth are to practice it because it is the truth. In the work of God in our institutions the truth is to be preserved in all its sacred influences.

Religious Principles to be Maintained

The medical practitioner should in all places keep his religious principles clear and untarnished. Truth should be paramount in his practice. He is to use his influence as a means of cleansing the soul by the healing beams of the Sun of Righteousness. When a time comes that physicians cannot do this, the Lord would have no more medical institutions established among Seventh-day Adventists. High prices are current in the world; but correct principles are to be brought into our work. The Bible standard is to be maintained. The way of the Lord, justice, mercy, and truth, is to be followed. No exorbitant bills are to be sent in for slight operations. The charges made are to be proportionate to the work done.

The work done in our medical institutions is to be true to the name, "Medical Missionary Work." We do not want the Lord to think ill of us because we misrepresent the work of Christ. God has not given us permission to do a work which will not bear the investigation of the judgment. He does not want any institution established by His people to bear a reputation similar to that borne by Ananias and Sapphira. Desiring to gain a reputation for self-sacrifice, liberality, and devotion to the Christian faith, Ananias and Sapphira sold their property, and laid part of the proceeds at the feet of the apostles, pretending they had given it all. They had not been urged to give all they had to the cause. God would have accepted part. But they desired it to be thought that they had given all. Thus they thought to gain the reputation they coveted, and at the same time keep back part of their money. They thought they had been successful in their scheme; but they were cheating the Lord, and He dealt summarily with this, the first case of deception and falsehood in the newly formed church. He slew them both, as a warning to all of the danger of sacrificing truth to gain favor.

We are not to misrepresent what we profess to believe in order to gain favor. God despises misrepresentation and prevarication. He will not tolerate the man who says, and does not. The best and noblest work is done by fair, honest dealing.—Manuscript 169, 1899.

The Percentage Plan a Snare

The Lord showed me that you made a decided mistake in taking, in addition to your regular wages, all the money that you obtained from your eye, ear, and throat work. This was a snare to you. It had a misleading influence upon you. Your great desire for display led you into extravagance....

Duty to be Holy and Uncorrupted

Only that which is pure and lovely and of good report is it safe for us to follow. Human beings are under the most sacred obligations to God to be holy and uncorrupted; for they have been bought with a price, even the precious blood of the Son of God. By their baptismal vows they are solemnly pledged to do nothing which will bring an evil report upon the Christian name. Before the Father, the Son, and the Holy Spirit, the professing Christian pledges himself to discourage pride, covetousness, unbelief. And as the true Christian seeks to fulfill this pledge, he grows in self-distrust. Constantly he places more dependence upon God. His reverence and love for the Saviour continually increase, and he is a living witness for his Master. He realizes what it means to be a child of God. He has a realizing sense that the cleansing blood of Christ secures for him pardon and elevation of character. In spirituality he grows like the lofty cedar. Daily he holds communion with God, and he has a treasure-house of knowledge from which to draw. He is mighty in the knowledge of the Scriptures. His fellowship is with the Father and the Son, and he knows more and still more of the divine will. He is filled with a constantly increasing love for God and for his fellowmen.—Letter 46, 1901.

Care in Expenditure

If physicians feel that they do not receive sufficient wages, their circumstances should be examined. If their work is too heavy, others should be brought in to share their responsibilities, and they should be given less to do. We are engaged in an important work, and great care must be exercised in the use of means. There is a world to receive the light. Souls unwarned are perishing. If increased wages are paid to those who ought to be satisfied, this will result in keeping out other laborers whose services are needed, but who, because of the lack of means, cannot be employed.—Manuscript 59, 1912.

The Policy Principle a Dishonor to God

There are those who will suggest to you that in order to be successful in your profession you must be a policy man; you *must* at times depart from strict rectitude. These temptations find a ready welcome in the heart of man; but I speak that which I know. Do not be deceived or deluded. Do not pamper self. Do not throw open a door through which the enemy may enter to take possession of the soul. There is danger in the first and slightest departure from the strictest rectitude. Be true to yourself. Preserve your God-given dignity in the fear of God. There is great need that every medical worker get hold and keep hold of the arm of Infinite Power.

The policy principle is one that will assuredly lead into difficulties. He who regards the favor of men as more desirable than the favor of God will fall under the temptation to sacrifice principle for worldly gain or recognition. Thus fidelity to God is constantly being sacrificed. Truth, God's truth, must be cherished in the soul and held in the strength of heaven, or the power of Satan will wrest it from you.

Never entertain the thought that an honest, truthful physician cannot succeed. Such a sentiment dishonors the God of truth and righteousness. He *can* succeed; for he has God and heaven on his side. Let every bribe to dissimulate be sternly refused. Hold fast your integrity in the strength of the grace of Christ, and He will fulfill His word to you.—Counsels to Parents, Teachers, and Students, 485-486

Promises for Self-Sacrificing Workers

Let everyone work on the principles of self-sacrifice. Work while the day lasts; for the night cometh, in which no man can work. As God's people work earnestly, humbly, self-sacrificingly, they will gain the rich reward of which Job speaks: "When the ear heard me, then it blessed me; ... the blessing of him that was ready to perish came upon me: and I caused the widow's heart to sing for joy." Christ will be acknowledged as the Creator and Redeemer. Those who are laborers together with God will be recognized and appreciated. The recognition of the faithful servants of God detracts not one iota from the gratitude and praise we offer to God and to the Lamb.

When the redeemed stand around the throne of God, those who have been saved from sin and degradation will come to those who worked for them with the words of greeting, "I was without God and without hope in the world. I was perishing in corruption and sin. I was starving for physical and spiritual food. You came to me in love and pity, and fed and clothed me. You pointed me to the Lamb of God, who taketh away the sin of the world."—Letter 74, 1901.

Prepare for Eternity

Make your life preparation for eternity. You have not a moment to lose. Do you keep God's commandments? Do you fear to offend Him? Do you feel your dependence on Christ? Do you realize that you must be kept every moment by His power? Is your life filled each day with submission, contentment, and gratitude?

Medical missionary workers are acknowledged by Christ, not because they bear the name they do, but because they are under the guardianship of the Chief Missionary, who left heaven to give His life for the life of the world. He says, "If ye love Me, keep My

[130] commandments.... He that hath My commandments, and keepeth them, he it is that loveth Me: and he that loveth Me shall be loved of My Father, and I will love Him, and will manifest Myself to Him."

Then, as witnesses for God, give proof that you are under the discipline and training of the great Medical Missionary; that you have placed yourself in His hands, to manifest His Spirit, to show to the world the sacred character of His great work, and to reveal to unbelievers the advantage of being under His guardianship.

A medical missionary is not of value to the cause of God unless all the principles embraced in the name that he bears are developed in his life. The gospel of Christ is to be brought into the daily life. We are to make our life in this world an example, as far as we possibly can, of what the life in heaven will be. This Christ expects of all who claim to be medical missionaries. They are not to cherish one principle that bears a taint of selfishness. They are to stand before the world as followers of Christ, partaking of His self-denial and humiliation and heralding His coming.—Letter 63, 1903.

Advice to a Young Physician

The Lord has given you your work. He expects you each week to interview yourself, to find out how you are trading on your Lord's goods. Are you putting to the tax your mental, moral, and physical powers in an effort to please the Lord, who desires you to accumulate talents by a correct use of those He has given you? Your being a physician in no case releases you from the necessity of practicing economy. There are new fields to be entered, and to enter these fields requires the closest economy. Will you enter these fields as you have entered -----, content to let others practice self-denial and lift the cross, while you indulge your fancies, spending money lavishly to make a show? God requires you to accomplish good with every jot of your influence. Then will be seen the most blessed results.

You need to learn the art of using your talents for the glory of Him who has lent them to you. This requires study and prayer and consecration. Some seem to have no idea of the science of handling money. They allow hundreds of dollars to pass through their hands without producing anything for God....

Cultivate Integrity, Self-Denial, and Humility

God calls upon you to straighten yourself out. Be a man. Put away your extravagance. Extravagant ideas must not be indulged under the name of medical missionary work. It is high time that we became Christians in heart. Integrity, self-denial, and humility should characterize our lives....

There is a great work to be done. Are you doing all you can to help? God has given us a commission which angels might envy. Medical missionary work is to be done. Thousands upon thousands of human beings are perishing. The compassion of God is moved. All heaven is looking on with intense interest to see what stamp medical missionary work will assume under the supervision of human beings. Will men make merchandise of God's ordained plan for reaching the dark parts of the earth with a manifestation of His benevolence?

Medical missionary work is a sacred thing of God's own devising. After Adam's transgression a costly price was paid to rescue the fallen race. Those who will cooperate with God in His effort to save, working on the lines on which Christ worked, will be wholly successful. The church is charged to convey to the world, without delay, God's saving mercy. We are not to cover mercy with selfishness and then call it medical missionary work.

The Church an Angel of Light

We have no time to waste. God has provided a means of recovery for sinners. By unselfish work His truth is to be represented. This is the trust He has given us, and it is to be faithfully executed.

When will the church do her appointed work? She is represented as an angel of light, flying through heaven with the everlasting gospel to be proclaimed to the world. This represents the speed and directness with which the church is to prosecute her work. In the medical missionary work Jesus is to behold the travail of His soul. Human beings are to be snatched as brands from the burning.

Heaven is Watching

But a change has come that has hindered the work which God designed to move forward without a trace of selfishness. All heaven is watching with intense anxiety to see what is to be the outcome of the work which is so large and so important. God is watching, the heavenly universe is watching; and souls are perishing. Is the enterprise of mercy through which in the past God has manifested His grace in rescuing and restoring, to become a matter of selfish merchandise? Shall the instrumentality ordained by heaven to bring good to man and glory to God be lost through improvident expenditure? Shall God's agency of blessing be used by those who profess to believe the truth in buying and selling and getting gain?

The experience of apostolic days will come to us if men will be worked by the Holy Spirit. The Lord will withdraw His blessing where selfish interests are indulged; but He will put His people in possession of good all through the world if they will use this for the uplifting of humanity. His work is to be a sign of His benevolence, a sign that will win the confidence of the world and bring in resources for the advancement of His kingdom.

A Contagious Example

God will test the sincerity of men. Those who will deny self, take up the cross, and follow Christ will have a continual work to do in the line of restoring the fallen human order. Those who sacrifice for truth make a great impression on the world. Their example is contagious and convincing. Men see that there is in the church that faith which works by love and purifies the soul. But when those who profess to be working for God seek to benefit themselves, they greatly retard the work and cast a reproach upon it....

Divine Authority to be Acknowledged

Never forsake the true standard, even though to cling to it makes you a beggar. God has set up a high standard of righteousness. He has made a plain distinction between human and divine wisdom. All who work on Christ's side must work to save, not to destroy. Worldly policy is not to become the policy of the servants of God. Divine authority is to be acknowledged. The church on earth is to be the representative of heavenly principles. Amid the awful confederacy of injustice, deception, robbery, and crime she is to shine with light from on high. In the righteousness of Christ she is to stand against the prevailing apostasy.—Letter 38, 1901.

As the Servants of Christ

Whatever work we do, we are to do it for Christ. There are many kinds of temporal work to be done for God. An unbeliever would do this work mechanically, for the wages he receives. He does not know the joy of cooperation with the Master Worker. There is no spirituality in the work of him who serves self. Common motives, common aspirations, common inspirations, a desire to be thought clever by men, rule in his life. Such a one may receive praise from men, but not from God. Those who are truly united with Christ do not work for the wages they receive. Laborers together with God, they do not strive to exalt self.

In the last great day decisions will be made that will be a surprise to many. Human judgment will have no place in the decisions then made. Christ can and will judge every case; for all judgment has been committed to Him by the Father. He will estimate service by that which is invisible to men. The most secret things lie open to His all-seeing eye. When the Judge of all men shall make His investigation, many of those whom human estimation has placed first will be placed last, and those who have been put in the lowest place by men will be taken out of the ranks and made first.—The Review and Herald, July 31, 1900.

Heart-Searching Questions

I ask those who live in the vanity of self-indulgence, Will you continue to act as if there rested on you no responsibility to practice self-denial? For what purpose are you living? What good are you accomplishing? Can you afford to live for self? Can you gain eternal life while you live thus? Has not God a place and a work for you? Is there not something more for you to do than merely to please and gratify self?—Letter 4a, 1902.

Two Classes of Servants

From a sermon, Grimsby, England, Sept. 19, 1886.

[134] In the last days there are to be only two parties, the one on the right hand and the other on the left, and Christ says unto one, "Come, ye blessed of My Father, inherit the kingdom prepared for you from the foundation of the world: for I was anhungered, and ye gave Me meat: I was thirsty, and ye gave Me drink: I was a stranger, and ye took Me in: naked, and ye clothed Me: I was sick, and ye visited Me: I was in prison, and ye came unto Me." And they answer, When saw we Thee thus and ministered unto Thee? And Christ says, "Inasmuch as ye have done it unto one of the least of these My brethren, ye have done it unto Me." But to those on the left He says, "Depart from Me, ye cursed, into everlasting fire, prepared for the devil and his angels."

The first class had Christ interwoven into their character, and they were not conscious of anything they had done. "Come, ye blessed of My Father," is the benediction, "inherit the kingdom prepared for you from the foundation of the world." So we see Christ identifies His interests with fallen man. He turns to those on the left hand and says, "I was an hungered, and ye gave Me no meat: I was thirsty, and ye gave Me no drink: I was a stranger, and ye took Me not in: naked, and ye clothed Me not: sick, and in prison, and ye visited Me not." And then they ask Him, "When saw we Thee an hungered, or athirst, or a stranger, or naked, or sick, or in prison, and did not minister unto Thee?" And the answer comes, "Inasmuch as ye did it not to one of the least of these, ye did it not to Me." Not the greatest but the least.

Well, now we want to bring Christ into our everyday life. Those who had not fed the hungry, or clothed the naked, or visited the sick, were not conscious of it, and why? Because they had educated and trained themselves in the school of self-indulgence, and the result was they lost heaven and the eternity of bliss which they might have had had they devoted their powers to God.—Manuscript 16, 1886.

A Commendation for Soul Winners

There will be a blessed commendation, a holy benediction, on the faithful winners of souls. They will join the rejoicing ones in heaven, who shout the harvest home. How great will be the joy when the redeemed of the Lord shall all meet, gathered into the mansions prepared for them! Oh, what rejoicing for all who have been impartial, unselfish laborers together with God in carrying forward His work in the earth! What satisfaction will every reaper have when the clear, musical voice of Jesus shall be heard, saying, "Come, ye blessed of My Father, inherit the kingdom prepared for you from the foundation of the world"! ...

The Redeemer is glorified because He has not died in vain. With glad, rejoicing hearts, those who have been colaborers with God see of the travail of their soul for perishing, dying sinners, and are satisfied. The anxious hours they have spent, the perplexing circumstances they have had to meet, the sorrow of heart because some refused to see and receive the things which make for their peace, are forgotten. The self-denial they have practiced in order to support the work is remembered no more. As they look upon the souls they sought to win to Jesus, and see them saved, eternally saved,—monuments of God's mercy and of a Redeemer's love,—there ring through the arches of heaven shouts of praise and thanksgiving.—The Review and Herald, October 10, 1907.

Gain That Is Loss

God will surely turn aside any advantage gained by selfish, unjust dealing. My brother, your senses must be cleansed and sanctified. We must reach a higher standard. We must watch, we must pray, always standing ready for action.—Letter 13, 1902.

*****

For Further Study

Fees and Wages:
Counsels on Health, 302-320 (Testimonies for the Church 7:206-209, Testimonies for the Church 8:142-144).

The Desire for High Wages:
Counsels on Health, 299.

A Lesson from Solomon's Reign:
Prophets and Kings, 61-65.

Remuneration for Physicians and Ministers Compared:
Testimonies For The Church 1:640, 641.

Institutional Wage Proportional to Prosperity:
Testimonies for the Church 8:142, 143.
"Not Bribed With Wealth or Frightened by Poverty":
Life Sketches of Ellen G. White, 302.
Simplicity and Economy:
Counsels on Health, 319, 320.
Equitable Wages for Women:
Counsels on Health, 365.

Section 8—Counsels and Cautions

Our Attitude Toward the Lord's Institutions

In past years I have written many things to our brethren and sisters in America, in Europe, and in Australia, regarding the attitude they should sustain toward our denominational institutions. I am now sending some of these things to you, as timely instruction.

From a letter written in 1889, I quote:

"Those who bear heavy responsibilities in our institutions should be strengthened and sustained by the knowledge that the members of every place are praying for the prosperity and success of these institutions. If the churches do not feel that the work done in our institutions is a most important work, and that the laborers need their sympathy and hearty, intelligent cooperation, this deficiency will retard the advancement of the work. Complaints are not infrequently made in regard to the men who carry a heavy load. Discouragements come upon these men because of the unconsecrated elements in the churches, who love to talk, and say, 'Report, and we will report it.' This makes more work for the men who are already overburdened.

"Those who daily consecrate themselves to God, and endeavor to hold up the hands of those who bear responsibilities, will be blessed of Heaven. We are engaged in a great work, and Satan will use all his power to win to his side the very men and women who could cooperate with God in doing a precious work if they were cleansed, sanctified, and guided by the Holy Spirit, if they had warm, true hearts of tender love and gave due respect to those whom God has appointed to carry on a great and important work. The men engaged in the Master's service have often been wounded by those who think and speak evil and create feelings of distrust and jealousy which should not be tolerated or kept alive by unsanctified tongues."

These same principles were brought to the attention of our brethren and sisters in the Iowa Conference in 1902. In a communication addressed to them is the following instruction:

Relation of Church Members to Medical Workers

"By baptismal vows church members have covenanted to remain under the control of the Father, the Son, and the Holy Spirit. Afterward under temptation some withdraw from the influence of the Spirit of God, and serve the enemy. They become vain talkers, mischief-makers. Instead of healing and restoring, they hurt and destroy.

"How careful every person who claims to love and fear God should be in regard to the reputation of the institutions that God Himself has established according to His word! How careful should every professing Christian be of the reputation of those whose work it is to bring relief to suffering human beings. The physician needs calm nerves. Cannot men and women be made to understand that when they are constantly endeavoring to injure and tear down the reputation of the Lord's appointed physicians, to whom a special work has been given, these servants of God feel keenly the wounds made by their unsanctified utterances? Their hearts are bruised and made sore by the criticizing spirit, the disparaging remarks, the unchristian example and practices of those who should stand as supporters of the men acting as God's helping hand.

Reckless and Cruel Criticism

"Many professing Christians have become the agents of Satan, who uses them to criticize and to discourage nigh unto death those whom God has appointed to do a most important work. Many words opposed to principles of truth and justice, many words creating suspicion and distrust, have been spoken. Cannot the poor souls who have been long in the way see that by their course of action they are ignorantly serving the enemy of all righteousness? Can they not see that they are driving successful laborers onto Satan's battleground, to become the sport of temptation?

"Many of these reckless talkers do not know what they are doing. They cannot see that their words discourage the ones whom God has appointed to represent Jesus Christ and His truth for this time. In relieving suffering humanity, consecrated physicians are doing the work of the Great Restorer, who has said, 'Inasmuch as ye have done it unto one of the least of these My brethren, ye have done it unto Me.' Matthew 25:40.

"Let those whose lips are unsanctified realize that for their own souls' interests they should now be converted in order that their words may be a savor of life unto life, and not of death unto death. It is time that the vain talkers reformed. Let each one begin to reform, and build over against his own house. Let every church member lighten the burdens and encourage the hearts of his brethren by holding up their hands and strengthening them to do God's will."—Series B, No. 5, pages 23-25.

Experience and Wisdom Needed

Plenty of physicians can be obtained who ceased to be students when they received their diplomas, who are self-inflated, who feel that they know all that is worth knowing, and what they do not know is not worth knowing. But this class are not the ones we want. When a physician enters upon his work as practitioner, the more genuine, practical experience he has, the more fully will he feel his want of knowledge.

If self-sufficient, he will read articles written in regard to diseases and how to treat them without nature's aid; he will grasp statements and weave them into his practice, and without deep research, without earnest study, without sifting every statement, he will merely become a mechanical worker. Because he knows so little, he will be ready to experiment upon human lives, and sacrifice not a few. This is murder, actual murder. He did not do this work with evil design, he had no malicious purposes; but life was sacrificed on account of his ignorance, because he was a superficial student, because he had not had that practice that would make him a safe man to be entrusted with human lives. It requires care-taking, deep, earnest taxation of the mind, to carry the burden a physician should carry in learning his trade thoroughly.

Every physician who has received a thorough education will be very modest in his claims. It will not do for him to run any risk in experimenting on human life, lest he be guilty of murder and this be written against him in the books of heaven. There should be a careful, competent physician who will deal scarcely ever in drugs,

[140] and who will not boast that powerful poisons are far more effective than a smaller quantity carefully taken.—Manuscript 22, 1887.

The Minister and His Wife

The minister and his wife who are truly converted and who give themselves wholly to the work of the Lord are daily becoming more and more intelligent and efficient in their labor for others. They can open the Scriptures to souls in such a way as to bring light to minds in darkness.

Women can learn what needs to be done to reach other women. There are women who are especially adapted for the work of giving Bible readings, and they are very successful in presenting the word of God in its simplicity to others. They become a great blessing in reaching mothers and their daughters. This is a sacred work, and those engaged in it should receive encouragement.

The Physician and His Wife

In the medical missionary work to be done, women should give treatment to women. A man and his wife who are both physicians can accomplish great good by laboring together. The wife can visit other women, and when she finds suffering and disease, she can consult with her husband as to the best method of helping the sufferers. We should have more women physicians than we have. When women who are sick are treated and cared for by women, a door through which Satan tries to enter is closed against him. Many cases have been presented to me where Satan has entered through this door to ruin families. Let him not obtain any advantage upon any point.

I wish all to understand this matter. There should be in our sanitariums women physicians who can stand by their husbands, and who can do the examining of women patients, and give them treatment. Many more sensible, thoroughly converted women should become intelligent physicians.

I am instructed that our sanitariums must have women physicians as well as men physicians.—Letter 108, 1910.

Subtle Temptations

Subtle, dangerous temptations will come to the physician who believes the truth for these last days. That which would be condemned in a worker of another class is supposed to be admissible in him. Thus a multitude of sins are covered up, sins which are registered in the books of heaven as a departure from Bible principles. Instead of being careless and familiar, he should act wisely, discreetly. Our sanitariums must not be made a subject of criticism because of a careless familiarity shown by the physicians and the nurses. Temptations of this kind the physician may resist if he understands his peril and clings to his Saviour, living out the word of God in every respect. If true to the word of God, we are on the side of Christ, on the side of the loyal, holy angels; we stand under the shield of Omnipotence. Of whom, then, should we be afraid?—Manuscript 162, 1897.

Maintaining a High Moral Standard

Some who have influence, who are apparently working for the interest of the sanitarium, encourage by their own course of action a disregard of rules and of order; and the influence of such persons goes a long way toward encouraging insubordination, especially in the direction of courtship and marriage. The parties are unfitted for their duties; they live an unreal life, indulge in too high and romantic visions of bliss, and in their desire to please each other they become unfaithful.

The ideas of courtship have their foundation in erroneous ideas concerning marriage. They follow impulse and blind passion. The courtship is carried on in a spirit of flirtation. The parties frequently violate the rules of modesty and reserve, and are guilty of indiscretion, if they do not break the law of God. The high, noble, lofty design of God in the institution of marriage is not discerned; therefore the purest affections of the heart, the noblest traits of character, are not developed.

Not one word should be spoken, not one action performed, that you would not be willing the holy angels should look upon and register in the books above. You should have an eye single to the glory of God. The heart should have only pure, sanctioned affection, worthy of the followers of Jesus Christ, exalting in its nature, and more heavenly than earthy. Anything different from this is debasing, degrading in courtship; and marriage cannot be holy and honorable in the sight of a pure and holy God unless it is after the exalted Scriptural principle.

[142]
Necessary Precautions

These precautions may be regarded as unnecessary. But those who will plead for greater liberty are not worthy to be connected with these institutions. Mild license is termed liberty and freedom, but those who are professedly sons and daughters of God should elevate the standard, and have no fellowship with the unruly who would have rules and regulations made to meet the cases of the disobedient.

The sanitarium, unless hedged about with vigilant rules and regulations, would soon become a hotbed of iniquity. There are those who would entrap and mislead souls; they have a spirit to revile, instead of showing respect for those who carry the burden and seek to keep up the standard. The fewer of such persons employed, the safer and purer will be the moral atmosphere of the sanitarium. There always will be persons who will find entrance to such an institution, whose influence will be for evil. They are of that class who are continually putting bitter for sweet, and sweet for bitter. There are professed Christians who will warp the conscience and becloud the mind, under the pretense of godliness; and those who do not see nor sense the danger are already the dupes or victims of Satan....

Instruction Regarding Association

It is not a time when marriage should be regarded in the light of felicity. It is uncertain business. More misery than happiness is the result; and yet marrying and giving in marriage is as it was in the days of Noah.

There seems to be no restraint; but passion and impulse have controlling power, and youth seems to be bewitched with lovesick sentimentalism. For this reason rules and regulations are highly essential to guard those connected with the sanitarium, the college, and the office of publication; and anyone who regards these restrictions as unnecessary has not spiritual discernment, and will prove a hindrance rather than a help....

The Sin of the Age

Sensuality is the sin of the age. But the religion of Jesus Christ will hold the lines of control over every species of unlawful liberty; the moral powers will hold the lines of control over every thought, word, and action. Guile will not be found in the lips of the true Christian. Not an impure thought will be indulged in, not a word spoken that is approaching to sensuality, not an action that has the least appearance of evil.

[143]

The senses will be guarded. The soul that has Jesus abiding in it will develop into true greatness. The intelligent soul who has respect unto all of God's commandments, through the grace of Christ, will say to the passions of the heart as he points to God's great moral standard of righteousness, "Hitherto shalt thou come, but no further: and here shall thy proud waves be stayed," and the grace of Christ shall be as a wall of fire round about the soul.

There are those who will say, "Oh, you need not be so particular. A little harmless flirtation will do no injury." And the carnal heart urges on to temptation, and to the practical sanctioning of indulgences which end in sin. This is a low cast of morality, not meeting the high standard of the law of God.

The vileness of the human heart is not understood. There are always individuals connected with our institutions whose characters are cast in an inferior mold, and they need but a word of encouragement from those in higher positions to take liberty to gratify the unholy heart. There are those at the sanitarium that are not open sinners; they hide their sins from human eyes; they have a fair outward morality; but the Lord's eye sees them. They find means to gratify the low sensual propensities; their lives are tarnished, and they are tarnishing others by their example....

Avoid the First Wrong Step

Do not see how close you can walk upon the brink of a precipice, and be safe. Avoid the first approach to danger. The soul's interests cannot be trifled with. Your capital is your character. Cherish it as you would a golden treasure. Moral purity, self-respect, a strong power of resistance, must be firmly and constantly cherished. There should not be one departure from reserve; one act of familiarity, one indiscretion, may jeopardize the soul, in opening the door to temptation, and the power of resistance becomes weakened.

The psalmist, when viewing the many snares and temptations to vice, inquires, "Wherewithal shall a young man cleanse his way?" This question is appropriate for everyone connected with our missions and every instrumentality of God. At this stage of our work, the answer comes, "By taking heed thereto according to Thy word." It is necessary to maintain a living connection with heaven, seeking as often as did Daniel—three times a day—for divine grace to resist appetite and passion. Wrestling with appetite and passion unaided by divine power will be unsuccessful; but make Christ your stronghold, and the language of your soul will be, "In all these things we are more than conquerors through Him that loved us." Said the apostle Paul, "I keep under my body, and bring it into subjection: lest that by any means, when I have preached to others, I myself should be a castaway."

Let no one think he can overcome without the help of God. You must have the energy, the strength, the power, of an inner life developed within you. You will then bear fruit unto godliness, and will have an intense loathing of vice. You need to constantly strive to work away from earthliness, from cheap conversation, from everything sensual, and aim for nobility of soul and a pure and unspotted character. Your name may be kept so pure that it cannot justly be connected with any thing dishonest or unrighteous, but will be respected by all the good and pure, and it may be written in the Lamb's book of life, to be immortalized among the holy angels.—Manuscript 4a, 1885.

Like Streams From a Pure Fountain

Directors and helpers, ... I speak to you as Christians, as to men and women whose souls are united to Christ as the branch is united to the living vine. If you have not been renewed in the spirit of your mind, for your soul's sake make no delay to have your life hidden with Christ in God. This is the first business of your life. When Christ is abiding in the heart, you will not be light, chaffy, and immodest, but circumspect, and reliable in every place, sending forth pure words like streams from a pure fountain, refreshing all with whom you come in contact.

If you decide to continue your idle talk and frivolous conduct, go into some other place where your influence and example will not be so widely felt, contaminating other souls. What you all need is such a sense of the purity and holiness of Christ as will lead you to despise this pretense of religion which blesses no one, gives no peace of conscience, no repose of faith.

[145]

Let all connected with these institutions that God has ordained for the saving of souls seek divine wisdom, heavenly grace, that they may have an elevating influence upon others. Unless they are constantly receiving strength from Jesus, looking to Him, trusting in Him, by faith drawing from His divine grace, they will become an easy prey to temptation.

There are so many forward misses, and bold, forward women, who have a faculty of insinuating themselves into notice, putting themselves in the company of young men, courting the attentions, inviting flirtations from married or unmarried men, that unless your face is set Christward, firm as steel, you will be drawn into Satan's net.

Educate to Purity of Thought

It is time that we as Christians reach a higher standard. God forbid that any institution that He has planted shall become a means of decoying souls, a place where iniquity is taught. Let all learn in the school of Christ, lowliness of heart; let them lean their helpless souls on Jesus. Live in the light from the oracles of God. Educate your minds and hearts to pure, elevated, holy thoughts; "be ye holy in all manner of conversation." Whatever influence you have, let it be directed to exalt Jesus. Unless you do this, you are a false guideboard, leading souls away from the truth, the life, the light of the world; and the more pleasing and attractive your manners, the greater injury you do to souls....

There will be no taste for trifling conversation in those who are looking to Jesus for strength, depending upon His righteousness for salvation. By faith they accept Jesus as their personal Saviour, and become partakers of the divine nature, having escaped the corruption that is in the world through lust.

While men and women in an institution for health should be kind and courteous, while they are required to be affable and congenial toward all, they should shun even the appearance of undue familiarity. And not only should they themselves observe the strictest propriety of conduct, but by precept and example they should educate others to be modest and to shun looseness, jesting, flattery, and nonsensical speeches.

Avoid Favoritism

Everything savoring of unbecoming familiarity should be discarded by physicians, superintendent, and helpers. There should be no giving of special favors or special attentions to a few, no preferring of one above another. This has been done, and it is displeasing to God. There are worthy persons who are afflicted and suffering, but do not complain, who are in need of special attentions. These men and women are often passed by with indifference and with a hardness of heart that is more like Satan's character than like Christ's, while young, forward misses, who in no way need or deserve favors, receive special attentions. All this neglect is written in the books of heaven. All these things are developing character.

Let all who are connected with the institution as helpers bear in mind the words of Inspiration: "The wisdom that is from above is first pure, then peaceable, gentle, and easy to be entreated, full of mercy and good fruits, without partiality, and without hypocrisy." When you pass by one who is in need of your sympathy, of your kindly acts, and give them not, but turn to the forward ones and bestow upon them your favors, remember that Jesus is insulted in the person of His afflicted ones. He says, "I was an hungered, and ye gave Me no meat: I was thirsty, and ye gave Me no drink: I was ... naked, and ye clothed Me not: sick, and in prison, and ye visited Me not." And when the surprised inquiry comes, When saw we Thee thus? the answer, "Inasmuch as ye did it not to one of the least of these [who were afflicted and needed your sympathy], ye did it not to Me." "They that be whole need not a physician, but they that are sick." They that are rich need not your favors, but they that are poor. The bruised and wounded, the lame of the flock, are among us, and these test the character of those who claim to be children of God.

Leading Others to Perdition

Angels of God are watching the development of character. They are weighing moral worth. If you bestow your attentions upon those who have no need, you are doing the recipients harm, and you will yourself receive condemnation, rather than reward. Remember that when by your conversation you descend to the level of frivolous characters, you are encouraging them in the path that leads to perdition. Your unwise attentions may prove the ruin of their souls. You degrade their conceptions of what constitutes Christian life and character. You confuse their ideas, and make impressions that may never be effaced. The harm thus done to souls that needed to be strengthened, refined, and ennobled, is often a sin unto death. They cannot associate these men with the sacred positions which they occupy. The ministers, the officers of the church, all are regarded as no better than themselves. Then where is their example?

God calls upon all who claim to be Christians to elevate the standard of righteousness, and to purify themselves even as He is pure. "Be ye holy in all manner of conversation." "If ye then be risen with Christ, seek those things which are above.... Set your affection on things above, not on things on the earth. For ye are dead, and your life is hid with Christ in God. When Christ, who is our life, shall appear, then shall ye also appear with Him in glory. Mortify therefore your members which are upon the earth; fornication, uncleanness, inordinate affection, evil concupiscence, and covetousness, which is idolatry: for which things' sake the wrath of God cometh on the children of disobedience." "Wherefore gird up the loins of your mind, be sober, and hope to the end for the grace that is to be brought unto you at the revelation of Jesus Christ; as obedient children, not fashioning yourselves according to the former lusts in your ignorance;" for you are to walk in the light, while you have the light; "but as He which hath called you is holy, so be ye holy in all manner of conversation; because it is written, Be ye holy; for I am holy."—Letter 6a, 1890.

An Appeal for More Sympathy

The Christian physician is a minister of the highest order. He is a missionary. Those who through their skill and faithful, earnest effort, by wisdom from God, can relieve bodily pain, place themselves in such a relation to their patients that they can point them to the Soul Healer, who can say, "Thy sins be forgiven thee." ...

Obtaining the Confidence of Patients

You are too reticent. It is in your power to bind the sick to your heart, and if you do not obtain the confidence of your patients, it is because you do not see the great need of tact, ingenuity, in ministering to the soul as well as to the body. I do not justify anyone in practicing deception upon the dying. In as mild a manner as possible tell them the truth in regard to their case (as I believe you do), and then point them to Jesus as their only hope.

You have no right to shut yourself up within yourself, and say scarcely anything to the patients. You should not keep patients waiting for your decision in their case. It is not right to cause them suffering of mind by unnecessary delay. Every case should receive prompt attention in its turn and according to its necessity. Negligence in this respect has hurt you from the very first of your medical practice. It need not and should not be.

I have been shown that this defect in your character has caused men and women to curse you in their hearts, and almost to blaspheme God. Now if I thought this could not be corrected, I would not write as I do. It is your duty as a Christian physician to educate your manners and your habits for the sickroom, to be cheerful and affable, to manifest tender sympathy, to converse freely on the subjects essential to your patients and which come within the sphere of your practice. You can reach a high standard in your practice.

Thinking of Disagreeable Matters

Do not, I beg of you, lay blame on others. You have pondered over disagreeable matters altogether too much. There are many things that you do not view in a correct light. Now, cease to think of disagreeable things; cease to talk of them; fix your mind on Jesus, your Helper, and work in faith and confidence. By disciplining yourself you can have greater success than you have ever yet had....

A physician needs to be in daily communion with God, that he may be a constant channel of light to his patients. He should be an imitator of the Lord Jesus Christ. While daily conversant with death, working for those on the verge of the grave, he requires a constant supply of the grace of God, for there is danger that he will become indifferent to eternal realities. His only safety is in keeping the Lord ever before him, his mind constantly under the influence of the Spirit of God.

Christian Courtesy and Delicacy

[149]

The physician should be governed by a strict sense of propriety at all times and on all occasions. I speak plainly, because I know that it is my duty to do this. You cannot be too chaste in your words or too modest in your examination of patients. Coarseness or indelicacy in the operating room, or by the bedside of the suffering, is a sin in the sight of God; and in the minds of the patients it will tell with power against the physician. Unless he constantly cherishes a strict sense of propriety, he will unguardedly shock sensitive patients who are modest and refined.

Above all other men who fill positions of responsibility, the physician needs to be connected with God, to be taught continually by Him, else there is danger that, under temptation, he will become unfaithful, coarse, and profligate. He needs a pure and undefiled religion. And those who stand as his assistants should be wise and calm, persons who fear God. You are safe only when connected with the Source of all power, of all purity and elevation of character.

There are coarse and even sensual minds among physicians. God forbid that this should be the character of one who claims to believe sacred truth. The Spirit of God will shield us from all evil, and will give us an appreciation of the reality of spiritual and eternal things.

The solemn truths which we profess will sanctify the soul if we bring them into the inner sanctuary of the heart. Oh, that every physician would be what God would have him—pure, holy, undefiled, shielded by the grace of God, knowing that Christ is his personal Saviour.

Ever bear in mind, Dr. -----, that the sickroom is a place where Christian courtesy, delicacy, and politeness should always be manifested. There should not be even an approach to commonness. The actions of the physician are making their impression; the tones of his voice, the expression of his countenance, the words he speaks, are weighed by the patient. Every movement is scrutinized.

Directing Gratitude to God

If the invalid is relieved from pain, and brought back, as it were, from death to life, he is inclined almost to worship the one who, he thinks, has saved his life. He seldom thinks that it is God who has done this work through His human agents. Now is the opportune moment for Satan to come in and lead the physician to exalt himself instead of Christ. Jesus says, "Without Me ye can do nothing."

You should lead the patient to behold Jesus as the physician of the body as well as of the soul. If the physician has the love of Christ in his own heart, he will use his influence to set the Mighty Healer before the afflicted one. He can direct the thoughts, the gratitude, and praise, to the Source of all power, mercy, and goodness. If he fails to do this, he is neglecting the most precious opportunities. Oh, what a chance for the Christian physician to exercise his talents to the glory of God, and thus put them out to the exchangers, to be multiplied, and send back to heaven a flood of light in praise and thanksgiving to God for His mercy and love. Oh, what opportunities to drop in the heart the seed which will bear fruit unto holiness!

He who loves God supremely, with all the heart, with all the soul, mind, might, and strength, will love his neighbor as himself, and will strive for his highest good. He will not lose one opportunity of setting the Lord before the afflicted one.

False Ideas of Etiquette

There are false ideas of consistency and etiquette, which lead to neglect of sacred duties. Worldly etiquette, which stands in the way of saving men's souls by lifting up Jesus before them, and of seeking to do them good, is to be discarded. It should be our constant study how we may best follow the example of Christ and promote His glory. Connection with God is everything. What physicians aim to do, Christ accomplished in the fullest sense. The physician labors with zeal to prolong life. Christ is the Giver of life.

Who has endowed the physician with reason and intelligence? He who is the truth and the life. He applies the balm of Gilead. He is the great Restorer. He is the one who has repeatedly vanquished death, and who grants eternal life—God over all. If the physician has learned in the school of Christ, he will, while ministering to the diseased bodies, watch for souls as one that must give an account.

The Unseen Witness [151]

Christian physicians need to pray—to watch unto prayer. Before them is opened a door for many temptations, and they need to be awakened to a lively sense that there is a Watcher by their side, as surely as there was a Watcher at that sacrilegious feast of Belshazzar, when men praised the gods of silver and gold and drank from the sacred vessels of the temple of God. When men take honor to themselves, they are dishonoring God.

Whenever one by any action leads men to be forgetful of God, or to neglect the plain injunctions of His word, the unseen Witness testifies, as in the writing on the walls of the palace, "Thou art weighed in the balances, and art found wanting." Daniel 5:27.—Manuscript 17, 1890.

Establishment of New Sanitariums

This morning I am writing before anyone else is astir. I am receiving letters from persons inquiring whether I have any light in regard to the establishment of new sanitariums.

For what purpose are our sanitariums established? How shall we relate ourselves to them?

Years ago light was given me in regard to the establishment of sanitariums. It is not after the Lord's mind to have sanitariums multiply too rapidly. It is not His plan for an institution to be in too close proximity to another one doing the same kind of work;

for an institution, wherever it may be, must have good facilities and experienced helpers. With it should be connected capable, God-fearing managers—men who are sound in the faith, who will exert an influence for good, and who are able to carry the heavy responsibilities entrusted to them without running behind and involving the institutions in debt.

He who begins to build a tower must first sit down and count the cost, to find out whether after beginning to build he will be able to finish. All who propose to establish a sanitarium should understand that it is a great undertaking. If they have not sufficient skill and adaptability successfully to build up a new sanitarium, let them connect with sanitariums already established, making the interests of these institutions their own....

Sanitariums for Personal Profit

Persons who feel at liberty to act from selfish impulse, and to establish an independent sanitarium for personal profit, have not considered the influence that such a course of action has on the world....

In times past Seventh-day Adventists have started out in this line with the selfish desire to acquire something that would benefit themselves. They have not been at all particular to take into consideration the effect their actions would have on the work of a similar institution, established in the order of God. If by misrepresentation of the institutions already in operation, such men can divert means to themselves for personal profit, they will be constantly tempted to do injustice to these institutions....

God will not bless those who work without taking counsel with their brethren. Any Seventh-day Adventist who supposes that in himself he is a complete whole, and that he can at all times safely follow his own mind and judgment, is not to be trusted; for he is not walking in the light as Christ is in the light. There will be many who have not a correct sense of what they are doing. Men need clear ideas, deep spirituality. In His service God desires every man to move sensibly, weighing the motives prompting his movements.

Among us will be irresponsible men who have no proper conception of the important work the Lord designs to have done in our institutions—the work of caring for the sick and of disseminating the precious, essential principles of health reform. Those who have failed of conforming their life practices to this important reform need to be thoroughly converted.

Spiritual Loss Through Selfish Aims

If men become so confused and unprincipled as to engage in sanitarium work for selfish personal profit, they will not be prospered in their spiritual life, and will be unable properly to influence others spiritually. Let those who have a great desire to distinguish themselves in some way, take up a work that does not involve the cause of God so much as does the establishment of a new sanitarium.—Manuscript 26, 1902.

In Wisdom and Equity

Yesterday afternoon [August 25, 1907], Dr. ----- visited me, and we had a long interview....

Dr. ----- asked me concerning the relation that we should sustain toward private medical work and private sanitariums. I could not say that there should be a binding about of men who are working privately in unselfish lines, although I know that in some cases the question involves great perplexity. Much depends on how these private sanitariums are conducted.—Letter 410, 1907.

Counting the Cost

Great care must be manifested in the establishing of sanitariums; for this is an important work. Those having the work in charge should counsel with experienced brethren regarding the best plans to follow. They should count the cost of every step taken. They should not launch out into the work without knowing how much money they have to invest.

The first question to be settled is, "Should there be a sanitarium in this locality?" If there should be, the path of duty is plain. But there is another question, and a very important one, to settle, "Are those who shall be entrusted with the work of planning and devising for the enterprise prepared to move cautiously, not in self-confidence, but in the fear of the Lord? Will they take counsel from those who have had experience in the work?"

A prevention of failure is worth far more than can be estimated. Let not the young men who have been placed in charge of certain lines of work become uneasy, restless, and venturesome. Let them learn wisdom from the failures of others.

Let no one suppose that it is an easy matter to manage an institution. I have seen so many take up this work and fail. A man is desirous of standing as the leader of some enterprise. A sanitarium is his choice. Taking up this work in his own strength, he makes an entire failure. Unless the men who stand as managers of our institutions are humble enough to be managed by the Lord Jesus, they will move unadvisedly. In order for men to strengthen the cause of God, their ability must be sanctified, that they may reason wisely from cause to effect.

The interests of our sanitariums must be guarded. All should feel it a privilege to do their best to advance medical missionary work. God requires His people to refrain from doing anything which will interfere with the work of another. It is not generous or right for a man to start sanitarium work on independent lines in a place where a sanitarium is already established. It is quite probable that the closest economy is required to conduct properly one sanitarium, furnishing proper facilities for treatment and healthful food for patients and helpers.

Every business transaction tells its story regarding the character of the individual. No haphazard work should be done. No movements should be made in a selfish spirit, irrespective of the rights and property of others.—Manuscript 93, 1901.

Sanitarium Work as a Speculation

At an early hour I am aroused by the word, Write out the things that I have presented to you.

In the building of the tabernacle, tact and skill were given to the Israelites. To His people today the Lord will give tact and skill to do His work. To all who have a part in His cause, He will impart wisdom. But they must depend wholly upon Him. They must be willing to be controlled and guided by Him. As a people we must walk and work as men and women accountable to God.

Some on their own responsibility have taken up sanitarium work. Some have entered into this work as a speculation, hoping to make money. Their principal aim was not so much to heal the bodies and souls of the sick as to make money. These have begun to learn that to engage in sanitarium work means much more than they anticipated.

Many unjust deeds are done in the hope of getting gain. The Lord has witnessed these deeds. No unrighteous act passes unnoticed. All that is gained in this way will be found to be loss, eternal loss.

God's Instrumentalities to be Pure, Holy, Elevated

Our sanitariums are God's instrumentalities, and they are to stand firmly in defense of the truth, making their influence a living demonstration of the power of the gospel. They are to be elevated, pure, holy, carrying forward the work in reformatory lines. Those connected with our sanitariums are to keep self in subordination, taking themselves to task, pruning from their practices all unrighteousness.

Not a thread of selfishness is to be drawn into the web. But this has been done, and will continue to be done unless God's professing people receive the new heart that makes the actions holy. Unless they reform, unless their characters are changed, they will be left outside the City of God; for within its gates can enter nothing that defiles. Only those who are without spot or wrinkle or any such thing will pass in the grand review. Unholy ambition will prove the ruin of many souls. This is the word that I am instructed to give to all who claim to believe present truth.

Departure from Correct Principles

Men have entered into the sanitarium work for the purpose of gain more than from a desire to do missionary work for Christ. They have not realized their responsibility to labor as consecrated, devoted believers seeking to impart light to those in darkness, showing the holiness that God accepts. They did not hold up the principles of health reform. Some were opposed to health reform; others were only half converted on the question of reform diet.

With some the chief thought in undertaking sanitarium work has been to show what "I can do." They did not first sit down and count the cost, asking themselves whether, after taking up the work, they would be able to carry it forward acceptably and successfully in the fear and love of God. Instead of moving cautiously, exercising the strictest economy at every step, they made investments on borrowed capital. They felt sure that they could carry forward the work without loss, and that their debts would soon be paid. They did not work out their plans with fear and trembling, and they brought trouble to the cause which their work was supposed to represent.

If our physicians would be willing to unite with men who have made a success of financial management; if they would cheerfully work in a humble way, until the earnings of their work enabled them to enlarge; if they would resolutely refuse to pile up debts, they would save themselves and their brethren from many sorrows. If they would depend on the help of God, putting their trust in Him and showing themselves willing to begin small and to let the merit of their work speak for itself, if they had sanctified motives, if they would make it their determination to exert a saving influence in the world, they would be blessed in their work, and many more sanitariums would be established as representatives of the truth.

A Solemn Warning

The Lord has instructed me to warn those who establish sanitariums in new places to begin their work in humility. They are to consecrate their abilities to God, to be used to the glory of His name.

The sanitariums established in the future are not to be immense, expensive buildings. Small local sanitariums are to be established in connection with our schools.

Many sanitariums are to be established in places outside the cities. Connected with them there are to be men and women of ability and consecration, who will conduct themselves in the love and fear of God. These institutions are to be training schools. Those who act a part in them are not to feel that they are prepared for graduation, that they know all they need to know. They are to study diligently and practice carefully the lessons Christ has given.—Manuscript 76, 1902.

Move Carefully

There are men who do not move wisely. They are anxious to make a large appearance. They think that outward display will give them influence. In their work, they do not first sit down and count the cost, to see whether they are able to finish what they have begun. Thus they show their weakness. They show that they have much to learn in regard to the necessity of moving carefully and guardedly. In their self-confidence they make many mistakes. Thus some have received harm from which they will never recover. This has been the case with several who have felt competent to establish and conduct sanitariums. Failure comes to them, and ... they find themselves involved in debt....

Contentment with Slow Growth

Men who might have done well if they had consecrated themselves to God, if they had been willing to work in a humble way, enlarging their business slowly and refusing to go into debt, have made a failure because they have not worked on right lines. And after getting into difficulty they have sold out as men incompetent to manage. They desired relief from financial pressure, and did not stop to think of the after results.

Those who help such ones out of difficulty are tempted to bind them with such strong cords in the shape of pledges that ever after they feel they are bondslaves. They seldom outgrow the reputation of poor management and failure.

To those who thus become involved in debt, I am instructed to say: Do not give up if you are moving in right lines. Work with all your power to relieve the situation yourselves. Do not throw an embarrassed institution upon an association that is already heavily burdened with debt. It is best for every sanitarium to stand in its own responsibility.

Those who have charge of our sanitariums should move guardedly. There are times when they will see little increase. Let them act with wisdom and tact and adaptability. Let them study and practice the instruction Christ gave in regard to building a tower. Forethought is of far more value than afterthought—when a neglect of wise calculation and careful management is plainly seen to result in failure.

Managers who are slack, who do not know how to manage, should be separated from the work. Secure the services of men and women who know how to bind about the edges so that the work shall not ravel out.

Let all who are connected with our institutions humble themselves before God. Let them ask God to help them to plan so wisely and economically that the institutions will take firm root and will bear fruit to God's glory. Depend not on men. Look to Jesus. Continue in prayer and watch unto prayer with thanksgiving. Be sure that you have a close connection with Christ.—Letter 12, 1902.

Honor Through Lowliness

Although having every necessary facility with which to work, the managers of some of our larger sanitariums have desired to make many improvements with money that is not their own, but the Lord's. Some neglect to perform deeds of mercy for the needy, and use for themselves the pittance saved in this way. Many commit act after act of complicated robbery of God in the person of His saints. In their business dealings, those connected with our institutions should always be actuated by noble principles, revealing by their example the pure, holy principles that govern every Christian....

The Saviour of mankind was born of humble parentage in a sin-cursed, wicked world. He was brought up in obscurity at Nazareth, a small town of Galilee. He began His work in poverty and without worldly rank. Thus God introduced the gospel in a way altogether different from the way in which many deem it wise to proclaim the same gospel in 1902. At the very beginning of the gospel dispensation He taught His church to rely, not on worldly rank and splendor, but on the power of faith and obedience. The favor of God is above the riches of gold and silver. The power of His Spirit is of inestimable value.

Never are we to rely upon worldly recognition and rank. Never are we, in the establishment of institutions, to try to compete with worldly institutions in size or splendor. The great desire of the managers of our sanitariums should be so to walk in obedience to the Lord that all the helpers connected with these institutions can by faith walk with God as did Enoch.

The Lord will guide all who humbly walk with Him. Humble men who trust in Him will be the most successful workers in His cause. We shall gain the victory, not by erecting massive buildings in rivalry with our enemies, but by cherishing a Christlike spirit of meekness and lowliness. Better far the cross and disappointed hopes, than to live with princes and forfeit heaven. Truth will be bitterly opposed, but never will it lose its vitality.—Manuscript 109, 1902.

Disadvantages of Large Institutions

"Break up the large centers," has been the word of the Lord. "Carry the light to many places." Those who are desirous of receiving a training for effective medical missionary work should understand that large sanitariums will be conducted so much like institutions of the world that students laboring in such sanitariums cannot obtain a symmetrical training for Christian medical missionary work.

The proclamation of the truth in all parts of the world calls for small sanitariums in many places, not in the heart of cities, but in places where city influences will be as little felt as possible.

I am obliged to say that the making of so large a plant in ----- and the calling together of those who should be engaged in medical missionary work in many places, is doing just what God has specified should not be done.

Danger in Separation From the Gospel

The fact that many patients are coming to the new sanitarium at ----- is not to be read as a sign that the planning for so large work there was for the best. To this large institution will come many men and women who are not really sick. Workers will be required to wait on them; our nurses will become the servants of worldly men and women who are not inclined to piety or religion. But this is not the work that God has given to His medical missionaries. Our charge has been given us by the greatest Medical Missionary that this world has ever seen.—Letter 210, 1903.

There is danger of Dr. -----'s seeking to meet the standard of the world in his ideas and practice. He needs to seek the Lord at every step. He should keep in view, not his own glory, but the glory of the

Lord.... And he is in danger of setting the medical missionary work first, making it the body instead of the arm. He will not succeed in this, and he must not attempt that which he cannot accomplish. He will be ambitious to do great things by separating the medical missionary work from the gospel ministry; but the Lord does not lead His physicians to separate the medical missionary work from the gospel ministry. Truth, present truth for this time, is to be believed and acted upon in connection with the principles of health reform.

The Sabbath a Test for this Time

The sanitariums which are established are to be closely and inseparably bound up with the gospel. The Lord has given instruction that the gospel is to be carried forward; and the gospel includes health reform in all its phases. Our work is to enlighten the world; for it is blind to the movements which are taking place, preparing the way for the plagues which God will permit to come upon the world. God's faithful watchmen must give the warning.

Dr. ----- has a desire to do large things. He is in danger of spending his energies outside the sanitarium, instead of devoting all his powers to making the institution a power in connection with the gospel message and the Sabbath reform. Dr. ----- needs to place himself where he will understand the truth for this time. This is his only safety as a physician. He needs to have his feet shod with the preparation of the gospel.

He is in danger of becoming confused and of failing to see the elevated, holy influence which the Sabbath question is to exert on the work for this time. He will consider it necessary to do on the Sabbath many things which should not be done on that day. If he seeks to embrace so many responsibilities, he will come to pay very little regard to the Sabbath. Such an influence will be a curse to the institution. Those who are connected with our sanitariums are to be taught to regard the Sabbath question as the great test for this time. God desires His people to bind medical missionary work up with the work of the third angel's message. This is the work that will restore the moral image of God in man....[See Observance of Sabbath, Section 11.]

Greater Power in Truth than in Worldly Show

Dr. ----- is not to study how he can best meet the requirements of the world. He is not to pattern after the world in his appearance and equipage, flattering himself that this is the way to meet the higher classes. The gospel forbids the cherishing of worldly ideas. You may ask where. I point you to the life of Christ. Think of what He was before He came to our world—Commander of all the heavenly intelligences. How did He come to this earth? We know Him as a poor man, who to the very close of His earthly history maintained His humility. The idea that outward show gives influence to a man or his position is one of Satan's lies. Let no man climb above the methods and example of our Lord. There is no higher standard than the life of Christ. As a people we are to shun the pretense of the world, which has made men and women what they are today. We are not to copy the customs and practices of worldly wisemen in order to gain favor or influence. Christlikeness is true Christianity. In the truth there is a power which no outward appearance or display can give, which no worldly suppositions or opinions can change or alter.—Manuscript 172, 1899.

[161]

No Compromise

To those who will engage in the medical missionary work, the temptation will come to exalt themselves, to put on an appearance for the sake of effect. Cut away everything of this character from your work. Let the whole burden of soul be to be just what Christ was in His work. We are to make no compromise with the habits and practices of the world. We are to stand upon the platform of eternal truth, pure, unadulterated truth. In this we may be considered singular, but this is the lot of all who make Christ their portion. Every worker in medical missionary lines is to make that work a success by living in connection with the Great Worker.—Manuscript 96, 1898.

* * * * *

For Further Study

Encourage One Another:
Counsels on Health, 242, 243.

Cooperation With Church Organization:
Counsels on Health, 519-52 (Testimonies for the Church 8:158-162).

Need of Mutual Counsel:
Counsels to Parents, Teachers, and Students, 92;
Life Sketches of Ellen G. White, 303.

Avoiding Unnecessary Responsibilities:
Testimonies for the Church 6:244-248, 252, 253;
Testimonies for the Church 8:189-191.

Holiness of Life:
Counsels on Health, 581-634.

Social Purity:
Counsels on Health, 567-57 (Testimonies for the Church 2:450-457).

Refinement and Delicacy:
Counsels on Health, 363-366.

Dealing With Sentimentalism:
Counsels on Health, 294, 295.

Mammoth Sanitariums:
Counsels on Health, 239 (Testimonies for the Church 7:102, 103).

Opposition to Be Expected:
Counsels on Health, 527.

Section 9—The Management of Sanitariums

A Noble Work

The management of our sanitariums involves a great deal. Those connected with them have a noble work to do, and right principles are to be strictly maintained. The workers are to labor for the establishment and support of the work of God in accordance with His appointment, and the spread of the principles of true temperance in eating, drinking, and dressing. To impart knowledge of this character and of the saving grace and mercy of God is the most honorable, noble work in which Seventh-day Adventists can engage. They thus honor God, and advance their own interests for this life and for the future, eternal life. Their example works for the saving of souls for whom Christ gave His life.

A High Standard

In our sanitariums we must seek to uplift a high standard. The banner of truth, goodness, and usefulness must ever be raised. The blessed fruits of the gospel tree are to be manifested in thorough consecration, in holy lives. Every true worker for the Master is to be as a city set on a hill, that cannot be hid. The physicians and managers in our medical institutions must be guarded; otherwise they will surely deny the principles of truth and righteousness, which exalt the Lord of heaven. They must have God dwelling in their hearts, or they will set an example to others that will be to their injury.

They will be tempted to cater to the tastes and habits of unconsecrated people by bringing in innovations, and the blessing of God will be removed from the work. Ever remember that in God's sight a heart that is meek and lowly constitutes true value, even the ornament of a meek and quiet spirit, which He regards as of great price. God can bless the meek and lowly. He can use them as honored instruments in blessing others; for they will give the glory to Him to whom belongs all greatness and power.

Tact and ingenuity will be required. It is necessary to be constantly on the alert to meet prejudice and to overcome difficulties. Unless this attitude is taken, there will be, not peace, but a sword, in our institutions. The workers are constantly brought in contact with others who also carry heavy burdens; and all need divine enlightenment. They need to manifest the unselfish, loving spirit of Christ. They will be tried. Their faith and love, patience and constancy, will be proved; but God is their Helper.—Manuscript 162, 1897.

Essential Qualifications for Management

Our health institutions are of value in the Lord's estimation only when He is allowed to preside in their management. If His plans and devisings are regarded as inferior to plans of men, He looks upon these institutions as of no more value than the institutions established and conducted by worldlings. God cannot endorse any institution unless it teaches the living principles of His law and brings its own actions into strict conformity to these precepts. Upon those institutions that are not maintained according to His law He pronounces the sentence, "Unaccepted; weighed in the balances of the sanctuary and found wanting."

The man at the head of any work in God's cause is to be a man of intelligence, a man capable of managing large interests successfully, a man of even temper, Christlike forbearance, and perfect self-control. He only whose heart is transformed by the grace of Christ can be a proper leader.

Those who act as managers and overseers in our sanitariums are not to make the world's policy their criterion; for the sign of God, as defined in Exodus 31:12-17, is to be revealed in all its comprehensive meaning. The proper observance of the Sabbath day by all connected with our sanitariums will exert an untold influence for good. Every medical institution established by Seventh-day Adventists is to bear God's sign before the world prominently, without disguising the facts in any way. We are to voice the message of the third angel flying in the midst of heaven with the everlasting gospel to proclaim to the world. We are to bear aloft the banner on which is inscribed,

"The Commandments of God and the faith of Jesus." [See Sabbath Observance, Section 11.]

The Use of Means

[165]

The men in positions of trust should regard the means they handle as God's revenue, and use it in an economical manner. When there is an abundance in the treasury, they are not to invest it in adding building to building in places already provided with memorials for God. Hundreds of other places are in need of this money, that they, too, may have something established to represent the truth. All parts of the Lord's vineyard are to be worked.

The power to use and disburse the Lord's money is not to be left to the judgment of any one man. An account must be given for every dollar expended. God's means is to be used at the proper times and in the right places, that it may be a blessing, and also an object lesson of how He works, in accordance with principles of equity, justice, and righteousness.

All Ye are Brethren

No one man is ever to set himself up as a ruler, as a lord over his fellowmen, to act out his natural impulses. No one man's voice and influence should ever be allowed to become a controlling power. Those who oppress their fellow workers in our institutions, and who refuse to change their manner of treating helpers under their charge, should be removed. As overseers, they should have exerted a superior, refining influence for the right. Their investment with power makes it all the more necessary for them to be models of true Christianity.

I am instructed by the Lord to say that position never gives a man grace or makes him righteous. "The fear of the Lord is the beginning of wisdom." Some men entrusted with positions of responsibility entertain the idea that position is for the aggrandizement of self. Let no manager think that all minds must be subjected to his mind, that all wills must be subordinate to his will, and that all methods must be laid aside for his methods. Greater injury cannot be done to any institution than by allowing such a man to remain in his position, after proper test and trial. It is a sin against God to permit unfaithful stewards to remain in positions of trust; for the Lord's people are liable to be misled by their unfaithfulness.—Manuscript 154, 1902.

[166]

Willing to Take Counsel

No one in an institution, not even the superintendent, should take the position that he is free to follow his own judgment in all things. Let no one think that he knows so much that he no longer needs to learn. Unless we are constantly learning of Christ, and unless we are willing to take counsel and advice from our brethren, we shall fail in our work; for we shall become self-sufficient, and with those who are self-sufficient God cannot work....

Quick to Discern

The man who occupies the position of superintendent must be brave and true, ready to stand fearlessly for what he knows to be right. He must be a man who is quick to discern and discriminate, a man who can make wrong right with as little friction as possible. A lack of discernment, a failure to reason from cause to effect, often brings about in our institutions a condition of things that is very displeasing to God.—Letter 30, 1887.

Unnecessary Debts

To the managers of all our sanitariums, I would say, Let no large debts be created. Make no unnecessary move. Set aside your desire for full equipment at once. Let the best possible use be made of fewer facilities, rather than to increase debt. All that is needed may in time be obtained, but all the furnishings and facilities need not be provided at once. Let reason, calm thought, and wise calculation be the rule of action. If success attends our institutions established for the care of the sick, it will be because the managers have preferred to get along with the most essential things rather than to pile up debts.

The Lord calls upon us to do a work in many places. We shall have sanitariums that can be carried on without involving our cause heavily in debt.—Letter 140, 1906.

Not With Outward Show

Our physicians are to show Christlike simplicity in every line of their work. If they are clothed with the panoply of heaven—Christlike meekness and lowliness—they will be truly successful. But conformity to the world, to gain its favor and recognition, will bring weakness. No such concession is to be made. Our hope and strength do not depend on outside appearances. Those who are influenced against the truth by a lack of extravagance in house, in furniture, in dress, in equipage, show that they are incapable of understanding the merit of truth. They are not capable of appreciating the gospel of Christ. God is dishonored when those connected with the work which is to prepare a people to stand the test of the time of trouble before us, forsake Him to follow the fashions of the world....

You are not to seek that popularity which has led far away from the simplicity of Christ. God is to be your Leader. Those who are Christians will stand in the strength of God. They will show in their lives the superiority which God gives to obedient subjects, those who are loyal to His commandments. Those who believe the truth will never be ashamed of the gospel of Jesus Christ. The principles of truth are to pervade our medical institutions. And then, as those who have followed the customs and fashions of the world shall in their suffering come to these institutions, they will see a simplicity that will charm their senses. They will feel the unseen presence of heavenly angels.—Manuscript 172, 1899.

Simplicity in Furnishing

Less expensively furnished rooms than you desire will be in accordance with the work God has given us to do in these last days. Your ideas are not molded and fashioned by a true practical idea of what it means to walk humbly with God. You look upon appearance as the great means of lifting you up to success. This is a delusion. You seek to make an appearance that is not in any way appropriate to the work God has given you to do, an appearance which it would require a large sum of money to keep up. We cannot consent to have the rooms of the sanitarium furnished in accordance with the idolatry of the age, even if this will bring an increase of patronage. Christian influence is of more value than this.

A desire for outside appearance is like a canker which is ever eating into the vitals. Appearance is a merciless tyrant. You need to guard against your inclination for show and entertainment. It is a mistake to suppose that by keeping up an appearance you will obtain more patients and therefore more means. The evils resulting from such a course have not yet appeared to you, but they will appear if you are not guarded....

God's Way is Best

God looks not upon outward display, but upon the heart. Well-advised movements must be made. Nothing must be invested extravagantly. It is not because we desire to exalt ourselves that we are seeking to build up a sanitarium, but because we desire to honor God and properly represent the truth, which has been misrepresented. In this institution our peculiar religious principles are to be magnified and exalted. Never are they to be hidden.

The Lord's way is always the best way. We are safe while we follow Him who says, "Learn of Me; for I am meek and lowly in heart." If Christ, the Majesty of heaven, is meek and lowly, how much more ought we to be, who are under sentence of death for disobedience. The influence of our physicians in the sanitarium should be such as to encourage meekness and lowliness. Men are not be exalted as great and wonderful. It is God who is to be magnified.—Letter 51, 1900.

The Ministry of Trials

In Christian experience, the Lord permits trials of various kinds to call men and women to a higher order of living and to a more sanctified service. Without these trials there would be a continual falling away from the likeness of Christ, and men would become imbued with a spirit of scientific, fanciful, human philosophy, which would lead them to unite with Satan's followers.

In the providence of God every good and great enterprise is subjected to trials, to test the purity and the strength of the principles of those who are standing in positions of responsibility and to mold and substantiate the individual human character after God's model. This is the highest order of education.

Perfection of character is attained through exercise of the faculties of the mind, in times of supreme test, by obedience to every requirement of God's law. Men in positions of trust are to be instrumentalities in the hands of God for promoting His glory; and in performing their duties with the utmost faithfulness they may attain perfection of character.—Manuscript 85, 1906.

Men of Discernment Needed

"You have," said our Instructor, "come to an important place in the history of your work. Who shall be chosen to carry responsibilities in the sanitarium at the beginning of its work? No mistake must be made in this matter. Men are not to be placed in positions of trust who have not been tested and tried. Men and women who understand the will of the Lord are to be chosen—men who can discern the work that needs to be done and prayerfully do it, that the mistakes and errors of the past need not be repeated."

"The one who is placed in the position of business manager," He said, "must daily be managed by the Lord. He occupies a very important place and he must possess the necessary qualifications for the work. He should have dignity and knowledge, blended with a clear sense of how to use his authority. Christ must be revealed in his life. He must be a man who can give religious instruction and exert a spiritual influence. He must know how to deal with minds, and he must allow his own mind to be controlled by the Spirit. Wisdom is to come forth from his lips in words of encouragement to all with whom he is connected. He must know how to discern and correct mistakes. He must be a man who will harmonize with his fellow workers, a man who possesses adaptability. He should be able to speak of the different points of our faith as occasion requires. His words and acts should reveal justice, judgment, and the love of God."

He who gave the Israelites instruction from the pillar of cloud and led them through the wilderness into the Promised Land is our Leader today. We are under divine guidance, and if we are obedient to God's commands we shall be in perfect safety and will receive distinguished marks of His favor.—Letter 325, 1904.

Moderation in Rates

In our sanitariums provision must be made for all classes. The Lord does not call upon our people to establish institutions where all who come can receive food and lodging free, and where the peculiar points of our faith must not be introduced. The Lord has not laid this work upon any Seventh-day Adventist. To do this would be a misuse of time and means.

The accommodation and treatment must be such that patients of the higher class will be attracted. Rooms must be fitted up for the use of those who are willing to pay a liberal price. But physicians are not to place too high an estimate on wealthy patients who can afford to pay high prices; neither is there to be an extravagant outlay of means with a view to gaining patronage. The charges for treatment and accommodations must not be so high that there will be a reluctance to keep to the simple, wholesome food that is essential to health. Ask a reasonable price for the treatment given. This course will recommend itself to all reasonable minds.

To set your price above what is true and honest may be in accordance with the custom of worldly physicians, but it will not redound to the glory of God. It is not His plan, and will not gain His approval. It will have an unfavorable influence upon the world. The charging of such high prices will bring a rebound, and will have an influence altogether different from what is expected. Exorbitant prices should never be charged.

A Change Called For

I am commissioned to speak to all who are engaged as physicians in our institutions. A reformation is required in regard to the management of these institutions. They are not to be conducted as the world would conduct them. While many who cannot afford to pay are treated free, others are charged exorbitant prices for operations which take but little time. The charges of worldly physicians are not to rule in our institutions....

Warnings and cautions have been given on these points from the Lord. He will not bless fraud in any phase of business transaction. The medical profession in general carries a heavy stock of unjust exactions; but shall we copy their sin? We are reformers. We are supposed to be pursuing a course that will represent the character of perfect humanity, the pure, elevated character of Christ. When this is true of us, a well-established purpose of strict integrity in things that are least will be carried by us into the larger responsibilities. Sanctified hearts will always reveal sanctified principles.—Manuscript 169, 1899.

To an Inexperienced Manager

You are to always place yourself in the position of the one with whom you deal, and see how you would feel under similar circumstances; then act as you would have others act toward you, that no shadow may be cast upon the precious cause of truth. It must not be reproached for the sake of gaining a few dollars or cents. Let no occasion ever be given for anyone to say that Seventh-day Adventists ever will do mean actions. Contempt will be what they will reap. Let all our business transactions stand in a pure, untarnished light before the world and with those of our faith. Do not let your course of action be of that character that it requires explanations in order to make it appear anyway in a favorable light.

Let all see this institution standing as an institution to promote the happiness and well-being of our fellowmen. Better, far better, to submit to some inconvenience and losses than to become mercenary and create angry feelings, and leave the unhappy impression on the minds that they have been taken advantage of and cheated, and they go away hostile to the institution. The principles and morals of the institution must ever be governed in all relations, to believers and unbelievers, with generous, well-defined principles of nobility and consideration, especially toward those who are suffering affliction.—Letter 26, 1888.

Consideration for an Injured Worker

When one of your number is injured at his work, as was the case some time ago, deal with him as you would like to be dealt with under similar circumstances. Show Christlike sympathy. This is God's way of dealing. Anything short of this is not true justice or nobility.

Special care should have been shown in dealing with the one hurt; for he was an unbeliever. You have reason to thank your heavenly Father that his life was spared.

If the one injured has to be taken to the sanitarium, the charge made for his treatment should be light, if any charge at all is made. And let it also be considered if justice does not require that his wages be paid during the time that he is away from his work because of the accident.

In no case is advantage to be taken of any worker; for all things are open before the eyes of Him with whom we have to do. He requires that integrity be cherished in the soul and revealed in the life.—Letter 58, 1902.

Be Kind to the Lowly

The desire to have one's own way, contrary to the judgment of co-workers, is to find no place in our institutions. "All ye are brethren." A spirit of love and tenderness is to be shown. In our sanitariums, and in any institution, kind words, pleasant looks, a condescending demeanor, are of great value. There is a charm in the intercourse of men who are truly courteous. In business transactions what power for good a little condescension has! How restoring and uplifting the influence of such dealing upon men who are poor and depressed, borne down to the earth by sickness and poverty! Shall we withhold from them the balm that such dealing brings? ...

Those in responsible positions will have to deal with those whose lot is far from easy. Toil and deprivation, with no hope for better things in the future, make their burden very heavy. And when pain and sickness are added, the load is almost greater than they have strength to bear. Let not God's stewards put sharpness into their dealing with such ones. This would be cruelty itself. Let them clothe themselves with courtesy as with a garment. Let them be kind and conciliatory in their dealing with the lowliest and poorest. God will see and reward such dealing.—Letter 30, 1887.

Sanctified Dignity to Be Preserved

I am instructed that our sanitariums are to be cleansed and purified from those persons whose course of action is a discredit to the sacred work of the sanitarium. Our health institutions should preserve a sanctified dignity. Let not helpers be employed here who have not a sense of true dignity. Employ those who give evidence that they are working to meet the standard of perfection, those in whose lives are seen the marks of the divine similitude.

Great wisdom should be exercised in selecting men and women as instructors in our sanitariums. They should be not only those who can speak intelligently on scientific questions, but men and women who have learned to be under the rule of the Spirit of God, and who obey the instructions of Christ. They should be able to give wise counsel in a kind and intelligent manner. Fretting and scolding will not benefit, but plain words spoken in a spirit of kindness will accomplish lasting results for good. The Lord will help all who truly desire to learn of Him.

Right impressions cannot be made upon the sick when those who compose the sanitarium family of helpers are disagreeable or uncouth in manner, or cherish a spirit of frivolity or are subject to jealous freaks. Such workers should not be retained in our institutions, for the enemy is always ready to work upon such minds and through their influence to drive souls away from Christ. Far better would it be to pay higher wages and secure good, sensible helpers in our institutions than to accept those whom you cannot discipline and train.

The Influence of a Beautiful Character

The pleasant disposition, the beautiful character, the Lord will use to bring blessing to the sick. The truths of the word of God possess a sanctifying, transforming power. If received into the heart and carried into the life, they will prove a savor of life unto life. Let those employed in our institutions be such as will let the light of truth shine forth in their daily words and actions. It is only such that Christ can accept as workers together with Him.

I write thus definitely that all may understand the importance of eradicating evil influences from our sanitariums, which are established for the purpose of bringing healing and blessing to suffering human beings who are sick in mind and body.—Manuscript 69, 1909.

Experienced Workers Needed

It is not the wisest course to connect with our sanitariums too many who are inexperienced, who come as learners, while there is a lack of experienced, efficient workers. We need more matronly women, and men who are sound and solid in principle—substantial men who fear God and who can carry responsibilities wisely. Some may come and offer to work for smaller wages because they enjoy being at a sanitarium or because they wish to learn; but it is not true economy to supply an institution largely with inexperienced helpers.

If the right persons are connected with our sanitariums, and if all will humble their hearts before God, although there may now be a heavy debt upon the institution, the Lord will work in such a way that the debt will be lessened, and souls will be converted to the truth, because they see that the workers are following in the way of the Lord and keeping His commandments.—Manuscript 57, 1909.

Wholly Devoted to God

I am very anxious that all those connected with our sanitariums shall be men whose lives are wholly devoted to God, free from all evil works. There are some who seem to have lost all sense of the sacred character of our institutions and the purpose for which they were established. A great dread has been upon my mind as to what the results will be of this lack of spirituality and clear discernment. There is a great need of loyalty to principle. The Lord calls for young men to work in our sanitariums who will not yield to temptation. The lives of the young people connected with our sanitariums should be such as to exert a convicting and converting power upon those who have not received the message for this time.

Our sanitariums are to be conducted in such a way that God will be honored and glorified. They are not to become a snare. But unless the human instrumentalities are under the guidance of the Holy Spirit, the enemy will use them to carry out his devisings for the hindrance of God's cause and for the destruction of their own souls. Many have already lost their first love for the great, grand, Bible truths concerning Christ's second coming.—Manuscript 63, 1908.

The Selection of Workers

Great care should be shown in choosing young people to connect with our sanitariums. Those who have not the love of the truth in the soul should not be chosen. The sick need to have wise words spoken to them. The influence of every worker should make an impression on minds in favor of the religion of Christ Jesus. Light has been given that the young people chosen to connect with our sanitariums should be those who have evidence that they have been apt learners in the school of Christ.—Letter 59, 1905.

Sanitariums and Education

Every sanitarium established by Seventh-day Adventists is to be conducted on educational lines. And constantly it is to advance to higher and still higher lines of work. Those who fill positions of responsibility should remember the influence that their words and actions have on those connected with them. They are to labor for the spiritual and physical health of those who are brought in connection with the institution. A far higher work is to be done in this line than has hitherto been done.

Those who occupy positions of responsibility in a sanitarium, either as manager or matron, should feel the importance of the responsibility resting on them to train those in their charge to do their work thoroughly and quickly. If they are true Christians, they will strive earnestly to achieve the best results for the present and eternal good of the learners. They will not betray sacred trusts by bringing into their instruction sentiments of their own that are not in harmony with the teaching of the word of God.

Those who take charge of this work are first to obtain Christlikeness. Daily they are to learn in the school of Christ. Then they will have wisdom to know how to deal with human minds. They will know how to carry on from stage to stage of true knowledge those

To Be Training Schools

All our institutions are to be training schools. Especially is this true with regard to our sanitariums. Wise counsel must be given to the youth. Neatness and thoroughness must be required from them. They are to be taught to make their motions as quick as possible as they work. Slowness should be treated as a disease that must be cured.

Every institution should have wise overseers over the inside and outside work, that the helpers may be trained to guard against shiftless, indolent habits. The matron should select from those under her those who can aid her in teaching the helpers to do their work with neatness and thoroughness. Slowness is never to be encouraged. Everyone should try to work quickly and at the same time with neatness and carefulness.

The matron is to show a motherly care for the girls in her charge. She is to show them the wisdom of putting by each month a portion of their wages, placing it in charge of faithful hands. She is to encourage them in neatness of dress, at the same time teaching them that their dress should always be neat and becoming. She is to discourage vanity and extravagance in any line.

The Elimination of Waste

The one who has charge of the finances should study how much he can save, instead of how much he can spend. All needless expense should be curtailed. Let the helpers understand that the consumption must not exceed the production. To waste in a sanitarium is a grave matter. There are so many who have to do with the different lines of work, and it is most essential that they understand the need of economy. Economy is a very valuable science. Many waste much by failing to save the odds and ends. In many a family as much is wasted as would support a small family. All these things are included in the education to be given in our sanitariums.

Money is a needed treasure; let it not be lavished on those who do not need it. Someone needs your willing gifts. Too often those who have means fail to consider how many in the world are hungry, starving for food. They may say, "I cannot feed them all." But by practicing Christ's lessons on economy you can feed one. It may be that you can feed many who are hungering for temporal food. And you can feed their souls with the bread of life. "Gather up the fragments that remain, that nothing be lost." These words were spoken by Him who had all the resources of the universe at His command; by His miracle-working power He supplied thousands with food, but He did not disdain to teach a lesson in economy.

The Spirit of Cheerful Service

The workers in our sanitariums are to be trained for the work for which they are best adapted. But when an emergency arises, and help is needed, no worker should say, That is not my work. The helper who has the idea that he is only to do the work assigned him, and no more, who feels no responsibility to help wherever and whenever help is needed, should at once dismiss this idea from his mind. He should never feel that a wrong is done him if in an emergency he is asked to work overtime. When extra help is needed, let the workers assist willingly, in Christian meekness, and they will receive a blessing.

It may be that some will rebel when they are asked to do the small, common duties. But these are the duties they need to know how to perform. It is faithfulness in little things that prepares us for usefulness in larger responsibilities. The most successful toilers are those who cheerfully take up the work of serving God in little things. Every human being is to work with his life thread, weaving it into the fabric to help to complete the pattern. Those who desire to be useful can always find employment. Time will never hang heavy on their hands....

No one is to spend his time longing to do the impossible, forgetting ordinary daily duties in a desire to do something great. Round after round, from the lowest round, the ladder must be climbed—it may be by painful effort. But success comes with diligent effort, and the progress made is of great value to the earnest striver for victory....

By their actions those connected with our institutions give proof of the worth, or worthlessness, of their judgment. Those who enter the service of the institution with a spirit of unwillingness to help, who do their allotted tasks with a feeling of compulsion, in sullen submission, who act as if they would gladly escape from the drudgery of the necessary daily duties which someone must do, are very little help to the institution. A mechanical obedience may hide the smoldering fire of rebellion, but it is ready to break out at any time against restraint. In the service of such there is no peace or light or love. The atmosphere surrounding their souls is not fragrant. The influence of their words and actions is felt by others, and this influence is a harm even to those who are trying to do their best in any position in which they are placed. Self-pity is deteriorating to the characters of those who cherish it, and it exerts an influence that spoils the happiness of others.

[178]
Patient Dealing with the Erring

The one who is placed in charge of such ones should in no case fret or scold. He should not give way to impatience or lose his self-control. Take them by themselves, and tell them that such exhibitions cannot be permitted, that their spirit must be changed. Tell them that to educate themselves to think that they need sympathy is the most foolish thing they can do. Pray with them; then give them their task, as God gives us our tasks. He has given to every man his work, according to his several ability.

If, after these youth have been fully and patiently tried, they make no change, let them be plainly told that they cannot be retained in the institution. Let their place be given to those who will not be such a burden to the institution....

There is to be no slavery. The service of all is to be cheerful and willing. But those who train the youth in our institutions have one disadvantage to work against. There are many who in the homelife have received an imperfect training. Often the mother makes herself the slave of her children, and in so doing neglects her most important work—the training of her children to wait on themselves, to follow habits of neatness, order, and thoroughness in the little things of life....

When such children reach the age of responsibility and caretaking, they are unsubdued and undisciplined. It may be that they have a desire to enter one of our sanitariums to take a nurse's training. They come, but the defects of their home training make their stay at the institution hard for themselves and for those who have charge of their education.

Overcoming Parental Neglect

Let there be in the institution no continuation of the spoiling received in the home. There will be no hope for these poor youth—wronged from childhood by unwise indulgence—if the policy followed in the home is followed in the institution. Let them be wisely and kindly disciplined, and when it is seen that they are trying to improve, trying to make themselves what they ought to be, let words of encouragement be spoken to them. But let them plainly understand that they cannot follow in the institution the course of self-pleasing that they followed in the home. If they are willing to begin at the beginning, if they are determined to master every problem, they will improve....

Their parents' neglect has made their training much harder than it otherwise would have been. Do not pass by any slighted work unnoticed; but do not blame or scold them. This will not overcome the difficulty, but will embarrass and discourage them. In the most kindly way tell them that the neglect of the past must be remedied, or they cannot be retained in the institution. The need for a reformation must be pointed out. They must be encouraged to change wrong habits and establish right ones.

Those who sympathize with the one who is causing great perplexity by his lack of determination to remedy the defects of his training are in need of being labored with. Show them that it is their duty to help those who have so much to overcome. Those in a position of responsibility in an institution can spoil young men and young women for a lifetime by unduly sympathizing with them, petting them, and listening to their complaints. Those who do this show that they themselves need to reform before they are prepared to take wise charge of a sanitarium or any other institution in which the youth are receiving a training.

This is one line of medical missionary work to be done in our sanitariums. And oh, how careful should those in charge be not to make any mistake. Those who, while occupying a position of trust, give wrong advice, are counterworking the work of the Lord Jesus.

Responsibilities of Leaders

Oh, what a work there is before those who are standing in responsible positions in our institutions! A great work is to be done. There are weighty responsibilities to be borne, and they must be borne by men who have a living experience in the things of God, who day by day seek Him with the whole heart. Solemn are the obligations resting on the physicians and managers of our sanitariums. They are to set an example worthy of their claim to believe the truth....

I desire if possible to impress the minds of our physicians and managers with the importance of giving so pure and righteous a representation of God that the world will see Him in His beauty. I desire them to be so filled with the Spirit that dwelt in Him that worldly policy will have no power to divert their minds from the work of presenting to men the grand, wonderful possibilities before every soul who receives and believes in Christ.—Manuscript 27, 1902.

Gentleness in Discipline

Into your discipline bring not a particle of harshness. Lay no rigid injunctions on the youth. It is these ironclad rules and commands that sometimes lead them to feel that they must and will do the thing they are charged not to do. When giving caution or reproof to the youth, do it as one who has a special interest in them. Let them see that you have an earnest desire for them to make a good record in the books of heaven....

By the words and works of this life is decided the eternal destiny of everyone; be very careful, therefore, not to drive a tempted soul onto the enemy's battleground. Provoke not the youth to wrath. Stir not up in them, by unjust charges and harsh treatment, the impulse to act rashly. Often those who ought to know how to deal with the youth drive them away from God by injudicious words and actions. God records such treatment of the youth as a sin against Himself.

Treat the tempted ones in a way that will draw them to you as a friend who will not misjudge or hurt them.

The admonitions God has given in His word are infinitely better than any words of reproof you can speak. Lead the youth to see that it is for their eternal good to follow the path the Lord has marked out for them. Tell them they must not sin, because it grieves the heart of the Redeemer. Tell them to fear to sin, because the wages of sin is death. In gentleness and love try to inspire in them an earnest purpose to do their whole duty to God and to their fellowmen. Remember that the future experience of these youth will bear the stamp of the teaching you have given them.

As you thus strive to educate the youth in your care you are educating yourselves, preparing yourselves to do better work for the Master. There is brought about in your character a reformation that makes you a safe example for the tempted and tried. In disciplining others you are disciplining and training yourselves....

Strive to Exemplify Christ

[181]

Let those who are placed in responsible positions beware lest, by defective characters and un-Christlike tempers, they work against God's plan. The glory of God and the good of human beings should lead every man to strive to be an example of what man may become through the grace of Christ. He is to rely wholly on the merits of the One who gave Himself as an offering that He might stand between God and man. The efforts of every one in whose heart the work of grace is daily done, will be a savor of life unto life to all who are under his watchcare. He will be successful in laboring for the saving of souls ready to perish. He will bring them to the Chief Shepherd, who alone can save to the uttermost all who come to Him.

The men who guide and instruct those who are ignorant and out of the way, need much of the patience and love of Christ. Many times their patience will be tried; those for whom they work will seem to be dull of understanding; it will be hard to lead them to act on correct principles. The truth must be brought to bear upon them to soften and subdue their hearts. Those who try to help them must have ability to lead them on step by step, realizing that they are to beseech sinners, not drive them, to be reconciled to God.

Christ says, My sheep hear My voice, and they follow Me away from the byways of sin. As Christ worked, so you are to work. In tenderness and love seek to lead the erring to the right way. This will call for great patience and forbearance, and for the constant manifestation of the forgiving love of Christ. Daily the Saviour's compassion must be revealed. The example He has left must be followed. He took upon His sinless nature our sinful nature, that He might know how to succor those that are tempted.

He who does this work must put into it his whole heart; for it is a work that requires all there is of a man. He who does it as a work that is done for wages, will make an utter failure....

It is not necessary to bring everything that needs to be corrected before the manager. When you see a worker in error, go to him, and talk with him kindly and tenderly, showing a sincere desire for his welfare. In nine cases out of ten your efforts will be successful. You will save a soul from death, and hide a multitude of sins.—Letter 67, 1902.

In the Place of a Father

All our institutions should be missionary agencies in every sense of the word. No work is to be allowed to hinder the work of soul saving. In every institution there is missionary work to be done. From the manager down to the humblest worker, all should feel a responsibility for the unconverted among their own number. They should put forth earnest efforts to win them to Christ. As a result of such effort many will be won to the Saviour and will become faithful and true in service to God. The consistent, religious life, the holy conversation, the unswerving integrity, the godly example—these are the means God uses to fasten conviction on the hearts and consciences of unbelievers.

My brethren, in the providence of God young men who have not accepted Christ as their Saviour have been brought into association, in business lines, with you. You have had years of experience in the truth. You have children of your own. You ought to know how to deal with these young men in a way that will draw them nearer to the Saviour. And yet, as the matter has been presented to me by the Lord, you have made little effort to win them, little effort to show love and respect for them. If converted, these young men could be used by the Lord in His work. But who of you who are so much older, so much more experienced, have carried on your hearts the burden of their salvation? Christ died to save them. Have you revealed for them a Christlike tenderness? Do you talk with them as if you thought them worth saving, or do you repulse them? Have you given them evidence that you have a loving, tender interest in them, or have you, by your attitude toward them, shown that you regarded them as beneath your notice?

God holds the managers of His institutions accountable to treat the youth in the employ of these institutions with courtesy, respect, and fatherly kindness. They are to deal with them as they themselves wish to be dealt with by Christ. Our first work, as the Lord has presented it to me, is to be so kind to the youth, so thoughtful of their interests, that they will feel at home in our presence.

Have you tried to be unselfish, to be kindly, to make your words and actions fragrant? Can those in your charge look up to you as true Christians? You are fathers. Will you ask yourselves if you would be willing to have your children treated as you have treated some of the youth in your charge? From the light given me, I know that there are some bearing responsibilities here who, unless converted, will never see the kingdom of heaven. It pains me to know that in the life practice they are not revealing wisdom, faith, and love for perishing souls. The treatment that some youth have received has given them hardly a ray of warm, genial friendship. They need an experience altogether different from the experience they are receiving in their association with men who ought to know God.

Just Dealing Regarding Wages

At times you have encouraged the workers to think that their wages would be raised, and then you have failed to fulfill the promise made. Is this letting your light shine forth in good works? Is such service acceptable to the Master? Is this kind of work to continue in God's institutions, which were established to do a work for the saving of the souls of those connected with them? You have restitution to make for wages as long as possible withheld. Did you not know when withholding these wages that you were not doing as you would be done by? Why will men profess to be Christians, and yet follow the sharp practices of the enemy? He will flatter your vanity. He will try to deceive you, to lead you to think that the course you are pursuing is the best course to follow in dealing with minds. But you will be without excuse in allowing him to deceive you; for God has marked out a plain path for you to follow....

Christ came to the world to seek and save the lost. When accused by the Pharisees of eating with publicans and sinners, He replied, "I am not come to call the [professedly] righteous, but sinners to repentance." He came to save, not to destroy. Souls are very precious in His sight; for by creation and by redemption they are His. Do not you realize that He holds you responsible for the salvation of those with whom you are dealing? Do you realize that He will require at your hands the souls you have not tried to save? Have you sought to outwit the enemy, who is constantly trying to lead the youth to think that the course of unbelievers is more nearly correct than the course of those who claim to believe the truth?

Unless managers cherish the love of God, young men and young women might better not be brought within the sphere of their influence....

The Heavenly Record

Remember that day by day the great Master Artist is taking a picture of your character. Your thoughts, your words, your actions, are transferred to His record book, as the features of the human countenance are transferred to the polished plate of the artist.

We are to be Christ's representatives on the earth—pure, kind, just, and merciful, full of compassion, showing unselfishness in word and deed. Avarice and covetousness are vices that God abominates. They are the offspring of selfishness and sin, and they spoil every work with which they are allowed to mingle. Roughness and coarseness of character are imperfections which the Scriptures decidedly condemn as dishonoring to God.

"Let your conversation"—your disposition and habits—"be without covetousness; and be content with such things as ye have: for He hath said, I will never leave thee, nor forsake thee." "Therefore as ye abound in everything, in faith, and utterance, and knowledge, and in all diligence, and in your love to us, see that ye abound in this grace also"—the grace of Christian liberality. "To do good and to communicate forget not: for with such sacrifices God is well pleased."

"Be Ye Clean"

The word of the Lord to those connected with His institutions is, "Be ye clean, that bear the vessels of the Lord." In all our institutions let self-seeking give place to unselfish love and labor. Then the golden oil will be emptied from the two olive branches into the golden pipes, which will empty themselves into the vessels prepared to receive it. Then the lives of Christ's workers will indeed be an exposition of the sacred truths of His word.

The fear of God, the sense of His goodness, His holiness, will circulate through every institution. An atmosphere of love and peace will pervade every department. Every word spoken, every work performed, will have an influence that corresponds to the influence of heaven. Christ will abide in humanity, and humanity will abide in Christ. In all the work will appear not the character of finite men, but the character of the infinite God. The divine influence imparted by holy angels will impress the minds brought in contact with the workers, and from these workers a fragrant influence will go forth to all who choose to inhale it. The goodly fabric of character wrought through divine power will receive light and glory from heaven, and will stand out before the world as a witness, pointing to the throne of the living God.

Then the work will move forward with solidity and double strength. A new efficiency will be imparted to the workers in every line. Men will learn of the reconciliation from iniquity which the Messiah has brought in through His sacrifice. The last message of warning and salvation will be given with mighty power. The earth will be lightened with the glory of God, and it will be ours to witness the soon coming, in power and glory, of our Lord and Saviour.—Letter 58, 1902.

* * * * *

For Further Study

Location of Sanitariums:
Counsels on Health, 265-270 (Testimonies for the Church 7:80-83; 85-89).

Economy in Buildings and Equipment:
Counsels on Health, 274-279 (Testimonies for the Church 7:90-94).

Operation:
Counsels on Health, 280, 28
Testimonies for the Church 4:571-573);
Counsels on Health, 305, 319, 320.

General Counsel Regarding Institutional Work:
Testimonies for the Church 5:549-563.

Not for Pleasure Seekers:
Counsels on Health, 271-27
Testimonies for the Church 7:95-97).

Commercial Gain:
Testimonies for the Church 3:169.

Danger in Worldly Prosperity:
Counsels on Health, 290, 291.

Sanitariums as a Refuge for Workers:
Testimonies for the Church 7:292-294.

Special Workers for Spiritual Work in Sanitariums:
Counsels on Health, 312, 31 (Testimonies for the Church 8:143, 144);
Counsels on Health, 29 (Testimonies for the Church 7:75).

Duty to the Poor:
Counsels on Health, 228-230 (Testimonies for the Church 4:550-552).

Businessmen, Integrity and Ability of:
Testimonies for the Church 7:247-249.

Business and Religion:
Testimonies for the Church 5:422-429.

Fair Dealings With Workers:
Counsels on Health, 314, 315.

Amusements in Sanitariums:
Counsels on Health, 240, 24
Testimonies for the Church 4:577-579).

Section 10—Opportunities for Ministry In Hospitals and Sanitariums

Restoration Through Reformation

The human family is suffering because of the transgression of the laws of God. Satan is constantly urging men to accept his principles, and thus he is seeking to counterwork the work of God. He is constantly representing the chosen people of God as a deluded people. He is an accuser of the brethren, and his accusing power he is constantly using against those who work righteousness. The Lord desires through His people to answer Satan's charges by showing the result of obedience to right principles.

He desires our health institutions to stand as witnesses for the truth. They are to give character to the work which must be carried forward in these last days in restoring man through a reformation of the habits, appetites, and passions. Seventh-day Adventists are to be represented to the world by the advance principles of health reform which God has given us.

Still greater truths are unfolding for this people as we draw near the close of time, and God designs that we shall everywhere establish institutions where those who are in darkness in regard to the needs of the human organism may be educated, that they in their turn may lead others into the light of health reform....

To Reveal the Principles of God's Kingdom

It is God's design to manifest through His people the principles of His kingdom. That in life and character they may reveal these principles, He desires to separate them from the customs, habits, and practices of the world. He seeks to bring them near to Himself, that He may make known to them His will....

A great work is to be accomplished in setting before men the saving truths of the gospel. This is the means ordained by God to stem the tide of moral corruption. This is His means of restoring His moral image in man. It is His remedy for universal disorganization. It is the power that draws men together in unity.

To present these truths is the work of the third angel's message. The Lord designs that the presentation of this message shall be the highest, greatest work carried on in our world at this time. That this work may be carried forward on correct lines He has directed the establishment of schools, sanitariums, publishing houses, and other institutions. In these institutions the attributes of God are to be unfolded, and the glory and excellence of the truth is to be made to appear more vivid.—Manuscript 166, 1899.

Opening Fast-Closed Doors

Every medical practitioner may through faith in Christ have in his possession a cure of the highest value—a remedy for the sin-sick soul. The physician who is converted and sanctified through the truth is registered in heaven as a laborer together with God, a follower of Jesus Christ.

Through the sanctification of the truth God makes physicians and nurses skillful in a knowledge of how to treat the sick, and this work is opening the fast-closed doors of many hearts. Men and women are led to see and understand the truth which is needed to save the soul as well as the body. This is an element that gives character to the work for this time.

The medical missionary work is as the right hand and arm to the third angel's message which must be proclaimed to a fallen world; and physicians, managers, and workers in any line, in acting faithfully their part, are doing the work of the message. From them the sound of the truth will go forth to every nation and kindred and tongue and people. In this work the heavenly angels bear a part. They awaken spiritual joy and melody in the hearts of those who have been freed from suffering, and joy and thanksgiving to God arise from many hearts that have received the precious truth....

Point to a Sin-Pardoning Saviour

The physician will find that it is for his present and eternal good to follow the Lord's way with suffering humanity. The mind that God has made, He can mold without the power of man; but He honors men by asking them to cooperate with Him in this great work. When the Spirit of God works on the mind of the afflicted one, and he inquires for truth, let the physician work for the precious soul as Christ would work for it. Do not urge upon him any special doctrine, but point him to Jesus as a sin-pardoning Saviour. Angels of God will make impressions on the human mind. Some will refuse to be illuminated by the light which God would let shine into the chambers of the mind and into the soul temple; but many will respond to the light, and from these minds every form of deception and error will be swept away.—Letter 205, 1899.

With Tenderness and Wisdom

The physician who proves himself worthy of being placed as leading physician in a sanitarium will do a grand work. But his work in religious lines should ever be of such a nature that the divine antidote for the relief of sin-burdened souls will be presented before the patients. All physicians should understand that such work should be done with tenderness and wisdom. In our institutions where mental patients are brought for treatment, the comforting words of truth spoken to the afflicted one will often be the means of soothing the mind and restoring peace to the soul.

When the leading physician passes by the spiritual part of the work, he is remiss in his duty, and gives a wrong example to the younger helpers who are learning to do the work of a Christian physician. These students neglect a part of the work that is most essential. This, I greatly fear, will result in a loss that can never be remedied.—Letter 20, 1902.

Learning to Work as He Worked

In all our sanitariums, God is to be acknowledged as the Master Workman. By becoming familiar with His life, the physicians and helpers are to learn how to work as He worked. He was the Majesty of heaven, the King of glory. But, clothed with the garb of humanity, He took His place at the head of the fallen race. He humbled Himself, and became obedient unto death, even the death of the cross. He assumed human nature to make it possible for man to be a partaker of the divine nature.

[190] The physician who strives to represent Christ will not assume prerogatives that the Master has not given him. He will not seek to rule over his fellowmen. He will remember that he is a laborer together with God. In spirit and word and act he will represent the Unseen One.—Manuscript 136, 1902.

Give Heed to Soul-Winning Effort

There are ministerial duties devolving upon the head physicians of our sanitariums outside of the purely medical work. They must give heed to the urgent calls that come for soul-winning efforts. Every jot of influence that the Lord has given them is to be used for Him. Our medical superintendents should so live and labor as to be recognized as men who place their trust in God, men who fear the Lord and depend upon His divine power.—Letter 158, 1909.

Daily Efforts in Soul Winning

Our faith in eternal realities is weak, our sense of duty small, in view of the opportunities that we have to point souls to the Saviour as their only hope. We are not to be cold and indifferent in regard to giving efficacious remedies for the healing of the soul. It is our duty to make known the truth, not in our own strength, but in the strong faith, assurance, and confidence that God imparts.

In our sanitariums no day should be allowed to pass without something being done for the salvation of souls. We are to offer special prayers for the sick, both when with them and when away from them. Then when they inquire about the remedy for sin, our own souls, softened by the Holy Spirit, will be all aglow with a desire to help them give their hearts to God....

Faithful Service

All the nurses and helpers are to give treatments and perform other kinds of service in such a delicate, reverential way—and withal so solidly, thoroughly, and cheerfully—that the sanitarium will prove a haven of rest.

The individual worker in any line in the treatment of the sick and the afflicted in a medical institution is to act as a Christian. He is to let his light shine forth in good works. His words are to magnify our Lord Jesus Christ. In the place of waiting for great opportunities to come before doing anything, he is to make the very best use of the talents lent him of God, in order that these talents may be constantly increased. He is not to think that he must be silent on religious subjects. Wherever he is, there is his field, in which he is earnestly to represent in word and deed the saving power of truth. He is not to wait to see what others do. He has a personality of his own, and he is responsible to Christ, whose servant he is, for every word and act. He is to be as attentive and faithful to duty as if he heard the Saviour's voice, "Verily I say unto you, Except ye be converted, and become as little children, ye shall not enter into the kingdom of heaven. Whosoever therefore shall humble himself as this little child, the same is greatest in the kingdom of heaven."

A Mouthpiece for God

It is highly important to know how to approach the sick with the comfort of a hope gained through faith in Christ Jesus and acceptance of His promises. When the awakened conscience cries out, "Lord, be merciful to me a sinner; make me Thy child," be ready to tell the sufferer, the once indifferent one, that there is hope for him, that in Jesus he will find a refuge.

The Saviour is inviting everyone, "Look unto Me, and live. Come unto Me, and find rest." Those who in meekness and love present the hope of the gospel to afflicted souls so much in need of this hope, are the mouthpiece of the One who gave Himself for all mankind that He might become a healer, a tender, sympathetic, compassionate Saviour. Let every means be devised to bring about the saving of souls in our medical institutions. This is our work. If the spiritual work is left undone, there is no necessity of calling upon our people to build these institutions. Those who have no burning desire to save souls are not the ones who should connect with our sanitariums.—Letter 159, 1902.

The Workers Needed

The Lord wants wise men and women acting in the capacity of nurses to comfort and help the sick and suffering. Through the ministrations of these nurses, those who have heretofore taken no interest in religious things will be led to ask, "What must I do to be saved?" The sick will be led to Christ by the patient attention of nurses who anticipate their wants, and who bow in prayer and ask the great Medical Missionary to look with compassion upon the sufferer and to let the soothing influence of His grace be felt and His restoring power be exercised....

Overcoming Nervous Timidity

The nervous timidity of the sick will be overcome as they are made acquainted with the intensive interest that the Saviour has for all suffering humanity. Oh, the depth of the love of Christ! To redeem us from death, He died on the cross of Calvary.

Let our physicians and nurses ever bear in mind the words, "We are laborers together with God." Let every physician and every nurse learn how to work for the alleviation of mental as well as physical suffering. At this time, when sin is so prevalent and so violently revealed, how important it is that our sanitariums be conducted in such a way that they will accomplish the greatest amount of good. How important that all the workers in these institutions know how to speak words in season to those who are weary and sin sick.

Physicians and nurses should ever be kind and cheerful, putting away all gloom and sadness. Let faith grasp the hand of Christ of His healing touch.

As our nurses minister patiently to those who are sick in body and soul, let them ask God to work for the suffering ones that they may be led to know Christ, and let them believe that their prayers will be answered. In all that is done let the love of Christ be revealed.—Letter 17, 1905.

Promptness in Meeting Appointments

There have been defects in the management at the sanitarium. The patients have felt that they were not treated as they should be. Appointments have been made which have not been filled. Such failures as these will greatly militate against the influence of a physician. The patients will not be often thus disappointed, without feeling bitterness of soul and mind....

The sick pay for their treatments in order that they may recover health; but if they are disappointed again and again, the reputation of the sanitarium will be imperiled. This evil must be corrected; the attention that has been promised must be given to the patients or the physician breaks the confidence of the patients in his word. If the leading physician cannot possibly meet the appointment, he should have his associate physician meet it for him, explaining to the patient the cause of his absence.

Unless the physicians in our sanitariums are men of thorough habits, unless they attend promptly to their duties, their work will become a reproach, and the Lord's appointed agencies will lose their influence. By a course of negligence to duty the physician humiliates the Great Physician, of whom he should be a representative. Strict hours should be kept with all patients, high or low. No careless neglect should be allowed in any of the nurses. Ever be true to your word, prompt in meeting your appointments; for this means much to the sick.—Letter 128, 1905.

Promptness and Efficiency

The sick should not be compelled to wait when they need advice and relief. Never should the physician neglect his patients. He should have quick, penetrating judgment, and should carry into the sickroom a genial atmosphere. He should not be cold, reticent, or hesitating, but should cultivate those qualities which exert a soothing influence over the suffering ones. They want more than looks; they want kind, hopeful words. The doctor should be ready to give them cheerful, reassuring words, words spoken from the heart in wisdom, showing that he understands the cases of those under his care. This will inspire a restfulness and confidence, even at the first interview.

The physician should be a man of pure mind. If his principles are uncorrupted, he will exert a telling influence in favor of the right. Physicians need to be constantly imbued with the Spirit of Christ, learning lessons from Him, the greatest Teacher the world ever knew;

then they will be pure in thought, in mind, in action. They will give no hint in word or manner that will lead them to impure thoughts.

Licentiousness is ruining many souls, and physicians especially need to watch and pray that they may not enter into temptation, and that they may have that grace which will make them examples of piety and purity. Their work is daily undergoing the close inspection of God, and their record will be accurately traced in the ledger of heaven.

[194] Physicians in our health institution have many and weighty responsibilities. Their only safety is in keeping their thoughts and impulses under the control of the Great Teacher. They have golden opportunities for doing good; they can guide and mold the many and varied minds with which they are brought in contact. They should take a stand for God. Show men and women connected with the Institute how pure and noble they may become; show them that you have firm confidence in God, and that He is your Source of strength, that you are resting wholly upon the promises. Fulfill your duty with promptness, while claiming your heavenly Father's help to overcome all weakness of character. With the hand of faith grasping the arm of divine power, put your whole being into your work.—Letter 6a, 1890.

The Privilege of Ministry

To the workers in our sanitariums I am instructed to say, Truth must be wisely, kindly, tenderly presented. In the fourteenth chapter of John there are precious lessons, valuable instruction, which should be appreciated by every child of God who desires to minister to others the comfort and grace of God. Let these lessons be impressed upon the mind; over and over again let them be repeated.

The Lord has brought us into possession of our health institutions that we may learn to bring to the sick, in the most attractive way, truths of heavenly origin. We must never lose sight of the fact that these institutions are instrumentalities in the hands of God for bringing the light of truth to those who are in darkness....

In His work of ministry for the sick and afflicted, Christ stands before the world as the greatest Medical Missionary the world has ever known, and the pattern for every Christian missionary worker.

He knew the right word to speak to each sufferer, and He spoke not only that which brought healing of body, but conviction of soul and spiritual enlightenment. He brought to the understanding of those who sought Him a knowledge of self, and of the soul's highest need.

Christ's discourses were the spiritual explanation of His ministry for the afflicted. He Himself was the great ideal of righteousness to those for whom He ministered. Thus He planted the seeds of truth in human hearts.

[195]

Prayer for the Sick

Often in the care of the suffering, much attention is given to minor matters, while the patients' need of the great all-saving truths of the gospel, which would minister to both soul and body, is forgotten. When you neglect to offer prayer for the sick, you deprive them of great blessings; for angels of God are waiting to minister to these souls in response to your petitions. In every possible and pleasant way, those who know the truth should seek to reveal the power of the grace of Christ. As they exemplify truth in their daily walk and conversation, they will exert a holy influence, and the grace of Christ will cooperate with human effort. Working intelligently for the recovery of body and soul from the results of sin, they will be true workers together with Christ and will be instruments in His hands to show forth His praise and salvation.

The Saviour's Love to be Experienced

The exercise of wisdom and good judgment will accomplish much for God. As His servants work out the requirements of the gospel according to their ability, God will make them a praise to His name. He purposes that through the exemplification of the truth in the lives of His followers, souls shall be won to Him.

All who profess godliness and a knowledge of the truth for this time are to communicate the same to those with whom they associate. But the fullness of a Saviour's love is not expressed as decidedly as it should be, and as a result in places where a rich harvest might be gathered for God there is seen a dearth. "Found wanting" are the words written against the names of many who might have done a work that would have won the approval of heaven. There is needed, to unite with human effort and ability, a larger measure of the grace of Christ.

It is God's purpose that our health institutions shall become very effectual means for bringing souls to the light of truth. Much more should be done to encourage. Only when we do our best for the upbuilding of Christ's kingdom can the words be spoken to us, Well done, good and faithful servant. Only as we exemplify the Spirit of truth in our lives can Christ's Spirit work with us to convict hearts and convert souls to the gospel.

To Teach and to Comfort

Christ desires to work in many ways through the men of His appointment. Every worker in our sanitariums should regard himself as Christ's minister to teach and to comfort, to let the light shine forth in word and deed. Those who are blessed with the light of truth are to reflect light. In taking the name of Christ upon them they have pledged themselves to become laborers together with God, and a spirit of consecrated labor should be manifest in working out the Lord's plans. They are to go into all the world, and preach the gospel to every creature, presenting the beauty of His life in their own example of earnest, self-sacrificing labor.

I pray that the Holy Spirit may lend its sanctifying power to the workers in our institutions. My brethren and sisters, arouse, and become laborers together with Him who gave His life for the saving of the world. We must not lessen our efforts at this time. Christ asks you to labor with all the energies of heart and soul and mind. If you will lend the aid of your influence and effort to the work of Christ, angels will unite with you, making you a saving power for Christ.—Manuscript 57, 1912.

A Winning Influence

In your care of the sick, act tenderly, kindly, faithfully, that you may have a converting influence upon them. You have need of the grace of Christ in order to properly represent the service of Christ. And as you present the grace of truth in true disinterested service, angels will be present to sustain you. The Comforter will be with you to fulfill the promise of the Saviour, "Lo, I am with you alway, even unto the end of the world."

I have a charge to give, a message to bear to our sanitarium workers. Keep your souls in purity. Do a work that will have a winning influence on those placed in your charge. You can speak often to the sick of the Great Physician who can heal the diseases of the body as verily as He heals the sickness of the soul. Pray with the sick, and try to lead them to see in Christ their Healer. Tell them that if they will look to Him in faith, He will say to them, "Thy sins be forgiven thee." It means very much to the sick to learn this lesson.—Letter 56, 1907.

Consecrated Nurses

Earnest, devoted young people are needed to enter the work of God as nurses. As these young men and women use conscientiously the knowledge they gain, they will increase in capability and become better and better qualified to be the Lord's helping hand. They may become successful missionaries, pointing souls to the Lamb of God, who taketh away the sin of the world, and who can save both soul and body.

The Lord wants wise men and women, acting in the capacity of nurses, to comfort and help the sick and suffering. Oh, that all who are afflicted could be ministered to by Christlike physicians and nurses who could help them to place their weary, pain-racked bodies in the care of the Great Healer, in faith looking to Him for restoration!

Many Converted and Healed

Every sincere Christian bows to Jesus as the true Physician of souls. When he stands by the bedside of the afflicted, there will be many not only converted, but healed. If through judicious ministration the patient is led to give his soul to Christ, and to bring his thoughts into obedience to the will of God, a great victory is gained.—The Review and Herald, May 9, 1912.

* * * * *

For Further Study

Spiritual Work for Patients:
Counsels on Health, 255.

Opening the Scriptures to the Sick:
Testimonies for the Church 7:103.

Contemplation of Encouraging Themes:
Testimonies for the Church 5:744, 745.

Religious Exercises at the Sanitarium:
Testimonies for the Church 4:565.

Avoiding Doctrinal Controversy:
Counsels on Health, 245, 246 (Testimonies for the Church 3:166, 167);
Counsels on Health, 255.

Human Hands Employed by Angels in Practical Ministry:
Testimonies for the Church 6:456, 457.

Untold Influence of Kindly Sympathy:
The Ministry of Healing, 158, 159.

Section 11—The Sanitarium Family

Christians to Be Light Bearers

Christians are to be light bearers, saying to all with whom they are brought in contact, Follow me as I follow Christ. They are to be examples of piety, representing Christ in word, in spirit, in action, in all business dealing with their brethren and with strangers. They are to show that their actions are a copy of the actions of their great Pattern. All this Christ enjoins upon His followers. They are to show the superiority of Heaven's principles over the principles of the world.—Letter 148, 1899.

To Send Forth Light and Knowledge

In every sanitarium there must be kept before all in the institution the principles of true service. From the institution is to go forth light and knowledge. All connected with it are to act their part intelligently, as representatives of the truth for this time. It is that they may be trained to do true missionary work, that young people are brought to our sanitariums.

If you will cooperate with God, He will go before you, and the glory of the Lord will be your rearward. Heavenly angels will break forth into singing as souls receive the great gift of God through Jesus Christ. You may assure the sick and afflicted that Christ is the Great Healer. They may believe on Him, and trust in His word; for it will never fail.—Letter 97, 1905.

Training for Various Lines of Work

In the sanitariums workers are to be trained, some of whom will be connected with the institution while others will go out as medical missionaries. These, in whatever line of work they are to labor, whether as physicians, nurses, or helpers, should be firm upon the principles of health reform and all the points of our faith, that as they come in contact with the patients, or go out into all the civilized world and to the regions that lie in heathen darkness, the truth of God on these subjects may be given to them. As these workers enter upon their duties, the efficiency of experienced men and women is increased a hundredfold, and the work for this time is far more rapidly accomplished.

Proper persons need to be selected and trained, persons who will do honor to every branch of the work. The consecration of their talents must be very real, and then God will bless their efforts. He is the source of all wisdom and grace. In His strength defects and ignorance may be overcome.

Every physician, every nurse, every helper, who has anything to do in God's service, must aim at perfection and under the discipline of the greatest Teacher the world has ever known, his course must ever tend upward toward this aim. All who are connected with the medical missionary work must be learners. No one must stop to think, I cannot do this. He must say instead, God requires me to be perfect. What did Christ say in regard to this matter?—"Be ye therefore perfect, even as your Father which is in heaven is perfect." Matthew 5:45.

No one who allows known defects to remain in his manners or his character is excused. Those connected with medical missionary work are connected with God's service, and they must try to reach His standard. He will give them wisdom and understanding. We are to show a superiority in intellect, in understanding, in skill, and knowledge, because we believe in God and in His power to work upon human hearts.

Read the history of Daniel. The Lord would have His people reach the highest round of the ladder, that they may glorify Him by possessing the ability He is willing to bestow. He has a treasure-house of knowledge from which we can all draw. Then let us realize our defects and improve under the instruction of God. Then the light and grace of God will be reflected to the world as the highest education, which sanctifies the receiver.

The religion of Jesus Christ never degrades; it never makes men and women coarse and rough. Incorrect speech, wrong habits, must be overcome. God would have every man correct in speech, correct in habits, possessing knowledge that will give him a standing place among men. I present this matter as the Lord has presented it to me. Let us determine to put ourselves to the task of learning in the school of Christ.

The Training of Nurses

In the training of nurses there must be an organized plan. They are learning a most valuable trade; and many temptations will come to them through offers of large wages and of places where they will have a better chance to earn money, if they will go with some patient. This point must be guarded, or there will surely be trouble....

Each one must have the spirit of self-sacrifice and self-denial, of which Christ has given us an example in His life. We are to feel our obligation to do the very best we can. Those who have many talents and those who have few are to work unitedly, as a wheel within a wheel. And if all feel their responsibility and accountability to God, they will do His will, acting their part according to His appointment.—Manuscript 162, 1897.

Put On Christ

There is not among us that simplicity that there should be. We should come to the Lord just as we are, humbling ourselves before Him, and wrestling earnestly until we receive the Holy Spirit. Why should we not do as the disciples did just before the Day of Pentecost? They sought the Lord earnestly, and when the Day of Pentecost was fully come, they were "all with one accord." Notwithstanding the opposition of the powers of darkness was so great that persecution arose, some even being put to death, the disciples witnessed for Christ, and large numbers were converted....

Will you not all put on Christ, not to lay Him off again, but to let His Spirit stamp your mind and character? When all in this institution are truly converted, there will be just as surely a wonderful work done as when on the Day of Pentecost the disciples received the outpouring of the Holy Spirit. The Lord Himself will be with you, to teach and to lead and to guide. You will see of the salvation of God. You may be disheartened at times. Discouragements will arise, but it is your privilege at all times to lay hold of the hope set before you in the gospel. Watch unto prayer. Believe that God will help you to speak words that will cheer and encourage and increase the faith of those with whom you associate....

No Haphazard Work

We cannot expect the blessing of God to rest upon us, if we serve God at will and let Him alone at pleasure. It is not necessary that we should cater to the world's demands for pleasure. There are other places in the world where people may find amusement. We need here substantial men and women; we need those who will reveal the simplicity of true godliness. We need men and women who are solid Christians, who will not feel that if they have had some experience they must therefore be highly honored. You may have a rich and living experience here; but the Lord cannot be honored by you while you think that it does not matter whether or not you are subdued in spirit, or whether you are really converted. If the work here is to be sustained, we must have those who will carry responsibilities in the fear of God. A preparation for the kingdom of God is no haphazard work. You cannot be religious at times and at other times irreligious.—Manuscript 57, 1909.

Regular Bible Instruction for Nurses

Nurses should have regular Bible instruction, that they may be able to speak to the sick words that will enlighten and help them. Angels of God are in the rooms where the suffering ones are to take treatment, and the atmosphere surrounding the soul of the one giving treatment should be pure and fragrant. In the lives of the physicians and nurses the virtues of Christ are to be seen. His principles are to be lived. Then, by what they do and say, the sick will be drawn to the Saviour.—Letter 59, 1905.

Laying Our Burdens at His Feet

The influence of the sanitarium family should be a united influence, each member seeking to become a power for good in that department in which he labors. If this result is obtained, there must first be a weeding out of every lame principle; then the workers can hope to succeed in perfecting themselves as Christian workers. It is only as they place themselves under the discipline of God, conforming their daily lives to the pattern that they have in the Saviour's earthly life, that they can become partakers of the divine nature and escape the corruption that is in the world through lust. As long as we are here in this world, we are on test and trial. We will be held accountable not only for the working out of our own salvation, but for the influence for good or evil that we exert on other souls.

He who is meek in spirit, who is purest and most childlike, will be made strong for the battle. He will be strengthened with might by His Spirit in the inner man. He who feels his weakness, and wrestles with God as did Jacob, and like this servant of old cries, "I will not let Thee go, except Thou bless me," will go forth with the fresh anointing of the Holy Spirit. The atmosphere of heaven will surround him. His influence will be a positive force in favor of the religion of Christ....

I am so glad that we can come to God in faith and humility, and plead with Him until our souls are brought into such close relationship with Jesus that we can lay our burdens at His feet, saying, "I know whom I have believed, and am persuaded that He is able to keep that which I have committed unto Him against that day". The Lord is able to do exceeding abundantly above all that we can ask or think. Our cold, faithless hearts may be quickened into sensibility and life, until we can say in faith, "The life which I now live in the flesh I live by the faith of the Son of God." Let us seek for the fullness of the salvation of Christ. Let us follow in the footsteps of the Son of God, for the promise is, "He that followeth Me shall not walk in darkness, but shall have the light of life."—Manuscript 63, 1908.

In the Daily Round of Duties

The manager of a sanitarium bears important responsibilities. Let his associates who are engaged in continuous, hard labor in the various handicrafts, keep their souls searched as with a lighted candle. Unity of action in diversity of labor must be maintained. The workers are to live out the prayer of Christ, who declares, "I sanctify Myself, that they also might be sanctified through the truth."

Let them read the word of the Lord, in order that they may have the wisdom that is unto salvation. The richest treasures are to be found by searching for them in the word. Some minds will be so impressed to seek these hidden treasures as to sell all that they have in order to buy the field and come into possession of the priceless jewels of truth. Ofttimes the most lowly are in possession of the hidden treasure which they may impart to others.

The truths of the word of God, applied to the heart and carried out with humility in the daily life practice, will make Christians strong in the strength of Jehovah and happy in His peace. Christian kindness and earnest consecration are constantly to be manifest in the life. We are not always engaged in special duties connected with sacred service; but the common, daily round of duties may be done in His spirit, and such labor will commend itself to every man, even to the unconverted who know not the doctrine. We may let our light so shine in good works that the truth which we cherish shall be, to unbelievers, spirit and life.—Letter 140, 1906.

Imitate God's Perfect Ways

Build for eternity. Christ's lessons are before us. We are to do carefully, neatly, and with exactitude whatever is to be done. We are to study economy in every line of work. Builders, gather up the fragments. Let nothing be lost. In all that there is to be done, in planting and building, imitate God's perfect ways.

Nurses and physicians, think of Jesus. How careful He was of the remnants of food left after feeding the five thousand! By His thoughtful care He would teach us order and economy. The great work of redemption weighed constantly upon His soul. As He was teaching and healing, all the energies of body and soul were taxed to the utmost, yet He noticed the most simple things in human life and in nature. His most instructive lessons were those in which He illustrated the kingdom of God by the simple things of nature. He did not overlook the needs of the humblest of His servants. His ear heard every needy cry. He was awake to the touch of the afflicted woman in the crowd. His divine nature, combined with the human, was so finely wrought that the least touch of faith brought a response.

When He raised from the dead the daughter of Jairus, He turned to the parents and reminded them that she must have something to eat.

The little things become great in accordance with the attention given them. The one talent is not to be wrapped in a napkin and hidden in the earth. Do what you can for the Master. "He that is faithful in that which is least" will be "faithful also in much." The Master will use every talent that we consecrate to Him. Your worth is determined by the faithfulness with which you do the little things. Everyone needs in the details of daily life to learn to build for time and for eternity. Then at last there will be written against his name in the books of heaven the most precious commendation, "Ye are complete in Him."—Manuscript 63, 1899.

A Sacred Responsibility

If those who hold positions of trust in the institution are persons who love and fear God, they will realize that a sacred responsibility is theirs because of the measure of authority and the consequent influence which their position gives them. They are dealing with human minds, being brought into connection with all classes of society; and they should move discreetly, for they are regarded as representatives of the institution. They should be kind and courteous, ever exercising Christian politeness to all with whom they are brought in contact, both believers and unbelievers. Brethren, you should watch for souls as they that must give an account. We should never forget that Jesus, in the infinite sacrifice He has made for them, has proved His love for these men, women, and children, and shown what value He sets upon them. They are the purchase of His blood. The rich and the poor are to be treated alike, with unvarying kindness.

Let your influence be persuasive, binding people to your heart because you love Jesus, and they are His. This is a great work. If, by your Christlike words and actions, you make impressions that will kindle in their hearts a hungering and thirsting after righteousness and truth, you are a colaborer with Christ. Your words and deportment are representing Jesus.

Those who have a leading influence in the institution should be men and women who possess devotion and piety; who are not narrow and selfish, but conscientious, self-denying, and self-sacrificing; who have an eye single to the glory of God. They should be in the world, but not of the world. Men of such a character will keep the way of the Lord, and they will be constantly teaching others by precept and example.

The Results of Right Principles

The patients and guests all need to have right principles placed before them. There will be men of investigating minds who will thus receive the key of knowledge, and will bring out treasures of thought for the enriching of other minds—thoughts that will be the saving of souls. Circumstances will call forth words, decisions in favor of the right, and many will be swayed in the right direction. Such is ever the result when the principles of right are implanted in minds by men who love righteousness, temperance, and truth. Words and works flowing from the love and fear of God become a widespread blessing—a blessing that is carried into the highways and byways of life.

Men who, like Enoch, are walking in the light of Christ, will exercise self-control, even under temptation and provocation. Although tried by the perversity and obstinacy of others, they dare not let impulse bear sway. If you are walking in the light, you will give evidence of divine power combined with human effort, and others will see that you are led and taught by God. You will feel that the Holy Watcher is by your side taking knowledge of your words.

Purity of thought must be cherished as indispensable to the work of influencing others. There must be a pure, holy atmosphere surrounding the soul, an atmosphere that will tend to quicken the spiritual life of all who inhale it.—Letter 6a, 1890.

Chosen for the Work

I wish to express to you some thoughts that should be kept before the sanitarium workers. That which will make them a power for good is the knowledge that the great Medical Missionary has chosen them for this work, that He is their chief instructor, and that it is ever their duty to recognize Him as their teacher.

The Lord has shown us the evil of depending upon the strength of earthly organizations. He has instructed us that the commission of the medical missionary is received from the very highest authority. He would have us understand that it is a mistake to regard as most essential the education given by physicians who reject the authority of Christ, the greatest Physician who ever lived upon the earth.—Letter 61, 1910.

Harmony Among Workers

It is of the utmost importance that harmony exist in our institutions. Better for the work to go crippled than for workers who are not fully devoted to be employed. It is unconsecrated, unconverted men who have been spoiling the work of God. The Lord has no use whatever for men who are not wholly consecrated to His service.—Letter 202, 1903.

Qualifications of the Matron

The nurses and student nurses should be under the charge of a matron who can be a guide and counselor to them. She should be capable of exercising wise supervision. She needs to be a woman of good health, not self-centered, but affectionate, unselfish, and sunny, one who can mold minds, not by being authoritative but by being kind and thoughtful, and yet firm to principle. She must forget herself in her interest for others. The simplicity of heart religion must be seen in those who perform the services required of a matron.—Manuscript 162, 1897.

A Woman of Experience

The one who occupies the position of matron in an institution should be a woman of experience, who in an emergency knows what needs to be done. She should be a woman of executive ability, a woman who is willing to bear burdens, and who daily goes to God for wisdom. She should be a woman who knows what the rules of propriety are, and who observes them.—Letter 30, 1887.

To Exalt the Word of God

The Lord calls for a solemn dedication to Him of the sanitariums that shall be established. Our object in the establishment of these institutions is that the truth for this time may through them be proclaimed. In order that this may be done, they must be conducted on right lines. In them business interests are not to be crowded in to take the place of spiritual interests. Every day devotional exercises are to be held. The word of God is in no case to be given a secondary place. Those who come to our sanitariums for treatment must see the word of God, which is the bread of life, exalted above all common, earthly considerations. A strong religious influence is to be exerted. It must be plainly shown that the glory of God and the uplifting of Christ are placed before all else.—Letter 183, 1905.

To Bring Comfort and Encouragement

In our sanitariums, of all places in the world, we need soundly converted physicians and wise workers—men and women who will not urge their peculiar ideas upon the sick, but who will present the truths of the word of God in a way that will bring comfort and encouragement and blessing to the patients. This is the work for which our sanitariums are established—to correctly represent the truths of the word of God, and to lead the minds of men and women to Christ.

Let the religious services held each day be short but educational in character. Present the Bible and its Author, the God of heaven and earth, and Christ the Son, the great Gift of God to the world. Tell the patients how the Saviour came to the earth to reveal the love of God for men. Present before them His great sacrifice in thus coming here to live and die. Let it be known that through faith in Christ every sinful human being may become a partaker of the divine nature, and learn to cooperate with God in the work of salvation.—Letter 112, 1909.

Consideration for the Thoughtless

Those who are connected with our sanitariums are to be educators. By pleasant words and kindly deeds they are to make the gospel attractive. As followers of Christ, they should seek to make the most favorable impression of the religion they profess, and to inspire noble thoughts. Some will be affected by their influence for time and for eternity.

In the work of helping others, we may gain most precious victories. We should devote ourselves with untiring zeal, with earnest fidelity, with self-denial, and with patience, to the work of helping those who need to develop. Kind, encouraging words will do wonders. There are many who, if a constant, cheerful effort is put forth in their behalf, without faultfinding or chiding, will show themselves susceptible of improvement. The less we criticize others, the greater will be our influence over them for good. To many, frequent, positive admonitions will do more harm than good. Let Christlike kindness be enjoined upon all.

There is a science in dealing with those who seem especially weak. If we would teach others, we ourselves must first learn of Christ. We need broad views, that we may do true medical missionary work, and show tact in dealing with minds.

Those who are really the least in need of help are likely to receive the most of our attention. But we need to show special wisdom in dealing with those who seem inconsiderate and thoughtless. Some do not comprehend the sacredness of the work of God. Those of the least ability, the thoughtless, and even the indolent, especially demand careful, prayerful consideration. We must exercise tact in dealing with those who seem to be ignorant and out of the way. By persevering effort in their behalf, we must help them to become useful in the Lord's work. They will respond readily to a patient, tender, loving interest.

We are to cooperate with the Lord Jesus in restoring the inefficient and the erring to intelligence and purity. This work ranks equally in importance with the work of the gospel ministry. We are called upon by God to manifest an untiring, patient interest in the salvation of those who need divine polishing.—Letter 113, 1905.

Dealing with the Unreasonable

When you jostle against the elements manifested by those who have no Bible religion, but only a profession, do not forget that you are a Christian. You greatly lower your influence and mar your own Christian experience when you lose your self-control and give them the least occasion to think that you have ill-treated them. Leave not this impression upon their minds if you can possibly avoid it. In this probationary time we are forming our characters for the future immortal life; but that is not all, for in this very process of character building we need to be extremely cautious how we build, for others will build after the pattern we give them.

We may never know until the judgment the influence of a kind, considerate course of action to the inconsistent, the unreasonable, and unworthy. If, after a course of provocation and injustice on their part, you treat them as you would an innocent person, you even take pains to show them special acts of kindness, then you have acted the part of a Christian; and they become surprised and ashamed, and see their course of action and meanness more clearly than if you plainly stated their aggravated acts to rebuke them.

If you had laid their wrong course of action before them, they would have braced themselves in stubbornness and defiance. But to be treated in tenderness and consideration they feel more deeply their own course of action, and contrast it with yours. Then ... you occupy vantage ground; and when you show a solicitude for their souls, they know that you are no hypocrite, but that you mean every word you say.

A few words spoken in a hasty manner, under provocation, and which seemed but a little thing—just what they deserved—often cut the cords of influence that should have bound the soul to your soul. The very idea of their being in darkness, under the temptation of Satan and blinded by his bewitching power, should make you feel deep sympathy for them, the same that you would feel for a diseased, sick patient who suffers, but on account of his disease is not aware of his danger.

Souls who have cost the life of God's only-begotten Son must be estimated in value by the immense ransom paid for them; and, rich or poor, black or white, must be treated in respect to the value Christ has placed upon the human soul.

These thoughts are worthy of solemn consideration. Any neglect on our part, any exaltation of self, any hasty, passionate exultations, may set a soul on the paths of destruction where he will never find the narrow path of holiness that leads heavenward.... There are grave mistakes made in dealing with unbalanced, diseased minds. They are sick. They need a physician, not to cut them off as a diseased limb, but to heal them. Jesus' course of management is given in the parable of the lost sheep. Should Jesus deal with us as we deal with one another, not one of us would be saved. Oh, how many will be lost because the words that should have been spoken in tender forbearance were left unsaid!—Letter 20, 1892.

The Dull Student

[211]

Students who at first may seem to be dull and slow, may in the end make greater progress than those who are naturally quicker. If they are thorough and systematic in their work, they will gain much that others will fail to gain. Those who form habits of patient, persevering industry will accomplish more than those of quick, vivacious, brilliant minds, who, though grasping a point quickly, lose it just as readily. The patient ones, though slower to learn, will stand ahead of those who learn so quickly that they do not need to study.—Manuscript 115, 1903.

Attitude of the Instructor

While the students must be ready to begin with lesser responsibilities and give evidence that they can be trusted, he [the instructor] should feel for them the tenderest affection. He should not become discouraged at their ignorance, but should give them credit for all the good qualities he sees in them. In educating himself in this direction, he is obtaining a valuable experience—an experience which he needs in order to be a practical Christian.

If the students make mistakes, let him not think them unworthy to be placed on trial again, as though they had committed sins that cannot be forgiven. He should kindly point out their errors, and they, in turn, should be grateful for a friend so faithful as to tell them their faults and how to correct them. To cast off the erring, or to treat them coldly, would not be doing as Christ has done for him. We are all fallible, and need the pity and consideration and forgiveness of one another. He cannot find perfection anywhere, and should not expect it, but he must bear with the perversity of men, and try to teach them.—Letter 1, 1885.

This World Not Heaven

Wherever persons of different stamps of character are associated together in any institution, there must be firm, determined effort to keep the institution pure, elevated, noble, that the wicked one shall not succeed in demoralizing it. There are unsanctified elements to meet, and if all are striving to do right and work righteousness and to be a blessing to each other, the objectionable features will be overcome. This world is not heaven. In our duties of life we are not associating with angels, but with human beings who are liable to err.—Manuscript 41, 1900.

Cultivate an Atmosphere of Praise

Do not allow the helpers to overwork. Let the patients see nurses that are cheerful and bright, not nurses who, because they are overworked, are discouraged and downhearted. It is most inconsistent with the principles on which our sanitariums are founded for the nurses to be allowed to break down in their work.

The workers are to practice the principles of health reform in all that they do—standing, walking, breathing, eating, and dressing. They are to surround themselves with an atmosphere of praise. They are to cultivate the voice, keeping it pleasant and sympathetic. No word of discouragement is to be heard. Let the nurses and physicians face the light. Let them open the windows of the heart heavenward, that it may be flooded with the beams of the Sun of Righteousness.—Letter 116, 1903.

Neatness and Order

Everything connected with a sanitarium should be neat and orderly. Neatness and order will often have more influence than mere words. In the bathroom everything should be so arranged as to make a favorable impression upon those who visit the institution.—Manuscript 57, 1909.

Gossip

There are some, both men and women, who gossip more than they pray. They have not clear spiritual discernment. They are far from God. When they talk with the patients, their attitude seems to say, Report and we will report it.

Helpers who follow this course are to be labored with and reproved. And if they refuse to change their course, let them be dismissed. If they are allowed to continue in the institution, they will bring about a condition of things that will separate the Lord from the institution. It is far better to send away the rebel workers than to shut the Lord out of the institution. Let the helpers, in whatever department they work, be discreet. If they repeat all they hear and talk of all they see, they will be a curse to the institution. There are those who find delight in telling things to create a sensation. This is demoralizing to an institution, and should not receive the least countenance.—Letter 30, 1887.

Rejoice in the Lord

The talent of speech is a precious talent. The riches of the grace of Christ which He is ever ready to bestow upon us, we are to impart in true, hopeful words. "Rejoice in the Lord alway: and again I say, Rejoice." If we would guard our words, so that nothing but kindness shall escape our lips, we will give evidence that we are preparing to become members of the heavenly family. In words and works we shall show forth the praises of Him who has called us out of darkness into His marvelous light. Oh, what a reformative influence would go forth if we as a people would value at its true worth the talent of speech and its influence upon human souls!

The Sabbath meetings, the morning and evening worship in the home, the services held in the chapel—all should be vitalized by the Spirit of Christ. Each member of the sanitarium family should confess Christ openly and with gladness, expressing the joy and comfort and hope that are written in the soul. Christ is to be set forth as the Chiefest among ten thousand, the One altogether lovely. He is to be set forth as the Giver of every good and perfect gift, the One in whom our hopes of eternal life are centered. If we would do this, all narrowness must be set aside, and we must call into exercise the love of Christ. The joy we experience in this love will be a blessing to others.

Deep Earnestness and Joy

I am bidden to say to the sanitarium family, Let your social meetings, and all your religious exercises, be characterized by a deep earnestness and a joy that expresses the love of God in the soul. Such meetings will be profitable to all; for they will bind heart to heart. Let there be earnest seasons of prayer; for prayer will give strength to the religious experience. Confess Christ openly and bravely, and manifest at all times the meekness of Christ.

The Lord would have the family of workers at Loma Linda channels of light. If we will keep the heart and mind opened heavenward, cherishing the comfort of His grace in the heart, the presence of Christ will be revealed. Let earnestness and zeal come into your lives. Make no backward movements. The Lord is our helper, our guide, our shield, our exceeding great reward. Do not allow levity to come into your experience, but cultivate cheerfulness; for this is an excellent grace. We cannot afford to be unmindful of our words and deportment....

We all have very much to be thankful for; let us open our lips in praise and thanksgiving to God. Let us come nearer to the Lord Jesus, and acknowledge our daily obligations to Him. He has made it possible for us to secure for ourselves a very happy life even in this world of sin, and holds out the hope of being continually in His presence in the kingdom He is preparing for His people. Should not these thoughts call forth from us praise and thanksgiving?—Letter 260, 1907.

The Observance of the Sabbath

Genuine medical missionary work is bound up inseparably with the keeping of God's commandments, of which the Sabbath is especially mentioned, since it is the great memorial of God's creative work. Its observance is bound up with the work of restoring the moral image of God in man. This is the ministry which God's people are to carry forward at this time. This ministry, rightly performed, will bring rich blessings to the church.—Testimonies for the Church 6:266.

The Physician Not Exempt

Often physicians are called upon on the Sabbath to minister to the sick, and it is impossible for them to take time for rest and devotion. The Saviour has shown us by His example that it is right to relieve suffering on this day; but physicians and nurses should do no unnecessary work. Ordinary treatment, and operations that can wait, should be deferred till the next day. Let the patients know that physicians must have one day for rest. The Lord says, "Verily My Sabbaths ye shall keep: for it is a sign between Me and you throughout your generations." Exodus 31:13.

Let no man, because he is a physician, feel at liberty to disregard this word of the Lord. He should plan his work so as to obey God's requirements. He should not travel on the Sabbath except when there is real suffering to be alleviated. When this is the case, it is not a desecration of the Sabbath for physicians to travel upon that day; but ordinary cases should be deferred.

God created the world in six days and rested upon the seventh. He sanctified and blessed the seventh day and made it His sacred memorial. "Wherefore," He declares, "the children of Israel shall keep the Sabbath, to observe the Sabbath throughout their generations, for a perpetual covenant." Exodus 31:16. Those who do this, keeping all of God's commandments, may claim the promises contained in Isaiah 58:11-14. The instruction given in this chapter is full and decided. Those who refrain from labor on the Sabbath may claim divine comfort and consolation. Shall we not believe God? Shall we not call holy the day which He calls holy? Man should not be ashamed to acknowledge as sacred that which God calls sacred. He should not be ashamed to do that which God has commanded. Obedience will bring him a knowledge of what constitutes true sanctification.

Let there be no robbery of God in tithes and offerings, no desecration of His holy time. Man is not to do his own pleasure on God's holy day. He has six days in which to work at secular business, but God claims the seventh as His own. "In it," He says, "thou shalt not do any work." Exodus 20:10. The servant of God will call sacred that which the Lord calls sacred. Thus he will show that he has chosen the Lord as his leader. The Sabbath was made in Eden, when the morning stars sang together and all the sons of God shouted for joy. God has placed it in our charge. Let us keep it pure and holy.—Manuscript 162, 1897.

At the Peril of the Soul

Those who, from whatever cause, are obliged to work on the Sabbath, are always in peril; they feel the loss, and from doing works of necessity, they fall into the habit of doing things on the Sabbath that are not necessary. The sense of its sacredness is lost, and the holy commandment is of no effect. A special effort should be made to bring about a reform in regard to Sabbath observance. The workers in the sanitarium do not always do for themselves what is their privilege and duty. Often they feel so weary that they become demoralized. This should not be. The soul can be rich in grace only as it shall abide in the presence of God....

If the rush of work is allowed to drive us from our purpose of seeking the Lord daily, we shall make the greatest mistakes; we shall incur losses, for the Lord is not with us. We have closed the door so that He cannot find access to our souls. But if we pray, even when our hands are employed, the Saviour's ear is open to hear our petitions.... God takes care of you in the place where it is your duty to be. But be sure, as often as possible, to go where prayer is wont to be made.—Counsels on Health, 422-424.

Sabbath Work

Physicians need to cultivate a spirit of self-denial and self-sacrifice. It may be necessary to devote even the hours of the holy Sabbath to the relief of suffering humanity. But the fee for such labor should be put into the treasury of the Lord, to be used for the worthy poor, who need medical skill but cannot afford to pay for it.—Health, Philanthropic, and Medical Missionary Work, page 42.

The Tithe

The men connected with the institutions of God's appointment should be careful to acknowledge Him in all their ways. To Him they owe their intellect and all their capabilities, and they are to acknowledge this. As did Abraham, they are to pay a faithful tithe of all they possess and all they receive. A faithful tithe is the Lord's portion. To withhold it is to rob God. Every one should freely, willingly, gladly, bring tithes and offerings into the storehouse of the Lord. In so doing he will receive a blessing. There is no safety in withholding from God His own portion.—Manuscript 162, 1897.

An Opportune Place for Backsliding

The sanitarium is a place which affords ample opportunity to backslide from God, to let self have the supremacy, and thus separate the soul from Christ and the holy angels.

Neither physicians nor helpers should attempt to perform their work without taking time to pray.—Health, Philanthropic, and Medical Missionary Work, page 16.

Build Harmoniously

None of us can afford to sin. It is expensive business. Sin so blinds the eyes that evil is not discerned, and by their indiscreet actions those thus blinded become instruments of unrighteousness to scatter for Satan....

Watch against habits of sin. Keep a watch over the tongue. Watch for opportunities to do good and bless others, ever looking to Jesus, growing in grace and in the knowledge of the truth. If you want the higher life, you must now live the higher life in the lower life of this world. We are working for time and for eternity. A well-built life is formed by living upon the plan of addition, laying up one grace after another in good deeds, in faith, patience, temperance, benevolence, courage, self-denial. Ye are God's husbandry. Ye are God's building. Learning of Christ, you will not be a jumble of opposites and inconsistencies—today sober and devout, tomorrow careless and frivolous.

Christ has made every provision that your character may be harmonious through the grace given you. Then build it harmoniously. Let the structure rise, stone on stone. Catch the rays of divine light from Jesus, and let them shine upon the pathway of others who are in darkness. All the universe of God is looking upon us with intense interest.—Letter 6a, 1890.

Changed Into the Divine Likeness

To the young men and young women who are being educated as nurses and physicians, I would say, Keep close to Jesus. By beholding Him you will become changed into His likeness.... You may have a theoretical knowledge of the truth, but this will not save you. You must know by experience how sinful sin is and how much you need Jesus as a personal Saviour. Only thus can you become sons and daughters of God. Your only merit is your great need.

Those selected to take the nurse's course in our sanitariums should be wisely chosen. Young girls of a superficial mold of character should not be encouraged to take up this work. Many of the young men who present themselves as desirous of being educated as physicians have not those traits of character which will enable them to withstand the temptations so common to the work of a physician. Only those should be accepted who give promise of becoming qualified for the great and sacred work of imparting the principles of true health reform.

Modesty in Deportment

The young ladies connected with our institutions should keep a strict guard over themselves. In word and action they should be reserved. Never when speaking to a married man should they show the slightest freedom. To my sisters who are connected with our sanitariums I would say, Gird on the armor. When talking to men, be kind and courteous, but never free. Observant eyes are upon you, watching your conduct, judging by it whether you are indeed children of God. Be modest. Abstain from every appearance of evil. Keep on the heavenly armor, or else for Christ's sake sever your connection with the sanitarium, the place where poor, shipwrecked souls are to find a haven. Those connected with these institutions are to take heed to themselves. Never, by word or action, are they to give the least occasion for wicked men to speak evil of the truth.

Not of the World

There are only two kingdoms in this world, the kingdom of Christ and the kingdom of Satan. To one of these kingdoms each one of us must belong. In His wonderful prayer for His disciples Christ said, "I pray not that Thou shouldest take them out of the world, but that Thou shouldest keep them from the evil. They are not of the world, even as I am not of the world. Sanctify them through Thy truth: Thy word is truth. As Thou hast sent Me into the world, even so have I also sent them into the world."

It is not God's will that we should seclude ourselves from the world. But while in the world we should sanctify ourselves to God. We should not pattern after the world. We are to be in the world as a corrective influence, as salt that retains its savor. Among an unholy, impure, idolatrous generation we are to be pure and holy, showing that the grace of Christ has power to restore in man the divine likeness. We are to exert a saving influence upon the world.

"This is the victory that overcometh the world, even our faith." The world has become a lazar house of sin, a mass of corruption. It knows not the children of God because it knows Him not. We are not to practice its ways or follow its customs. Continually we must resist its lax principles. Christ said to His followers, "Let your light so shine before men, that they may see your good works, and glorify your Father which is in heaven." It is the duty of physicians and nurses to shine as lights amid the corrupting influences of the world. They are to cherish principles which the world cannot tarnish....

The blessing of grace is given to men that the heavenly universe and the fallen world may see, as they could not otherwise, the perfection of Christ's character. The Great Physician came to our world to show men and women that through His grace they may so live that in the great day of God they can receive the precious testimony, "Ye are complete in Him."—Manuscript 24, 1900.

* * * * *

For Further Study

Successful Institutional Work:
Counsels on Health, 255-320 (Testimonies for the Church 4:586, 587).

High Calling of Sanitarium Workers:
Counsels on Health, 250-254 (Testimonies for the Church 7:68-71).

Duties and Privileges of Sanitarium Workers:
Counsels on Health, 398-411, 420-424.

Faithfulness Among Workers:
Testimonies for the Church 4:554-564.

Christian Influence:
Testimonies for the Church 4:565-570.

Moral and Intellectual Culture of Workers:
Counsels on Health, 257-260 (Testimonies for the Church 4:454-459).

Workers to Be Health Reformers:
Counsels on Health, 261.

The Choice of Associates:
Counsels on Health, 414-419 (Testimonies for the Church 4:587-591).

Sharing Responsibilities:
Counsels on Health, 338, 339;
Testimonies for the Church 8:231-235.

Adherence to Principle:
Counsels on Health, 287, 288 (Testimonies for the Church 4:576, 577).

Cheerfulness:
Counsels on Health, 406, 407 (The Ministry of Healing, 222-224).

Criticism and Faultfinding:
Counsels on Health, 296, 297.

Frivolity and Criticism:
Counsels on Health, 412, 413.

Conscientious Attention to Little Things:
Testimonies for the Church 4:572.

Sabbath Observance in Sanitariums:
Counsels on Health, 234-239 (Testimonies for the Church 7:104-

109);
Counsels on Health, 422.
The Head Physician:
Counsels on Health, 337-339.
The Chaplain:
Counsels on Health, 289 (Testimonies for the Church 4:546, 547.)

Section 12—The Prevention of Disease and Its Cure by Rational Methods

Prevention of Disease

The distinction between prevention and cure has not been made sufficiently important. Teach the people that it is better to know how to keep well than how to cure disease. Our physicians should be wise educators, warning all against self-indulgence, showing that abstinence from the things that God has prohibited is the only way to prevent ruin of body and mind.—Manuscript 99, 1902.

Early Teaching of Physiology

The Creator of man has arranged the living machinery of our bodies. Every function is wonderfully and wisely made. And God has pledged Himself to keep this human machinery in healthful action if the human agent will obey His laws and cooperate with God. Every law governing the human machinery is to be considered just as truly divine in origin, in character, and in importance as the word of God. Every careless, inattentive action, any abuse put upon the Lord's wonderful mechanism by disregarding His specified laws in the human habitation, is a violation of God's law. We may behold and admire the work of God in the natural world, but the human habitation is the most wonderful.

From the first dawn of reason the human mind should become intelligent in regard to the physical structure. Here Jehovah has given a specimen of Himself; for man was made in the image of God. It is Satan's determined work to destroy the moral image of God in man. He would make the intelligence of man, his highest, noblest gift, the most destructive agent to pollute with sin everything he touches.—Manuscript 3, 1897.

Educate the Sick

The first labors of a physician should be to educate the sick and suffering in the very course they should pursue to prevent disease. The greatest good can be done by our trying to enlighten the minds of all we can obtain access to, as to the best course for them to pursue to prevent sickness and suffering, and broken constitutions, and premature death. But those who do not care to undertake work that taxes their physical and mental powers will be ready to prescribe drug medication, which lays a foundation in the human organism for a twofold greater evil than that which they claim to have relieved.

[222]

A physician who has the moral courage to imperil his reputation in enlightening the understanding by plain facts, in showing the nature of disease and how to prevent it, and the dangerous practice of resorting to drugs, will have an uphill business, but he will live and let live.... He will, if a reformer, talk plainly in regard to the false appetites and ruinous self-indulgence, in dressing, in eating and drinking, in overtaxing to do a large amount of work in a given time, which has a ruinous influence upon the temper, the physical and mental powers....

Right and correct habits, intelligently and perseveringly practiced, will be removing the cause for disease, and the strong drugs need not be resorted to. Many go on from step to step with their unnatural indulgences, which is bringing in just as unnatural [a] condition of things as possible.

Stimulants and Narcotics

Diseases of every stripe and type have been brought upon human beings by the use of tea and coffee and the narcotics, opium, and tobacco. These hurtful indulgences must be given up, not only one, but all; for all are hurtful, and ruinous to the physical, mental, and moral powers, and should be discontinued from a health standpoint. The common use of the flesh of dead animals has had a deteriorating influence upon the morals as well as the physical constitution.

Ill health in a variety of forms, if effect could be traced to the cause, would reveal the sure result of flesh eating. The disuse of meats, with healthful dishes nicely prepared to take the place of flesh-meats, would place a large number of the sick and suffering ones in a fair way of recovering their health, without the use of drugs. But if the physician encourages a meat-eating diet to his invalid patients, then he will make a necessity for the use of drugs....

[223] Drugs always have a tendency to break down and destroy vital forces, and nature becomes so crippled in her efforts that the invalid dies, not because he needed to die, but because nature was outraged. If she had been left alone, she would have put forth her highest efforts to save life and health. Nature wants none of such help as so many claim that they have given her. Lift off the burdens placed upon her, after the customs of the fashion of this age, and you will see in many cases nature will right herself. The use of drugs is not favorable or natural to the laws of life and health. The drug medication gives nature two burdens to bear, in the place of one. She has two serious difficulties to overcome, in the place of one.

There is now positive need even with physicians, reformers in the line of treatment of disease, that greater painstaking effort be made to carry forward and upward the work for themselves, and to interestedly instruct those who look to them for medical skill to ascertain the cause of their infirmities. They should call their attention in a special manner to the laws which God has established, which cannot be violated with impunity. They dwell much on the working of disease, but do not, as a general rule, arouse the attention to the laws which must be sacredly and intelligently obeyed to prevent disease.

The Physician's Example an Educating Influence

If the physician has not been correct in his dietetic practices, if his own appetite has not been restricted to a plain, wholesome diet, in a large measure discarding the use of the flesh of dead animals, ... he will as soon educate and discipline the taste and appetite of his patients to love the things that he loves, as to give them the sound principles of health reform. He will prescribe for sick patients flesh-meats, when it is the very worst diet that they can have. It stimulates, but does not give strength.

Nature will want some assistance to bring things to their proper condition, which may be found in the simplest remedies, especially in the use of nature's own furnished remedies—pure air, and with a precious knowledge of how to breathe; pure water, with a knowledge how to apply it; plenty of sunlight in every room in the house if possible, and with an intelligent knowledge of what advantages are to be gained by its use. All these are powerful in their efficiency, and the patient who has obtained a knowledge of how to eat and dress healthfully may live for comfort, for peace, for health, and will not be prevailed upon to put to his lips drugs, which, in the place of helping nature, paralyzes her powers. If the sick and suffering will do only as well as they know in regard to living out the principles of health reform perseveringly, then they will in nine cases out of ten recover from their ailments.

Obedience to Nature's Laws

The feeble and suffering ones must be educated line upon line, precept upon precept, here a little and there a little, until they will have respect for and live in obedience to the law that God has made to control the human organism. Those who sin against knowledge and light, and resort to the skill of a physician in administering drugs, will be constantly losing their hold on life. The less there is of drug dosing, the more favorable will be their recovery to health. Drugs, in the place of helping nature, are constantly paralyzing her efforts....

They do not inquire into their former habits of eating and drinking, and take special notice of their erroneous habits which have been for many years laying the foundation of disease. Conscientious physicians should be prepared to enlighten those who are ignorant, and should with wisdom make out their prescriptions, prohibiting those things in their diet which he knows to be erroneous.

He should plainly state the things which he regards as detrimental to the laws of health, and leave these suffering ones to work conscientiously to do those things for themselves which they can do, and thus place themselves in right relation to the laws of life and health. When from an enlightened conscience they do the very best they know how to do to preserve themselves in health, then in faith they may look to the Great Physician, who is a healer of the body as well as of the soul.

We are health reformers. Physicians should have wisdom and experience, and be thorough health reformers. Then they will be constantly educating by precept and example their patients from drugs. For they well know that the use of drugs may produce for the time being favorable results, but will implant in the system that which will cause great difficulties hereafter, which they may never recover from during their lifetime. Nature must have a chance to do her work. Obstructions must be removed and opportunity given her to exert her healing forces, which she will surely do, if every abuse is removed from her and she has a fair chance.

Confidence in Nature's Remedies to be Cultivated

The sick should be educated to have confidence in nature's great blessings which God has provided; and the most effective remedies for disease are pure soft water, the blessed God-given sunshine coming into the rooms of the invalids, living outdoors as much as possible, having healthful exercise, eating and drinking foods that are prepared in the most healthful manner....

There are many, many afflicted in our world with tobacco poison.... The physician, if he is not a novice, can trace the effects back to the true cause, but he dares not forbid its use, because he indulges in it himself. Some will in an undecided, halfway manner advise the tobacco users to take less of this narcotic; but they do not say to them, This habit is killing you. They prescribe drugs to cure a disease which is the result of indulging unnatural appetites, and two evils are produced in the place of removing one.

Thousands need to be educated patiently, kindly, tenderly, but decidedly, that nine tenths of their complaints are created by their own course of action....

Self-indulgence a Cause of Disease

Some have not the moral courage to keep right on in the fear of the Lord. There is even among those who have intelligence in regard to the laws of life and health, a constant selfish indulgence in those things which are injurious to both soul and body. There is intemperance in eating and in the many varieties of food taken at one meal. In the preparation of food there are unhealthful mixtures which ferment in the stomach and cause great distress. And yet these go on, continuing their indulgence, which lays the foundation for numerous difficulties. If these would have self-control, and educate their taste to eat only those things which the abused stomach can and will assimilate, they would save large expense in doctor bills and avoid great sufferings....

It is the work of the physician to educate those who are ignorant in regard to these things. There should be training schools to educate nurses and prepare the minds to sense the danger and to see the importance of bringing in skill and tact in the preparation of foods which shall be substituted for the meat diet. This kind of education will pay in the end. Wisdom should be used not to remove meat all at once from those who have been in the habit of using it, but educate the mind to see the importance of the use of healthful food.—Manuscript 22, 1887.

The Law of Faith and Works

The grace of God is always reformatory. Every human being is in a school, where he is to learn to give up hurtful practices, and to obtain a knowledge of what he can do for himself. Those who ignore these things, who take no precautions in regard to getting pure air to breathe and pure water to drink, cannot be free from disease. Their systems are defiled and the human structure injured.

Such people are careless, reckless, presumptuous, and self-destroying. Knowledge is strewn along their pathway, but they refuse to gather up the rays of light, saying that they depend on God. But will God do those things that He has left for them to do? Will He supply their neglect? Will He wink at their willing ignorance, and do great things for them, by restoring soul, body, and spirit, while they ignore the most simple agencies, the use of which would bring them their health? While day by day they indulge their appetite by eating that which brings disease, can they expect the Lord to work a miracle to restore them? This is not the Lord's way of working. By doing this, they make the Lord altogether such an one as themselves. Faith and works go together....

Let all examine their own hearts, to see if they are not cherishing that which is a positive injury to them, and in the place of opening the door of the heart to let Jesus, the Sun of Righteousness in, are complaining of the dearth of the Spirit of God. Let these search for their idols, and cast them out. Let them cut away every unhealthful indulgence in eating or drinking. Let them bring their daily practice into harmony with nature's laws. By doing, as well as believing, an atmosphere will be created about the soul that will be a savor of life unto life.—Manuscript 86, 1897.

Combat Disease by Simple Methods

Our people should become intelligent in the treatment of sickness without the aid of poisonous drugs. Many should seek to obtain the education that will enable them to combat disease in its varied forms by the most simple methods. Thousands have gone down to the grave because of the use of poisonous drugs, who might have been restored to health by simple methods of treatment. Water treatments, wisely and skillfully given, may be the means of saving many lives.

Let diligent study be united with careful treatments. Let prayers of faith be offered by the bedside of the sick. Let the sick be encouraged to claim the promises of God for themselves. "Faith is the substance of things hoped for, the evidence of things not seen," Christ Jesus, the Saviour of men, is to be brought into our labors and councils more and more.—Manuscript 15, 1911.

Hygienic Principles

Our sanitariums are to be conducted on hygienic methods. The light God has given on the subject of disease and its causes needs to be dwelt upon largely; for it is wrong habits in the indulgence of appetite and inattention to the care of the body that tells upon people. Habits of cleanliness, care in regard to that which is introduced into the mouth, should be observed.

It is not best to tell patients that flesh-meats shall never be used; but reason and conscience are to be awakened in regard to self-preservation and purity from every perverted appetite. They can learn to relish a diet that is healthful and abstemious, consisting of fruits, grains, and vegetables.

Drug Medication

Drug medication is to be discarded. On this point the conscience of the physician must ever be kept tender and true and clean. The inclination to use poisonous drugs, which kill if they do not cure, needs to be guarded against. Matters have been laid open before me in reference to the use of drugs. Many have been treated with drugs and the result has been death. Our physicians, by practicing drug medication, have lost many cases that need not have died if they had left their drugs out of the sickroom.

[228]

Fever cases have been lost, when, had the physicians left off entirely their drug treatment, had they put their wits to work and wisely and persistently used the Lord's own remedies, plenty of air and water, the patients would have recovered. The reckless use of these things that should be discarded has decided the case of the sick.

Experimenting in drugs is a very expensive business. Paralysis of the brain and tongue is often the result, and the victims die an unnatural death, when, if they had been treated perseveringly, with unwearied, unrelaxed diligence with hot and cold water, hot compresses, packs, and dripping sheet, they would be alive today.

Nothing should be put into the human system that will leave a baleful influence behind. And to carry out the light on this subject, to practice hygienic treatment, is the reason which has been given me for establishing sanitariums in various localities.

I have been pained when many students have been encouraged to go where they would receive an education in the use of drugs. The light I have received on the subject of drugs is altogether different from the use made of them at these schools or at the sanitariums. We must become enlightened on these subjects.

The intricate names given medicines are used to cover up the matter, so that none will know what is given them as remedies unless they consult a dictionary....

Patients are to be supplied with good, wholesome food; total abstinence from all intoxicating drinks is to be observed; drugs are to be discarded, and rational methods of treatment followed. The patients must not be given alcohol, tea, coffee, or drugs; for these always leave traces of evil behind them. By observing these rules, many who have been given up by the physicians may be restored to health.

In this work the human and divine instrumentalities can cooperate in saving life, and God will add His blessing. Many suffering ones not of our faith will come to our institutions to receive treatment. Those whose health has been ruined by sinful indulgence, and who have been treated by physicians till the drugs administered have no effect, will come; and they will be benefited.

The Lord will bless institutions conducted in accordance with His plans. He will cooperate with every physician who faithfully and conscientiously engages in this work. He will enter the rooms of the sick. He will give wisdom to the nurses.—Manuscript 162, 1897.

Seeds of Death

When you understand physiology in its truest sense, your drug bills will be very much smaller, and finally you will cease to deal out drugs at all. The physician who depends upon drug medication in his practice shows that he does not understand the delicate machinery of the human organism. He is introducing into the system a seed crop that will never lose its destroying properties throughout the lifetime. I tell you this because I dare not withhold it. Christ paid too much for man's redemption to have his body so ruthlessly treated as it has been by drug medication.

Years ago the Lord revealed to me that institutions should be established for treating the sick without drugs. Man is God's property, and the ruin that has been made of the living habitation, the suffering caused by the seeds of death sown in the human system, are an offense to God.—Letter 73, 1896.

Thousands Might Recover

Thousands who are afflicted might recover their health if, instead of depending upon the drugstore for their life, they would discard all drugs and live simply, without using tea, coffee, liquor, or spices, which irritate the stomach and leave it weak, unable to digest even simple food without stimulation. The Lord is willing to let His light shine forth in clear, distinct rays to all who are weak and feeble.

Vegetables, fruits, and grains should compose our diet. Not an ounce of flesh-meat should enter our stomachs. The eating of flesh is unnatural. We are to return to God's original purpose in the creation of man.—Manuscript 115, 1903.

What We Can Do for Ourselves

In regard to that which we can do for ourselves: There is a point that requires careful, thoughtful consideration. I must become acquainted with myself. I must be a learner always as to how to take care of this building, the body God has given me, that I may preserve it in the very best condition of health. I must eat those things which will be for my very best good physically, and I must take special care to have my clothing such as will conduce to a healthful circulation of the blood. I must not deprive myself of exercise and air. I must get all the sunlight that it is possible for me to obtain. I must have wisdom to be a faithful guardian of my body.

I should do a very unwise thing to enter a cool room when in a perspiration; I should show myself an unwise steward to allow myself to sit in a draft and thus expose myself so as to take cold. I should be unwise to sit with cold feet and limbs and thus drive back the blood from the extremities to the brain or internal organs. I should always protect my feet in damp weather. I should eat regularly of the most healthful food which will make the best quality of blood, and I should not work intemperately if it is in my power to avoid doing so. And when I violate the laws God has established in my being, I am to repent and reform, and place myself in the most favorable condition under the doctors God has provided—pure air, pure water, and the healing, precious sunlight.

Presumption and Indolence

If we neglect to do that which is within the reach of nearly every family, and ask the Lord to relieve pain when we are too indolent to make use of these remedies within our power, it is simply presumption. The Lord expects us to work in order that we may obtain food. He does not propose that we shall gather the harvest unless we break the sod, till the soil, and cultivate the produce. Then God sends the rain and the sunshine and the clouds to cause vegetation to flourish. God works and man cooperates with God. Then there is seedtime and harvest. God has caused to grow out of the ground herbs for the use of man, and if we understand the nature of these roots and herbs, and make a right use of them, there would not be a necessity of running for the doctor so frequently, and people would be in much better health than they are today.—Letter 35, 1890.

Instruction for Missionaries

Those who desire to become missionaries are to hear instruction from competent physicians, who will teach them how to care for the sick without the use of drugs. Such lessons will be of the highest value to those who go out to labor in foreign countries. And the simple remedies used will save many lives.—Manuscript 83, 1908.

Sunlight, Ventilation, and Temperature

To afford the patient the most favorable conditions for recovery, the room he occupies should be large, light, and cheerful, with opportunity for thorough ventilation. The room in the house that best meets these requirements should be chosen as the sickroom. Many houses have no special provision for proper ventilation, and to secure it is difficult; but every possible effort should be made to arrange the sickroom so that a current of fresh air can pass through it night and day.

So far as possible, an even temperature should be maintained in the sickroom. The thermometer should be consulted. Those who have the care of the sick, being often deprived of sleep or awakened in the night to attend to the patient, are liable to chilliness, and are not good judges of a healthful temperature.—The Ministry of Healing, 220-221.

Nature's Great Medicinal Resources

In the efforts made for the restoration of the sick to health, use is to be made of the beautiful things of the Lord's creation.

Seeing the flowers, plucking the ripe fruit from the trees, hearing the happy songs of the birds, have a peculiarly exhilarating effect on the nervous system. From out-of-door life, men, women, and children will gain the desire to be pure and guileless. By the influence of the quickening, reviving, life-giving properties of nature's great medicinal resources, the functions of the body are strengthened, the intellect awakened, the imagination quickened, the spirits enlivened. The mind is prepared to appreciate the beauties of God's word.

Why should not the young men and women who are seeking to obtain a knowledge of how to care for the sick, have the advantage of nature's wonderful resources? ... [232]

God helping me, I will do my utmost to show the life-giving power of sunshine and fresh air. How much better it is for the sick to be in the open air than within four walls, decorated though these walls may be with many pictures!—Letter 71, 1902.

Healing Power in Outdoor Life

The surroundings of a sanitarium should be as attractive as possible. Out-of-door life is a means of gaining health and happiness. As the sick look upon the beautiful scenery, as they see the flowers in their loveliness, they will venture to take a few steps outdoors to gather some of the flowers—precious messengers of God's love to His family in affliction here below. In flower garden and orchard, the sick will find health, cheerfulness, and happy thoughts....

What an influence an outdoor life among the flowers and fruit-laden trees has upon those who are sick both in body and in mind! After they stay for a short time at a sanitarium situated in the midst of the beauties of nature, hope begins to take the place of despair. The heart is softened by the objects of beauty in nature, that the great Master Artist has given to mankind as pictures in which are portrayed His goodness and love....

Encourage the patients to live out of doors. Devise plans to keep them outdoors, where they will become acquainted with God through nature. As they take exercise in the open air, restoration will begin in body, mind, and soul. Life in the open air, away from the congested cities, is health-restoring. The pure air has in it health and life. As it is breathed in, it has an invigorating effect on the whole system....

Those who are connected with our sanitariums should make every effort to encourage the patients to live an outdoor life, so far as it is possible for them to do so. Nature is the great physician that will heal them of all their maladies, both spiritual and physical. Everything that can be done should be done to give those who come to our sanitariums for treatment the opportunity of living as much as possible in the open air. The patients should have the advantages that are given by natural surroundings. Nature is the great restorer of both soul and body.—Manuscript 43, 1902.

An Elixir of Life

When a sanitarium is established in the country, the sick can breathe the pure air of heaven. As they walk among the flowers and trees, joy and gladness fill their hearts. It is as if the smile of God were upon them, as they look upon the beautiful things He has created to bring joy to their sad hearts.

Life in the open air is good for body and mind. It is God's medicine for the restoration of health. Pure air, good water, sunshine, beautiful surroundings—these are His means for restoring the sick to health in natural ways.

The fact that in the country all these advantages can be obtained is a powerful incentive to the establishment of a sanitarium in the country. There the institution can be surrounded by flowers and trees, orchards and vineyards. The effect of such surroundings is as it were an elixir of life.

It is worth more than silver or gold to sick people to lie in the sunshine or in the shade of the trees. And whenever opportunity offers, let those in charge of them draw lessons teaching the love of God from the things of nature, from the lofty trees, the springing grass, and the beautiful flowers. Every opening bud and blossoming flower is an expression of God's love for His children. Point them upward to Him whose hand has made the beautiful things of nature....

Life Only in Christ

The fruit of the tree of life in the Garden of Eden possessed supernatural virtue. To eat of it was to live forever. Its fruit was the antidote of death. Its leaves were for the sustaining of life and immortality. But through man's disobedience death entered the world. Adam ate of the tree of the knowledge of good and evil, the fruit of which he had been forbidden to touch. This was his test. He failed, and his transgression opened the floodgates of woe upon our world.

The tree of life was a type of the one great Source of immortality. Of Christ it is written, "In Him was life; and the life was the light of men." He is the fountain of life. Obedience to Him is the life-giving, vivifying power that gladdens the soul. Through sin man shut himself off from access to the tree of life. Now, life and immortality are brought to light through Jesus Christ....

Benefits of Open-Air Exercise

Why deprive the patients of the health-restoring blessing to be found in out-of-door life? I have been instructed that as the sick are encouraged to leave their rooms and spend time in the open air, tending the flowers, or doing some other light, pleasant work, their minds will be called from self to something more health-giving. Open-air exercise should be prescribed as a beneficial, life-giving necessity. The longer patients can be kept out of doors, the less care they will require.

The more cheerful their surroundings, the more hopeful they will be. Surround them with the beautiful things of nature, place them where they can see the flowers growing and hear the birds singing, and their hearts will break into a song in harmony with the song of the birds. Shut them in rooms, and, be those rooms ever so elegantly furnished, they will grow fretful and gloomy. Give them the blessing of outdoor life; for thus their souls will be uplifted, unconsciously, and, in a large sense, consciously. Relief will come to body and mind....

Health and Joy in Field and Orchard

Our Redeemer is constantly working to restore in man the moral image of God. And although the whole creation groans under the curse, and fruit and flowers are nothing in comparison with what they will be in the earth made new, yet even today the sick may find health and gladness and joy in field and orchard. What a restorative this is! What a preventive of sickness! The leaves of the tree of life are for the healing of the believing, repenting children of God who avail themselves of the blessing to be found in tree and shrub and flower, even marred as nature is by the curse.—Manuscript 41, 1902.

Awaken Faith in the Great Healer

The soothing power of pure truth seen, acted, and maintained in all its bearings is of a value no language can express to people who are suffering with disease. Keep ever before the suffering sick the compassion and tenderness of Christ, and awaken their conscience to a belief in His power to relieve suffering, and lead them to faith and trust in Him, the Great Healer, and you have gained a soul and ofttimes a life.

Therefore personal religion for all physicians in the sickroom is essential to success in giving the simple treatment without drugs. He who is a physician and guardian of the health and body, God would have in every way educated to learn lessons of the Great Teacher how to work in Christ and through Christ to save the souls of the sick. How can any physician know this until the Saviour shall be received as a personal Saviour to him who administers to suffering humanity?

Religion should be made prominent in a most tender, sympathetic, compassionate way. No one of all the parties with whom he is acquainted can do as much for the sick one as a truly converted nurse and physician. Actions of purity and refinement in looks and words, and above all the sweet words of prayer, though few, yet if sincere, will be a sure anchor to the suffering ones.—Letter 69, 1898.

* * * * *

For Further Study

In the Sickroom:
The Ministry of Healing, 219-224.
The Use of Rational Remedies:
The Ministry of Healing, 234-240.
Hygienic Principles:
The Ministry of Healing, 271-294.
Pure Air and Sunshine:
Counsels on Health, 55-60.
Benefits of Outdoor Life:
Counsels on Health, 162-183 (The Ministry of Healing, 51-58, 112, 113; Christ's Object Lessons, 24-27; Testimonies for the Church 2:525-527; Testimonies for the Church 3:135-138; Testimonies for the Church 7:76-79, 85-87; Counsels to Parents, Teachers, and Students, 187);
The Ministry of Healing, 261-268.
Benefits of Physical Exercise:
Counsels on Health, 52-54 (Testimonies for the Church 2:528-533);
Counsels on Health, 189-192 (Education, 210-213);
Counsels on Health, 199, 200 (Testimonies for the Church 3:78).
Cleanliness:
Counsels on Health, 61-63;
Counsels on Health, 101-104 (Testimonies for the Church 3:70, 71).

Section 13—Medical Missionary Work and the Gospel Ministry

A United Work

I wish to speak about the relation existing between the medical missionary work and the gospel ministry. It has been presented to me that every department of the work is to be united in one great whole. The work of God is to prepare a people to stand before the Son of man at His coming, and this work should be a unit. The work that is to fit a people to stand firm in the last great day must not be a divided work.

The ministry of the gospel is to present the truth which must be received in order for people to be sanctified and made ready for the coming of the Lord. And this work is to embrace all that was embraced in Christ's ministry. Gospel workers are to minister on the right hand and on the left, doing their work intelligently and solidly.

There is to be no division between the ministry and the medical work. The physician should labor equally with the minister, and with as much earnestness and thoroughness for the salvation of the soul as well as for the restoration of the body....

The Body—the Arm—the Head

The medical missionary work has never been presented to me in any other way than as bearing the same relation to the work as a whole as the arm does to the body. The gospel ministry is an organization for the proclamation of the truth and the carrying forward of the work for sick and well. This is the body, the medical missionary work is the arm, and Christ is the head over all. Thus the matter has been presented to me.

It has been urged that because the medical missionary work is the arm of the body, there should be a oneness of respect shown. This is so. The medical missionary work is the arm of the body, and God wants us to take a decided interest in this work.

Christ was bound up in all branches of the work. He did not make any division. He did not feel that he was infringing on physicians when He healed the sick. He proclaimed the truth, and when the sick came to Him for healing, He asked them if they believed that He could make them whole. He was just as ready to lay His hands in healing on the sick and afflicted as He was to preach the gospel. He was just as much at home in this work as in proclaiming the truth; for healing the sick is a part of the gospel.

To take people right where they are, whatever their position, whatever their condition, and help them in every way possible—this is gospel ministry. It may be necessary for ministers to go into the homes of the sick and say, "I am ready to help you, and I will do the best I can. I am not a physician, but I am a minister, and I like to minister to the sick and afflicted." Those who are sick in body are nearly always sick in soul, and when the soul is sick, the body is made sick.—Manuscript 62, 1900.

To Open Doors

The right hand is used to open doors through which the body may find entrance. This is the part the medical missionary work is to act. It is to largely prepare the way for the reception of the truth for this time. A body without hands is useless. In giving honor to the body, honor must also be given to the helping hands, which are agencies of such importance that without them the body can do nothing. Therefore the body which treats indifferently the right hand, refusing its aid, is able to accomplish nothing....

All through this country a work must be done that has not yet been done. The medical missionary work must be recognized. Those who go forth to engage in the work of the ministry must be intelligent upon the subject of health reform. Those men who after many years' experience have yet no appreciation of the medical missionary work, should not be appointed to preside over our churches. They are not walking in the light of present truth for this time. Those who love the truth and appreciate the question of temperance in all its bearings should not be placed in the charge of a minister who has not heeded the light God has given upon health reform. What help can a man be to a church if he is not walking in the light?

No Other Work So Successful

In new fields no work is so successful as medical missionary work. If our ministers would work earnestly to obtain an education in medical missionary lines, they would be far better fitted to do the work Christ did as a medical missionary. By diligent study and practice they can become so well acquainted with the principles of health reform that wherever they go they will be great blessing to the people they meet.

For thirty years the necessity of health reform has been held before our people. By the practice of its simple principles the sick and suffering are relieved, and fields otherwise unapproachable become most interesting fields of action. The seeds of truth, cast into good ground, produce an abundant harvest....

A Revelation of Christ's Compassion

Medical missionary work brings to humanity the gospel of release from suffering. It is the pioneer work of the gospel. It is the gospel practiced, the compassion of Christ revealed. Of this work there is great need, and the world is open for it. God grant that the importance of medical missionary work shall be understood, and that new fields may be immediately entered. Then will the work of the ministry be after the Lord's order; the sick will be healed, and poor, suffering humanity will be blessed.

Begin to do medical missionary work with the conveniences which you have at hand. You will find that thus the way will open for you to hold Bible readings. The heavenly Father will place you in connection with those who need to know how to treat their sick ones. Put into practice what you know regarding the treatment of disease. Thus suffering will be relieved, and you will have opportunity to break the bread of life to starving souls....

Brings Rays of Heavenly Brightness

The doing of medical missionary work brings rays of heavenly brightness to wearied, perplexed, suffering souls. It is as a fountain open for the wayworn, thirsty traveler. At every work of mercy, every work of love, angels of God are present. Those who live nearest to heaven will reflect the brightness of the Sun of Righteousness....

This is True Ministry

Read the Scriptures carefully, and you will find that Christ spent the largest part of His ministry in restoring the suffering and afflicted to health. Thus He threw back upon Satan the reproach of the evil which the enemy of all good had originated. Satan is the destroyer; Christ is the Restorer. And in our work as Christ's colaborers, we shall have success if we work on practical lines. Ministers, do not confine your work to giving Bible instruction. Do practical work. Seek to restore the sick to health. This is true ministry. Remember that the restoration of the body prepares the way for the restoration of the soul.—Manuscript 55, 1901.

An Effective Instrument

When connected with other lines of gospel effort, medical missionary work is a most effective instrument by which the ground is prepared for the sowing of the seeds of truth, and the instrument also by which the harvest is reaped. Medical missionary work is the helping hand of the gospel ministry. So far as possible, it would be well for evangelical workers to learn how to minister to the necessities of the body as well as the soul; for in doing this, they are following the example of Christ. Intemperance has well-nigh filled the world with disease, and the ministers of the gospel cannot spend their time and strength in relieving all in need of help. The Lord has ordained that Christian physicians and nurses shall labor in connection with those who preach the word. The medical missionary work is to be bound up with the gospel ministry.—The Review and Herald, September 10, 1908.

Encourage the Workers

We now ask those who shall be chosen as presidents of our conferences to make a right beginning in places where nothing has been done. Recognize the medical missionary work as God's helping hand. As His appointed agency it is to have room and encouragement. Medical missionaries are to have as much encouragement as any accredited evangelist. Pray with these workers. Council with them if they need counsel. Do not dampen their zeal and energy. Be sure by your own consecration and devotion to keep a high standard before them. Laborers are greatly needed in the Lord's vineyard, and not a word of discouragement should be spoken to those who consecrate themselves to the work.—Manuscript 33, 1901.

The Worst Evil

My brethren, the Lord calls for unity, for oneness. We are to be one in the faith. I want to tell you that when the gospel ministers and the medical missionary workers are not united, there is placed on our churches the worst evil that can be placed there. Our medical missionaries ought to be interested in the work of our conferences, and our conference workers ought to be as much interested in the work of our medical missionaries.—Manuscript 46, 1904.

A Means of Entrance to Hearts

Medical missionary work must have its representatives in our cities. Centers must be made and missions established on right lines. Ministers of the gospel are to unite with the medical missionary work, which has ever been presented to me as the work which is to break down the prejudice which exists in our world against the truth.

The medical missionary work is growing in importance, and claims the attention of the churches. It is a part of the gospel message, and must receive recognition. It is the heaven-ordained means of finding entrance to the hearts of people. It is the duty of our church members in every place to follow the instruction of the Great Teacher. The gospel message is to be preached in every city; for this is in accordance with the example of Christ and His disciples. Medical missionaries are to seek patiently and earnestly to reach the higher classes. If this work is faithfully done, professional men will become trained evangelists.—Manuscript 33, 1901.

Earnest Appeal to Physicians

I am concerned because so many things engage the minds of our physicians which keep them from the work that God would have them do as evangelists. From the light that God has given me I know that the living preacher who is consecrated and devoted, and knows how to put his trust in God, is greatly needed. We need one hundred workers where now we have one. There is a great work to be done before satanic opposition shall close up the way and our present opportunities for labor shall be lost. Time is rapidly passing. Our publications are numerous, but the Lord calls for the men and women in our churches who have the light to engage in genuine missionary work. Let them in all humility exercise their God-given talents in proclaiming the message that should come to the world at this time.

I hope you will exercise all your capabilities in this work. Present the importance of present truth from the physician's standpoint. The Lord has declared that the educated physician will find entrance in our cities where other men cannot. Teach the message of health reform. This will have an influence with the people.

Let us study our Bibles, and teach the words of truth. Let us do as Christ's apostles did; let us offer prayer for the sick, for there are many who cannot have the advantages of our sanitariums. The Lord will remove infirmities in answer to prayer. Gospel ministers should be able to present the subject of health reform in its simplicity. If this phase of present truth is presented in a clear, simple, Christlike manner, it will have an effect upon the people. There will be a response from many hearts.—Letter 128, 1909.

Many Saved From Degradation

I have been shown that the medical missionary work will discover, in the very depths of degradation, men who once possessed fine minds, richest qualifications, who will be rescued by proper labor from their fallen condition. It is the truth as it is in Jesus that is to be brought before human minds after they have been sympathetically cared for and their physical necessities met. The Holy Spirit is working and cooperating with the human agencies that are laboring for such souls, and some will appreciate the foundation upon a rock for their religious faith.

There is to be no startling communication of strange doctrine to these subjects whom God loves and pities; but as they are helped physically by the medical missionary workers, the Holy Spirit cooperates with the minister of human agencies to arouse the moral powers. The mental powers are awakened into activity, and these poor souls will, many of them, be saved in the kingdom of God.—Special Testimonies for Ministers and Workers, No. 11, page 32.

The Poor Not to Be Neglected

We are living in the last days of this earth's history, and medical missionary work is to be all that the name signifies. To the poor the gospel is to be preached. The poor man as well as the rich man is the object of God's special care and attention. Take away poverty, and we should have no way of understanding the mercy and love of God, no way of knowing the compassionate and sympathetic heavenly Father.

Those who have the truth for these last days will bear a message adapted to the poor. One would think that the gospel was inspired in order to reach this class. Christ came to the earth to walk and work among the poor. To the poor He preached the gospel. His work is the gospel worked out on medical missionary lines—in justice, mercy, and the love of God which is the sure fruit borne because the tree is good. And today in the person of His believing, working children, who move under the guidance of the Holy Spirit, Christ visits the poor and the needy, relieving want and alleviating suffering.—Letter 83, 1902.

Labor for the Wealthy

Those who will exercise their God-given ability for the conversion to the truth of the intellectual, the refined, and the world-absorbed wealthy class, are doing a good and essential work. Many look upon this class as hopeless, and they do little to open the eyes of those who, blinded and dazed by the power of Satan, have lost eternity out of their reckoning. But here is a field of labor that should not be neglected. These persons are stewards to whom God has committed important trusts. We should come close to this class, for I know that many of them are soul burdened; they long for something, they know not what.

If saved to Jesus Christ, they will be useful agents in the hands of God to communicate the light to others. If converted to the truth, they will have a special burden to draw other souls of this neglected class to the light. They will feel that a dispensation of the gospel is committed to them for those who have made the world their god. They need the awakening which the Holy Spirit of God can give them, and those who have an experimental knowledge of the truth are under obligation to God to communicate the precious light to the world-absorbed, world-loving soul.

Some will be convicted and will heed the words spoken to them in love and tenderness. They will acknowledge that the truth is the very thing they need to set them free from the slavery of sin and the bondage of worldly principles. There are opened before them themes of thought, fields for action, that they had never comprehended.

In Jesus the Redeemer they discern infinite wisdom, infinite justice, infinite mercy—depths, heights, lengths, and breadths of love which passeth knowledge. Beholding the perfection of Christ's character, contemplating His mission, His love, His grace, His truth, they are charmed; the great want of the soul is met, and they will say with the psalmist, "I shall be satisfied, when I awake, with Thy likeness." The divine object of faith and love they see to be Jesus Christ; with them the love of the world, the worshiping of earthly treasures, has come to an end....

By Personal Efforts and Living Faith

God would have the truth opened to the men to whom He has given special endowments but who are ignorant of the soul's great necessity. There are some who are especially fitted to engage in this work; there are those who should seek the Lord daily, making it a study how to reach persons of this class, not to have merely a casual acquaintance with them, but to lay hold of them by personal effort and living faith, manifesting a deep love for their souls, a real concern that they shall have knowledge of the truth as it is presented in the word of God....

This class have been sadly neglected. The workers have judged from appearance, and have taken it as a certainty that they would labor in vain. But these persons whom God has gifted, ministers and people, are to be laid hold of by the hand of living faith. Let the workers grasp the promises of God, saying, "Thou hast promised,

'Ask, and ye shall receive.' I must have this soul converted to Jesus Christ." Solicit prayer for the souls for whom you labor; present them before the church as objects for the supplication. It will be just what the church needs, to have their minds called from their little, petty difficulties, to feel a great burden, a personal interest, for a soul that is ready to perish. Select another and still another soul, daily seeking guidance from God, laying everything before Him in earnest prayer, and working in divine wisdom. As you do this, you will see that God will give the Holy Spirit to convict, and the power of the truth to convert, the soul.

I have been shown that thousands of wealthy men have gone to their graves unwarned, because they have been judged from appearance, and passed by as hopeless subjects. The Lord would have this order of things changed. Let judicious men enter upon the work, men who as yet have done nothing in this line because it has seemed forbidding and hopeless. It is a great and important work, and God will endow men with wisdom to undertake it.

It will be by no casual, accidental touch that these wealthy, world-loving, world-worshiping souls will be drawn to Christ. Decided personal effort must be put forth by men and women imbued with the missionary spirit, who will not fail nor be discouraged. The messenger of God is ever to bear in mind that the universe of heaven have long been waiting to cooperate with the human agents in this work which has been shunned and neglected.—Letter 47, 1894.

The Value of Medical Work

Some utterly fail to realize the importance of missionaries' being also medical missionaries. A gospel minister will be twice as successful in his work if he understands how to treat disease. Continually increasing light has been given me on this subject. Some, who do not see the advantage of educating the youth to be physicians both of the mind and of the body, say that the tithe should not be used to support medical missionaries, who devote their time to treating the sick. In response to such statements as these, I am instructed to say that the mind must not become so narrowed down that it cannot take in the truth of the situation. A minister of the gospel who is also a medical missionary, who can cure physical ailments, is a much more efficient worker than one who cannot do this. His work as a minister of the gospel is much more complete....

Will Break Down Prejudice [246]

As the medical missionary cares for the sick, if he is well equipped with knowledge and with instruments for putting that knowledge into practice, he will surely break down prejudice. Women should be educated in medical missionary lines, that as they go forth to heathen countries they may help those of their sisters who need help. In His service the Lord will open doors whereby His word can find entrance.

Living the gospel, maintaining its principles—this is a savor of life unto life. Doors that have been closed to him who merely preaches the gospel, will be opened to the intelligent medical missionary. God reaches hearts through the relief of physical suffering. A seed of truth is dropped into the mind, and is watered by God. Much patience may be required before this seed shows signs of life, but at last it springs up, and bears fruit unto eternal life.

How slow men are to understand God's preparation for the day of His power! God works today to reach hearts in the same way that He worked when Christ was upon this earth. In reading the word of God, we see that Christ brought medical missionary work into His ministry. Cannot our eyes be opened to discern Christ's methods? Cannot we understand the commission He gave to His disciples and to us?—Manuscript 58, 1901.

What the Missionary Nurse Can Do

There are many lines of work to be carried forward by the missionary nurse. There are openings for well-trained nurses to go among families and seek to awaken an interest in the truth. In almost every community there are large numbers who do not attend any religious service. If they are reached by the gospel, is must be carried to their homes. Often the relief of their physical needs is the only avenue by which they can be approached. As missionary nurses care for the sick and relieve the distress of the poor, they will find many opportunities to pray with them, to read to them from God's word, to speak of the Saviour. They can pray with and for the helpless ones who have not strength of will to control the appetites that passion has degraded. They can bring a ray of hope into the lives of the defeated and disheartened. Their unselfish love, manifested in acts of disinterested kindness, will make it easier for these suffering ones to believe in the love of Christ.

With No Inducement of Praise or Compensation

Many have no faith in God and have lost confidence in man. But they appreciate acts of sympathy and helpfulness. As they see one with no inducement of earthly praise or compensation coming to their homes, ministering to the sick, feeding the hungry, clothing the naked, comforting the sad, and tenderly pointing all to Him of whose love and pity the human worker is but the messenger—as they see this, their hearts are touched. Gratitude springs up, faith is kindled. They see that God cares for them, and as His word is opened they are prepared to listen.—The Review and Herald, May 9, 1912.

Efficiency and Power

The presenting of Bible principles by an intelligent physician will have great weight with many people. There is efficiency and power with one who can combine in his influence the work of a physician and of a gospel minister. His work commends itself to the good judgment of the people.—Counsels on Health, 546.

An Example of Healing and Soul-Winning Work

Christ has given us an example. He taught from the Scriptures the gospel truths, and He also healed the afflicted ones who came to Him for relief. He was the greatest physician the world ever knew, and yet He combined with His healing work the imparting of soul-saving truth.

And thus should our physicians labor. They are doing the Lord's work when they labor as evangelists, giving instruction as to how the soul may be healed by the Lord Jesus. Every physician should know how to pray in faith for the sick, as well as to administer the proper treatment. At the same time he should labor as one of God's ministers, to teach repentance and conversion, and the salvation of soul and body. Such a combination of labor will broaden his experience, and greatly enlarge his influence.

One thing I know, the greatest work for our physicians is to get access to the people of the world in the right way. There is a world perishing in sin, and who will take up the work in our cities? The greatest physician is the one who walks in the footsteps of Jesus Christ.—Counsels on Health, 544.

A Blended Ministry

The physician should reveal the higher education in his ability to point to the Saviour of the world as one who can heal and save the soul and the body. This gives the afflicted an encouragement that is of the highest value. The ministry to the physical and the spiritual are to blend, leading the afflicted ones to trust in the power of the heavenly Physician. Those who, while giving the proper treatments, will also pray for the healing grace of Christ, will inspire faith in the minds of the patients. Their own course will be an inspiration to those who supposed their cases to be hopeless.

This is why our sanitariums were established—to give courage to the hopeless by uniting the prayer of faith with proper treatment, and instruction in physical and spiritual right living. Through such ministrations many are to be converted. The physicians in our sanitariums are to give the clear gospel message of soul healing.—Letter 146, 1909.

Physicians as City Evangelists

Those who are Christian physicians may do a precious work for God as medical missionaries. Too often so many things engage the minds of physicians that they are kept from the work that God would have them do as evangelists. Let the medical workers present the important truths of the third angel's message from the physician's viewpoint. Physicians of consecration and talent can secure a hearing in large cities at times when other men would fail. As physicians unite with ministers in proclaiming the gospel in the great cities of the land, their combined labors will result in influencing many minds in favor of the truth for this time.

From the light that God has given me, I know that His cause today is in great need of the living representatives of Bible truth. The ordained ministers alone are not equal to the task. God is calling not only upon the ministers, but also upon physicians, nurses, canvassers, Bible workers, and other consecrated laymen of varied talent who have a knowledge of present truth, to consider the needs of the unwarned cities. There should be one hundred believers actively engaged in personal missionary work where now there is but one. Time is rapidly passing. There is much work to be done before satanic opposition shall close up the way. Every agency must be set in operation, that present opportunities may be wisely improved.—The Review and Herald, April 7, 1910.

A Twofold Service

You greatly need divine wisdom to enable you to serve in two positions of responsibility—as skillful physician, and also as a preacher of the gospel. There must be a daily conversion in order to blend successfully the work for the body and soul. I cannot tell you in detail just how this should be done, but I know that you can do an important work in the ministry of the word, in instructing the souls for whom you labor to believe in Jesus Christ.—Letter 64, 1910.

Sent Forth Two and Two

It is medical missionaries that are needed all through the field. Canvassers should improve every opportunity granted them to learn how to treat disease. Physicians should remember that they will often be required to perform the duties of a minister. Medical missionaries come under the head of evangelists. The workers should go forth two by two, that they may pray and consult together. Never should they be sent out alone. The Lord Jesus Christ sent forth His disciples two and two into all the cities of Israel. He gave them the commission, "Heal the sick that are therein, and say unto them, The kingdom of God is come nigh unto you."

We are instructed in the word of God that an evangelist is a teacher. He should also be a medical missionary. But all are not given the same work. "He gave some, apostles; and some, prophets; and some, evangelists; and some, pastors and teachers; for the perfecting of the saints, for the work of the ministry, for the edifying of the body of Christ." ...

Those who labor in our conferences as ministers should become acquainted with the work of ministering to the sick. No minister should be proud that he is ignorant where he should be wise. Medical missionary work connects man with his fellowmen and with God. The manifestation of sympathy and confidence is not to be limited by time or space.—Manuscript 33, 1901.

Cooperation

God has given direction as to how the work is to be done. In our camp meetings we meet all classes of people, high and low, rich and poor. None are excluded. It is the Lord's desire that the very best of medical missionary physicians shall hold themselves in readiness to cooperate with the ministers of the gospel. They are to be one with Christ, men through whom God can work. The Lord desires His work to advance in reformatory lines. During our camp meetings genuine medical missionary work is to be done.

No line is to be drawn between the genuine medical missionary work and the gospel ministry. These two must blend. They are not to stand apart as separate lines of work. They are to be joined in an inseparable union, even as the hand is joined to the body. Those in our institutions are to give evidence that they understand their part in the genuine gospel medical missionary work. A solemn dignity is to characterize genuine medical missionaries. They are to be men who understand and know God and the power of His grace.

Stripped of All Selfishness

Whatever may be our ingathering or increase, the conference is to be kept free from every thread of selfishness. So also should the medical missionary work be stripped of all selfishness, and carried forward after the order of God. The different lines of work are to sustain one another.—Letter 102, 1900.

Not by Proxy

Holy and devout persons, both men and women, are wanted now to go forth as medical missionaries. Let them cultivate their physical and mental powers and their piety to the uttermost. Every effort should be made to send forth intelligent workers. The same grace that came from Jesus Christ to Paul and Apollos, which caused them to be distinguished for their spiritual excellences, can be received now, and will bring into working order many devoted missionaries.

Let not a large number fold their hands, saying, "Oh, yes, let such and such ones go into untried fields," while they themselves put forth no interested, devoted, self-denying labor, and expect the work the Lord has committed to them to be done by proxy. There are those who, if they will deny self and lift the cross, will find that God will communicate with them as verily as He did with Paul and Barnabas. These are representatives of what very many should be. "The scripture saith, Whosoever believeth on Him shall not be ashamed. For there is no difference between the Jew and the Greek: for the same Lord over all is rich unto all that call upon Him."—Special Testimonies Relating to Medical Missionary Work, page 8 (1893).

The Distinguishing Sign

True sympathy between man and his fellowman is to be the sign distinguishing those who love and fear God from those who are unmindful of His law. How great the sympathy that Christ expressed in coming to this world to give His life a sacrifice for a dying world! His religion led to the doing of genuine medical missionary work. He was a healing power. "I will have mercy, and not sacrifice," He said. This is the test that the great Author of truth used to distinguish between true religion and false. God wants His medical missionaries to act with the tenderness and compassion that Christ would show were He in our world.—Manuscript 117, 1903.

True Charity

It is only by an unselfish interest in those in need of help that we can give a practical demonstration of the truths of the gospel.

"If a brother or sister be naked, and destitute of daily food, and one of you say unto them, Depart in peace, be ye warmed and filled; notwithstanding ye give them not those things which are needful to the body; what doth it profit? Even so faith, if it hath not works, is dead, being alone." "And now abideth faith, hope, charity, these three; but the greatest of these is charity." Much more than mere sermonizing is included in preaching the gospel. The ignorant are to be enlightened; the discouraged are to be uplifted; the sick are to be healed. The human voice is to act its part in God's work. Words of tenderness, sympathy, and love are to be witness to the truth. Earnest, heartfelt prayers are to bring the angels near.—An Appeal for a Medical Missionary College, pages 13, 14.

The Atmosphere of Love

Visiting the sick, comforting the poor and the sorrowful for Christ's sake, will bring to the workers the bright beams of the Sun of Righteousness, and even the countenance will express the peace that dwells in the soul. The faces of men and women who talk with God, to whom the invisible world is a reality, express the peace of God. They carry with them the soft and genial atmosphere of heaven, and diffuse it in deeds of kindness and works of love. Their influence is of a character to win souls to Christ. If all could see and understand, and be doers of the words of God, what peace, what happiness, what health of body and peace of soul, would be the result! A warm, kindly atmosphere of love, the pitying tenderness of Christ in the soul, cannot be estimated. The price of love is above gold and silver and precious stones, and makes human agents like Him who lived not to please Himself.—Letter 43, 1895.

Sowing and Reaping

Not one word too much has been said in vindication and praise of genuine medical missionary work. Connected with other lines of gospel work, medical missionary work is the instrument by which the ground is prepared for the sowing of the seed of truth, and the instrument also by which the harvest is reaped. If all our ministers had received and practiced the light that God had given on health reform, the needy and the outcasts would be embraced in every evangelistic effort to as much larger extent than they have been. With medical missionary work acting as the helping hand of the gospel ministry, the sick would be restored to health, and many souls would be led into the light....

The gospel of Christ is to be bound up with medical missionary work, and medical missionary work is to be bound up with the gospel ministry. The world needs the efforts of medical missionaries who are bound up with the gospel message. The ministers of the gospel cannot spend their time and strength in doing the work that needs to be done in this line, but by the influence of pen and voice they can strengthen this work. They are to look upon it as the helping hand of the gospel, regarding it with great appreciation as the means of preparing hearts for the sowing of the seed of truth, and of bringing many to Christ.

Ministers to Combat Disease

The minister will often be called upon to act the part of a physician. He should have a training that will enable him to administer the simpler remedies for the relief of suffering. Ministers and Bible workers should prepare themselves for this line of work, for in doing it they are following the example of Christ. They should be as well prepared by education and practice to combat disease of the body as they are to heal the sin-sick soul by pointing to the Great Physician. They are fulfilling the commission Christ gave to the Twelve and afterward to the Seventy, "Into whatsoever city ye enter, ... heal the sick that are therein, and say unto them, The kingdom of God is come nigh unto you." Christ stands by their side, as ready to heal the sick as when He was on this earth in person.—Manuscript 88, 1902.

As He Is Perfect

Our work is to strive to attain in our sphere of action the perfection that Christ in His life on the earth attained in every phase of character. He is our example. In all things we are to strive to honor God in character. In falling day by day so far short of the divine requirements, we are endangering our soul's salvation. We need to understand and appreciate the privilege with which Christ invests us, and to show our determination to reach the highest standard. We are to be wholly dependent on the power that He has promised to give us.

Just before making this requirement, the Saviour said to His disciples: "Love your enemies, bless them that curse you." We are to love our enemies with the same love that Christ manifested toward His enemies by giving His life to save them. Many may say, "This is a hard commandment; for I want to keep just as far as I can from my enemies." But acting in accordance with your own inclination would not be carrying out the principles that our Saviour has given. "Do good," He says, "to them that hate you, and pray for them which despitefully use you, and persecute you; that ye may be the children of your Father which is in heaven: for He maketh His sun to rise on the evil and on the good, and sendeth rain on the just and on the unjust." This scripture illustrates one phase of Christian perfection. While we were yet enemies of God, Christ gave His life for us. We are to follow His example.

Love Your Enemies

I must write still more of the scripture, "Love your enemies, bless them that curse you, do good to them that hate you, and pray for them which despitefully use you, and persecute you; that ye may be the children of your Father which is in heaven: for He maketh His sun to rise on the evil and on the good, and sendeth rain on the just and on the unjust.... Be ye therefore perfect, even as your Father which is in heaven is perfect." I have been deeply impressed by these words. We must understand their real meaning. If we would represent Christ's character by obeying this requirement, there would be a great change in evildoers. Many souls would be convicted of their sinfulness and converted through the impressions made upon them by our refusal to resent the evil actions of those controlled by satanic agencies. We must prayerfully and determinedly work on the Lord's side. In all the issues that provoke the soul we should resist the evil and refuse to abuse the evildoer.

Let us daily represent Christ's great love by loving our enemies as Christ loves them. If we would thus represent the grace of Christ, strong feelings of hatred would be broken down and into many hearts genuine love would be brought. Many more conversions than are now seen would follow. True, it will cost us something to do this. If the ministers who preach the word, and those who occupy prominent positions in the medical missionary work, would regard it as their special duty to practice the teachings of the word in the daily life, bringing themselves under the discipline of the requirements of Christ and working under His authority, their consistent course would lead many to break away from the tyranny of Satan's service and to take their stand under the bloodstained banner of Prince Immanuel.

An Enlarged Experience

Again my mind is exercised much in regard to our behavior and formation of character in this life. Professedly we have taken our stand on the Lord's side, to represent in this evil generation the close relationship that Christians enjoy with God, and with Jesus Christ whom He hath sent. It is certainly our privilege to enlarge our experience, to deepen our consecration, and to come into closer contact with our heavenly Father, bringing our will and way into conformity with His will and way.

My prayer this morning is most earnest and importunate, that in the Christian warfare we shall not fail nor be discouraged. "There is light above," a Voice says to me, and in response I withdraw my eyes from the earthly and the discouraging and look to the heavenly, praying earnestly that God's people may more distinctly and forcibly realize the dignity that our heavenly Father has conferred upon us in calling us to represent before the world, in sinful flesh, His goodness and mercy. Upon us, as well as upon the unthankful and the unholy, He pours unnumbered blessings. We are to express our thankfulness to Him that we are accepted as workers to cooperate with the Lord Jesus Christ.

Those who preach the word of the Lord must live that which they teach. If we receive the grace of God in the heart, we must reveal to others this grace in every word and act. Those who dwell upon the long-sufferance and mercy of Christ must practice His patience and forbearance, and never reveal a spirit of high-handed injustice toward their brethren or others.

Do Right Regardless of Results

Some will say, "How can we do this? We should be taken advantage of by the unprincipled and designing." Remember that a disciple is to do the will of his master. We are not to reason in regard to results; for then we should be kept ever busy, and ever in uncertainty. We must take our stand to acknowledge fully the power and authority of God's word, whether or not it agrees with our preconceived opinions. We have a perfect Guidebook. The Lord has spoken to us; and whatever may be the consequences, we are to receive His word and practice it in daily life, else we shall be choosing our own version of duty and shall be doing exactly the opposite of that which our heavenly Father has appointed us to do.

[256]

We are not our own, to act as we choose. We are called to be representatives of Christ. We are bought with a price. As the chosen sons and daughters of God, we should be obedient children, acting in accordance with the principles of His character as revealed through His Son.

Jesus has said, "Do good to them that hate you." How much we can accomplish by following this instruction we can never estimate. "Pray for them which despitefully use you, and persecute you; that ye may be the children of your Father which is in heaven: for He maketh His sun to rise on the evil and on the good, and sendeth rain on the just and on the unjust."

Are not the principles here brought to view often overlooked? The amount of evil that might be avoided by following them is by no means small: for sometimes the hearts of persecutors are susceptible of divine impressions, as was the heart of the apostle Paul before his conversion. It is always best to endeavor to carry out the whole will of God as He has specified. He will take care of the results.—Manuscript 148, 1902

Zeal and Perseverance in Medical Missionary Work

Could I arouse our people to Christian effort, could I lead them to engage in medical missionary work with holy zeal and divine perseverance, not in a few places, but in every place, putting forth personal effort for those out of the fold, how grateful I should be! This is true missionary work. In some places it is attended with little success, apparently; but again, the Lord opens the way, and signal success attends the effort. Words are spoken which are as nails fastened in a sure place. Angels from heaven cooperate with human instrumentalities, and sinners are won to the Saviour.—Letter 43, 1903.

In Excellent Company

The spirit of persecution will not be excited against those who have no connection with God, and so have no moral strength. It will be aroused against the faithful ones, who make no concessions to the world and will not be swayed by its opinions, its favor, or its opposition. A religion that bears a living testimony in favor of holiness, and that rebukes pride, selfishness, avarice, and fashionable sins, will be hated by the world and by superficial Christians.... When you suffer reproach and persecution you are in excellent company; for Jesus endured it all, and much more. If you are faithful sentinels for God, these things are a compliment to you. It is the heroic souls, who will be true if they stand alone, who will win the imperishable crown.—The Youth's Instructor, May 28, 1884

A Revival Will Come

If the workers will humble their hearts before God, the blessing will come. They will all the while be receiving fresh, new ideas, and there will be a wonderful revival of gospel medical missionary work.—Testimonies for the Church 9:219.

* * * * *

For Further Study

Medical Missionaries and Their Work:
The Ministry of Healing, 161-216.
The Pioneer Work:
Counsels on Health, 497-502.
A Plea for Medical Missionaries:
Counsels on Health, 392-397 (Testimonies for the Church 9:167-172).

A Call for Gospel Medical Missionaries:
The Desire of Ages, 821-828.
Counsels to Medical Missionaries:
Testimonies for the Church 8:201, 202.
The Gospel, "In Illustration":
Testimonies for the Church 6:241;
"In Practice":
Counsels on Health, 532.
Neglect by the Church and the Ministry:
Testimonies for the Church 6:294-304.
Ministers to Be Medical Missionaries:
Counsels on Health, 533.
Physicians as Evangelists:
Counsels on Health, 535, 536, 543-548.
Opportunities for Consecrated Nurses:
Counsels on Health, 387-390 (Testimonies for the Church 6:83, 84).
Gospel Workers to Teach Health Reform:
Counsels on Health, 43 (Testimonies for the Church 6:376, 377).
Diet, a Proper Subject for the Evangelist:
Counsels on Health, 44 (Testimonies for the Church 9:112, 113).
A United Work:
Counsels on Health, 513, 518 (Testimonies for the Church 6:288-293);
Counsels on Health, 516, 517 (Testimonies for the Church 6:291-292);
Counsels on Health, 519, 520 (Testimonies for the Church 8:158, 159);
Counsels on Health, 524, 525 (Testimonies for the Church 6:240-242);
Counsels on Health, 534, 550 (Testimonies for the Church 7:111);
Counsels on Health, 557, 558.
A Combined Work as Physician and Minister in Christ's Work:
Counsels on Health, 528.
Words of Caution to a Physician:
Counsels on Health, 519-52 (Testimonies for the Church 8:158-162).
House-to-Tiouse Work by Medical Missionaries:
Counsels on Health, 538.

"Teaching and Healing":
The Ministry of Healing, 139-160.
Work for the Poor:
Counsels on Health, 14 (Testimonies for the Church 6:255);
Testimonies for the Church 6:83-85;
The Ministry of Healing, 183-208.
Work Supported by Converted Men of Wealth:
Testimonies for the Church 9:114, 115.
Ministry to the Rich:
Counsels on Health, 15-18 (Testimonies for the Church 6:256-258);
Testimonies for the Church 6:80-83;
The Ministry of Healing, 209-216.

Section 14—Teaching Health Principles

The Gospel of Health

The principles of health reform are found in the word of God. The gospel of health is to be firmly linked with the ministry of the word. It is the Lord's design that the restoring influence of health reform shall be a part of the last great effort to proclaim the gospel message. Our physicians are to be God's workers. They are to be men whose powers have been sanctified and transformed by the grace of Christ. Their influence is to be knit up with the truth that is to be given to the world. In perfect and complete unity with the gospel ministry the work of health reform will reveal its God-given power. Under the influence of the gospel great reforms will be made by medical missionary work.—Manuscript 172, 1899.

The First Work

If we would elevate the moral standard in any country where we may be called to go, we must begin by correcting their physical habits. Virtue of character depends upon the right action of the powers of the mind and body.—Counsels on Health, 505.

Educate in the Laws of Life

God's blessing will rest upon every effort made to awaken an interest in health reform; for it is needed everywhere. There must be a revival on this subject; for God purposes to accomplish much through this agency. Present temperance with all its advantages in reference to health. Educate people in the laws of life so that they may know how to preserve health. The efforts actually put forth at present are not meeting the mind of God. Drug medication is a curse to this enlightened age.

Educate away from drugs. Use them less and less, and depend more upon hygienic agencies; then nature will respond to God's physicians—pure air, pure water, proper exercise, a clear conscience.

Many might recover without one grain of medicine, if they would live out the laws of health. Drugs need seldom be used. It will require earnest, patient, protracted effort to establish the work and to carry it forward upon hygienic principles. But let fervent prayer and faith be combined with your efforts, and you will succeed. By this work you will be teaching the patients, and others also, how to take care of themselves when sick, without resorting to the use of drugs.—Letter 6a, 1890.

The Science of Self-Denial

Should all the sick be healed by prayer, very few would improve their opportunities to become acquainted with right ways of eating, drinking, and dressing. Those connected with our sanitariums should realize the duty resting upon them to give the patients an education in the principles of healthful living.

The sick have their lesson to learn. They must be denied those preparations of food that would retard or prevent their recovery to health. They must learn the science of self-denial, eating simple food prepared in a simple way. They should live much in the sunlight, which should find its way to every room of the building. Lectures on health topics should be given. These lectures will open the blinded understanding, and truths never before thought of will be fastened on the mind.—Letter 63, 1905.

Counsel to a Sanitarium Physician

In the night season I was talking with you. I had some things to say to you on the diet question. I was talking freely with you, telling you that you would have to make changes in your ideas in regard to the diet to be given those who come to the sanitarium from the world. These people have lived improperly, on rich food. They are suffering as a result of indulgence of appetite.

A reform in their habits of eating and drinking is needed. But this reform cannot be made all at once. The change must be made gradually. The health foods set before them must be appetizing. All their lives, perhaps, they have had three meals a day, and have eaten rich food. It is an important matter to reach these people with the truths of health reform.

But in order to lead them to adopt a sensible diet, you must set before them an abundant supply of wholesome, appetizing food. Changes must not be made so abruptly that they will be turned from health reform instead of being led to it. The food served to them must be nicely prepared, and it must be richer than either you or I would eat....

I write this because I am sure that the Lord means you to have tact in meeting the people where they are, in their darkness and self-indulgence. As far as I am concerned personally, I am decidedly in favor of a plain, simple diet. But it will not be best to put worldly, self-indulgent patients on a diet so strict that they will be turned from health reform. This will not convince them of the need of a change in their habits of eating and drinking. Tell them the facts. Educate them to see the need of a plain, simple diet, and make the change gradually. Give them time to respond to the treatment and the instruction given them. Work and pray, and lead them along as gently as possible.—Letter 331, 1904.

How to Present the Principles of Healthful Diet

The Lord desires every minister, every physician, every church member, to be careful not to urge those who are ignorant of our faith to make sudden changes in diet, thus bringing them to a premature test. Hold up the principles of health reform, and let the Lord lead the honest in heart. They will hear and believe. The Lord does not require His messengers to present the beautiful truths of health reform in a way that will prejudice the minds of others. Let no one place stumbling blocks before those who are walking in the dark paths of ignorance. Even in praising a good thing, it is well not to be too enthusiastic, lest you turn out of the way those who come to hear. Present the principles of temperance in their most attractive form.

Lead the People

We must not move presumptuously. The laborers who enter new territory to raise up churches must not create difficulties by attempting to make prominent the question of diet. They should be careful not to draw the lines too closely. Impediments would thus be thrown on the pathway of others. Do not drive the people. Lead them. Preach the word as it is in Christ Jesus. The health journal will help you to learn not only how to prepare healthful food and how to give treatment to the sick, but also how to instruct others in these lines. Workers must put forth resolute, persevering effort, remembering that everything cannot be learned at once. They must have a fixed determination patiently to teach the people.

Wherever the truth is carried, the people should be given instruction in regard to the preparation of healthful foods. God desires that in every place the people should be taught by skillful teachers how to utilize wisely the products that they can raise or readily obtain in their section of the country. Thus the poor, as well as those in better circumstances, can be taught to live healthfully.—Letter 135, 1902.

Labor Lost Without Instruction

It is labor lost to teach people to go to God as a healer of their infirmities unless they are educated to lay aside every wrong practice and cease to indulge perverted appetite. They must be taught to use the provisions God has given. To refuse the remedies which they may as well have as not without paying a doctor's fee, to neglect to let into every room in the house God's pure air and sunshine, shows a lack of faith in Him. Faith in God's power to heal infirmities is dead unless the one diseased improves the light God has given him by bringing his habits into harmony with right principles.—Manuscript 86, 1897.

Educate, Educate, Educate

We must educate, educate, educate, pleasantly and intelligently. We must preach the truth, pray the truth, and live the truth, bringing it with its gracious, health-giving influences within the reach of those who know it not. As the sick are brought into touch with the

Life-giver their faculties of mind and body will be renewed. But in order for this to be, they must practice self-denial, and be temperate in all things. Thus only can they be saved from physical and spiritual death and restored to health.

When the human machinery moves in harmony with the life-giving arrangements of God, as brought to light through the gospel, disease is overcome and health springs forth speedily. When human beings work in union with the Life-giver, who offered up His life for them, happy thoughts fill the mind. Body and mind and soul are sanctified. Human beings learn of the Great Teacher, and all upon which they look ennobles and enriches the thoughts. The affections are drawn out in gladness and thankfulness to the Creator. The life of the man who is renewed in the image of Christ is as a light shining in darkness.—Letter 83, 1905.

Deeds of Ministry

To teachers in our schools, to ministers and physicians and nurses, I would say, If you will, you can succeed in revealing the truths of the third angel's message. This will not be done merely by preaching the word, but by the deeds of loving ministry. It is the spirit of the word that we so greatly need. Those who have the spirit of Christ will work His works.

I have been instructed to refer our people to the fifty-eighth chapter of Isaiah. Read this chapter carefully and understand the kind of ministry that will bring life into the churches. The work of the gospel is to be carried by means of our liberality as well as by our labors. When you meet suffering souls who need help, give it them. When you find those who are hungry, feed them. In doing this you will be working in lines of Christ's ministry. The Master's holy work was a benevolent work. Let our people everywhere be encouraged to have a part in it.—Manuscript 7, 1908.

Teach Self-Denial

The work you have been doing in the cities is meeting heaven's approval.... What you have done demonstrates that if our physicians and our ministers can work together in the presentation of truth to the people, more can be reached than could be influenced by the minister laboring alone....

Present before the people the need of resisting the temptation to indulge appetite. This is where many are failing. Explain how closely body and mind are related and show the need of keeping both in the very best condition. The health talks which you give in the meetings will be one of the best ways of advertising our sanitariums....

Abstinence and Health

The minds of the suffering ones must be led to grasp the hope of deliverance from special peril. Speak to them hopeful words, words of courage. There are those patronizing our sanitariums whom the Lord will heal if they will abstain from the use of liquor and drugs and will use simple and safe remedies to counteract disease brought on through perverted appetite. If they will act their part to break the spell of the enemy by firmly resisting temptation, and will surrender themselves to the One who gave His life for sinful souls, they will become sons and daughters of God.

All who indulge the appetite, waste the physical energies, and weaken the moral power, will sooner or later feel the retribution that follows the transgression of physical law.

Christ gave His life to purchase redemption for the sinner. The world's Redeemer knew that indulgence of appetite was bringing physical debility and deadening the perceptive faculties so that sacred and eternal things could not be discerned. He knew that self-indulgence was perverting the moral powers, and that man's great need was conversion—in heart and mind and soul, from the life of self-indulgence to one of the self-denial and self-sacrifice....

Christ's Victory a Lesson for Us

Christ entered upon the test upon the point of appetite, and for nearly six weeks resisted temptation in behalf of man. That long fast in the wilderness was to be a lesson to fallen man for all time. Christ was not overcome by the strong temptations of the enemy, and this is encouragement for every soul who is struggling against temptation. Christ has made it possible for every member of the human family to resist temptation. All who would live godly lives may overcome as Christ overcame, by the blood of the Lamb and the word of their testimony. That long fast of the Savior's strengthened Him to endure. He gave evidence to men that He would begin the work of overcoming just where ruin began—on the point of appetite....

Responsibility of Physicians and Ministers

We need the influence of the right example of our physicians and our ministers. Let them exercise their powers for the control of appetite, that mental and moral powers may be strengthened. As far as possible, let them adopt such habits of life that the physical and mental powers shall be equally taxed. The exercise of the voice in speaking is a healthful exercise. Teach and live carefully. Hold firmly to the position that all, even our leading men, need to exercise good common sense in the care of their health, securing equal taxation of the body and the brain.—Letter 158, 1909.

Hygienic Restaurants as Schools

Interested workers will be led to offer themselves for various lines of missionary effort. Hygienic restaurants will be established. But with what carefulness should this work be done!

Every hygienic restaurant should be a school. The workers connected with it should be constantly studying and experimenting, that they may make improvement in the preparation of healthful foods. In the cities this work of instruction may be carried forward on a much larger scale than in smaller places. But in every place where there is a church, instruction should be given in regard to the preparation of simple, healthful foods for the use of those who wish to live in accordance with the principles of health reform. And the church members should impart to the people of their neighborhood the light they receive on this subject.—Testimonies for the Church 7:112, 113.

Instruction in Homes and in Schools

In San Bernardino Dr. ----- has found many openings for educational work. About three months ago she began to conduct studies in cooking, healthful dress, and general hygiene, with some of the families of our own church. She was assisted in her work by some of the helpers from the sanitarium who were able to give practical demonstrations in healthful cooking and in simple nursing.

Neighbors were invited to attend these demonstrations, and some who were present by invitation requested that similar studies be given in their homes, to which they might invite some of their friends. Thus the work grew rapidly, until Dr. ----- was unable to respond to all the requests she received. Her work was brought to the attention of the superintendent of public schools, and at his invitation she gave health talks before as many as fifteen hundred children in the schools of the city. Her cooperation with the Women's Christian Temperance Union has enabled her to become acquainted with many excellent ladies. Such efforts as these are powerful factors in removing from the minds of many the prejudice that exists against our people.—The Review and Herald, August 1, 1907.

Cooperation With Other Temperance Workers

We should do all in our power to cooperate with heavenly agencies for the promulgation of truth and righteousness in the earth. We cannot do a better work than to unite, so far as we can do so without compromise, with the W.C.T.U. workers. Years ago we regarded the spread of the temperance principles as one of our most important duties. It should be so today. Our schools and sanitariums are to reveal the power of the grace of Christ to transform the life. They should be important factors in the temperance cause.—Letter 274, 1907.

Educate the Poor

Questions [in vision] were asked as to the advisability of educating others to supply the place of meat and tea and coffee with a more healthful diet. Should we make known our methods, and thus cut off from ourselves the benefits we might receive in establishing the trade in the colonies? Should we give away the science of how to make these healthful foods? Should we teach the poor people how they can live without using the flesh of dead animals? Should we teach the poor people who come into the truth how to plant and raise nuts, how to produce for themselves those things which would cost too much if they bought them prepared by other hands? Should we teach them how to prepare these foods for themselves?

The Voice of Wisdom

These seemed to be important questions, and hard to solve. Then the voice of wisdom was heard; the subject of health reform is a great subject, an important subject, and this missionary work is to be carried into the highways and byways of life. The third angel's message is present truth for 1898, and the health question is as closely connected with that message as the arm is with the body. Therefore light must be given as to the best methods of introducing health reform. Meat is the greatest disease breeder that can be introduced into the human system. But you cannot teach health reform unless you present the most inexpensive methods of living. The enemy must have no advantage in any line. The Lord can only bless those who are keeping every precept He has given in relation to this life.—Manuscript 105, 1898.

Purpose of Health-Food Work

According to the light given me of God, the food business should be carried on for the purpose of educating people to live healthfully and economically, not for financial gain. Each one should learn what foods are best adapted to his own necessities.—Letter 82, 1903.

Like the Manna

The light that God has given and will continue to give on the food question is to be to His people today what the manna was to the children of Israel. The manna fell from heaven, and the people were told to gather it and prepare it to be eaten. So in the different countries of the world light will be given to the Lord's people, and health foods suited to these countries will be prepared.

The members of every church are to cultivate the tact and ingenuity that God will give them. The Lord has skill and understanding for all who will use their ability in striving to learn how to combine the productions of the earth so as to make simple, easily prepared, healthful foods, which will take the place of flesh-meat, so that the people will have no excuse for eating flesh-meat.—Manuscript 78, 1902.

The Lord Will Teach the Obedient

In grains, fruits, vegetables, and nuts are to be found all the food elements that we need. If we will come to the Lord in simplicity of mind, He will teach us how to prepare wholesome food free from the taint of flesh-meat.—Manuscript 27, 1905.

Instruction in the Art of Cooking

We need a genuine education in the art of cooking.... Form classes where you may teach the people how to make good bread and how to put together ingredients to make healthful food combinations from the grains and the vegetables. Such an education will assist in creating a desire among our people to move out of the cities, to secure land in the country, where they can raise their own fruit and vegetables.—Manuscript 150, 1905.

United Action Necessary

It is the Lord's design that in every place men and women shall have the privilege of developing their talents by preparing healthful foods from the natural products of their section of their country. No man is to forbid them. If they look to God, exercising their skill and ingenuity under the guidance of His Spirit, they will learn how to prepare natural products into healthful foods. Thus they will be able to teach the poor how to prepare foods that will take the place of flesh-meat.

Those thus helped can in turn instruct others. Such a work will yet be done. If it had been done before, there would today be many more people in the truth than there are, and we should have had many more who could give instruction than we have. Let us learn what our duty is, and then do it. We are not to be dependent and helpless, trusting in human beings.—Manuscript 85, 1902.

Incentives to Activity

Some may say, "If the Lord is coming soon, what need is there to establish schools, sanitariums, and food factories? What need is there for our young people to learn trades?"

It is the Lord's design that we shall constantly improve the talents He has given us. We cannot do this unless we use them. The prospect of Christ's soon coming should not lead us to idleness. Instead, it should lead us to do all we possibly can to bless and benefit humanity. No idler is guiltless in the Lord's sight.

Bible religion never makes men idlers. We believe that Christ's coming is near. Then let everyone make the most of his God-given time in seeking to prepare himself and others for this great event. Teach the importance of life's duties to those who are wasting their opportunities.

Work for the intemperate man and the tobacco user, telling them that no drunkard shall inherit the kingdom of God and that "there shall in no wise enter into it anything that defileth." Show them the good they could do with the money they now spend for that which does them only harm.—Letter 25, 1902.

Tolerance for Others' Opinions

[269]

We must remember that there are a great many different minds in the world, and we cannot expect everyone to see exactly as we do in regard to all questions of diet. Minds do not run in exactly the same channel. I do not eat butter, but there are members of my family who do. It is not placed on my table; but I make no disturbance because some members of my family choose to eat it occasionally. Many of our conscientious brethren have butter on their tables, and I feel under no obligation to force them to do otherwise. These things should never be allowed to cause disturbance among brethren. I cannot see the need of butter where there is an abundance of fruit and of sterilized cream. Those who love and serve God should be allowed to follow their own convictions. We may not feel justified in doing as they do, but we should not allow differences of opinion to create disunion. May the Lord help us to be as firm as a rock to the principles of the law spoken from Sinai, and may He help us not to allow differences of opinion to be a barrier between us and our brethren.—Letter 331, 1904.

Teaching Extreme Views

It is the desire and plan of Satan to bring in among us those who will go to great extremes—people of narrow minds, who are critical and sharp, and very tenacious in holding their own conceptions of what the truth means. They will be exacting, and will seek to enforce rigorous duties, and go to great lengths in matters of minor importance, while they neglect the weightier matters of the law—judgment and mercy and the love of God. Through the work of a few of this class of persons, the whole body of Sabbath keepers will be designated as bigoted, pharisaical, and fanatical. The work of the truth, because of these workers, will be thought to be unworthy of notice.—The Review and Herald, May 29, 1888.

Good Cooking a Science

Some are called to what are looked upon as humble duties—it may be to cook. But the science of cooking is not a small matter. The skillful preparation of food is one of the most essential arts, standing above music teaching or dressmaking. By this I do not mean to discount music teaching or dressmaking, for they are essential. But more important still is the art of preparing food so that it is both healthful and appetizing. This art should be regarded as the most valuable of all the arts, because it is so closely connected with life. It should receive more attention; for in order to make good blood, the system requires good food. The foundation of that which keeps people in health is the medical missionary work of good cooking.

Often health reform is made health deform by the unpalatable preparation of food. The lack of knowledge regarding healthful cookery must be remedied before health reform is a success.

Good cooks are few. Many, many mothers need to take lessons in cooking, that they may set before the family well-prepared, neatly served food.

Before children take lessons on the organ or the piano they should be given lessons in cooking. The work of learning to cook need not exclude music, but to learn music is of less importance than to learn how to prepare food that is wholesome and appetizing.

Cooking Schools

Connected with our sanitariums and schools there should be cooking schools, where instruction is given on the proper preparation of food. In all our schools there should be those who are fitted to educate the students, both men and women, in the art of cooking. Women specially should learn how to cook.

It is a sin to place poorly prepared food on the table, because the matter of eating concerns the well-being of the entire system. The Lord desires His people to appreciate the necessity of having food prepared in such a way that it will not make sour stomachs and in consequence sour tempers. Let us remember that there is practical religion in a loaf of good bread.

A Talent of the Highest Value

Let not the work of cooking be looked upon as a sort of slavery. What would become of those in our world if all who are engaged in cooking should give up their work with the flimsy excuse that it is not sufficiently dignified? Cooking may be regarded as less desirable than some other lines of work, but in reality it is a science above all other sciences. Thus God regards the preparation of healthful food. He places a high estimate on those who do faithful service in preparing wholesome, palatable food.

The one who understands the art of properly preparing food, and who uses this knowledge, is worthy of higher commendation than those engaged in any other line of work. This talent should be regarded as equal in value to ten talents; for its right use has much to do with keeping the human organism in health. Because so inseparably connected with life and health, it is the most valuable of all gifts.—Manuscript 95, 1901.

Many Will Be Rescued

The Lord has presented before me that many, many will be rescued from physical, mental, and moral degeneracy through the practical influence of health reform. Health talks will be given, publications will be multiplied. The principles of health reform will be received with favor, and many will be enlightened. The influences that are associated with health reform will commend it to the judgment of all who want light, and they will advance step by step to receive the special truths for this time.—Testimonies for the Church 6:378, 379.

* * * * *

For Further Study

Sanitarium Work to Be Educational:
Counsels on Health, 221-223, 248, 469, 470.
The Physician an Educator:
The Ministry of Healing, 125-136.
Ministers to Teach Health Reform:
Counsels on Health, 43 (Testimonies for the Church 6:376, 377).
The Church to Study Health Principles:
Counsels on Health, 425-430 (Testimonies for the Church 7:62-67).
Continual Reform to Be Advocated:
Counsels on Health, 445-453.
Tact in Teaching Health Principles:
Counsels on Health, 438, 442 (Testimonies for the Church 3:20, 21).
The Use of Health and Temperance Literature:
Counsels on Health, 445-447, 462-466, 479 (Testimonies for the Church 7:136).
Teaching Temperance Reform:
Counsels on Health, 432-437.
Teaching Health Principles at Camp Meeting:
Counsels on Health, 433, 467, 468.

Section 15—Diet and Health

Important Principles

Seventh-day Adventists are handling momentous truths. On the subject of temperance they should be in advance of all other people. The question of how to preserve the health is one of primary importance. When we study this question in the fear of God we shall learn that it is best, both for our physical health and for our spiritual advancement, to observe simplicity in diet. Let us patiently study this question. We need knowledge and judgment in order to move wisely in this matter. Nature's laws are not to be resisted, but obeyed.

Only when we are intelligent in regard to the principles of health reform can we be fully aroused to see the evils resulting from an improper diet. Those who, after seeing their mistakes, have courage to change their habits, will find that the reformatory process requires a struggle and much perseverance. But when correct tastes are formed, they will realize that the use of food which they have formerly regarded as harmless was slowly but surely laying the foundation for dyspepsia and other diseases.

Provide Nourishing Food

Some of our people conscientiously abstain from eating improper food, and at the same time neglect to eat food that would supply the elements necessary for the proper sustenance of the body. Let us never bear a testimony against health reform by failing to use wholesome, palatable food in place of the harmful articles of diet that we have discarded. Much tact and discretion should be employed in preparing nourishing food to take the place of that which has constituted the diet of many families. This effort requires faith in God, earnestness of purpose, and a willingness to help one another. A diet lacking in the proper elements of nutrition brings reproach upon the cause of health reform. We are mortal, and must supply ourselves with food that will give proper sustenance to the body.

Those who do not know how to cook hygienically should learn to combine wholesome, nourishing articles of food in such a way as to make appetizing dishes. Let those who desire to gain knowledge in this line subscribe for our health journals....

Without continually exercising ingenuity, no one can excel in healthful cookery; but those whose hearts are open to impressions and suggestions from the Great Teacher will learn many things, and will be able also to teach others; for He will give them skill and understanding.

Careful attention should be given to the proper use of nut foods. Some kinds of nuts are not so wholesome as others. Do not reduce the bill of fare to a few articles composed largely of nut foods. These foods should not be used too freely. If they were used more sparingly by some, the results would be more satisfactory. As combined in large proportions with other articles in some of the recipes given, they make the food so rich that the system cannot properly assimilate it.

Intelligent Advancement

Let us make intelligent advancement in simplifying our diet. In the providence of God, every country produces articles of food containing the nourishment necessary for the upbuilding of the system. These may be made into healthful, appetizing dishes.

Let those who advocate health reform strive earnestly to make it all that they claim it is. Let them discard everything detrimental to health. Use simple, wholesome food. Fruit is excellent, and saves much cooking. Discard rich pastries, cakes, desserts, and the other dishes prepared to tempt the appetite. Eat fewer kinds of food at one meal, and eat with thanksgiving.

Concerning flesh-meat we can all say, Let it alone. And all should bear a clear testimony against tea and coffee, never using them. They are narcotics, injurious alike to the brain and to the other organs of the body. The time has not yet come when I can say that the use of milk and of eggs should be wholly discontinued. Milk and eggs should not be classed with flesh-meats. In some ailments the use of eggs is very beneficial.

Let the members of our churches deny every selfish appetite. Every penny expended for tea, coffee, and flesh-meat is worse than wasted, for these things hinder the best development of the physical, mental, and spiritual powers.—Letter 135, 1902.

Sanctification and Self-Mastery

God's people are to learn the meaning of temperance in all things. They are to practice temperance in eating and drinking and dressing. All self-indulgence is to be cut away from their lives. Before they can really understand the meaning of true sanctification and of conformity to the will of Christ, they must, by cooperating with God, obtain the mastery over wrong habits and practices.—Manuscript 16, 1902.

Show the Value of Health Reform

Keep the work of health reform to the front, is the message I am given to bear. Show so plainly the value of health reform that a widespread need for it will be felt. But never advocate a starvation diet. It is possible to have a wholesome, nutritious diet without using flesh-meat.—Letter 49, 1902.

To the Glory of God

By the inspiration of the Spirit of God, Paul the apostle writes that "whatsoever ye do," even the natural act of eating or drinking, should be done, not to gratify a perverted appetite, but under a sense of responsibility; "do all to the glory of God." Every part of the man is to be guarded; we are to beware lest that which is taken into the stomach shall banish from the mind high and holy thoughts.

Individual Rights

"May I not do as I please with myself?" ask some, as if we were seeking to deprive them of a great good when we present before them the necessity of eating intelligently and conforming all their habits to the laws God has established. There are rights which belong to every individual. We have an individuality and an identity that is our own. No one can submerge this identity in that of another. All must act for themselves, according to the dictates of their own conscience.

As regards our responsibility and influence, we are amenable to God as deriving our life from Him. This we do not obtain from humanity, but from God only. We are His by creation and by redemption. Our very bodies are not our own, to treat as we please, to cripple by habits that lead to decay, making it impossible to render to God perfect service. Our lives and all our faculties belong to Him. He is caring for us every moment; He keeps the living machinery in action; if we were left to run it for one moment, we should die. We are absolutely dependent upon God.

A great lesson is learned when we understand our relation to God and His relation to us. The words, "Ye are not your own," "ye are bought with a price," should be hung in memory's hall, that we may ever recognize God's right to our talents, our property, our influence, our individual selves. We are to learn how to treat this gift of God, in mind, in soul, in body, that as Christ's purchased possession we may do Him healthful savory service.

Integrity of Daniel

Why did Daniel and his companions refuse to eat at the king's table? Why did they refuse his meats and wines? Because they had been taught that this class of food would not keep the mind and the physical structure in the very best condition of health to do God's service....

They were very careful to keep themselves in touch with God. They prayed and studied, and brought into their practical life strictly conscientious, humble minds. They walked with God as did Enoch. The word of the Lord was their meat and their drink. "And in all matters of wisdom and understanding, that the king inquired of them, he found them ten times better than all the magicians and astrologers that were in all his realm."

In the light of this Scripture history, all the testimony of man as to the advantages of a meat diet, or of a great variety of food, should not have the least weight with any human being. When the children of faith shall with earnest prayer dedicate themselves to God without reserve, the Lord will honor their faith and will bless them with a clear mind.—Letter 73, 1896.

Appeal to a Physician

You cannot understand how much more effectual your services in the religious interest would be, and how much more satisfactory to yourself, if you would follow the light which has been given you.... Shall your appetites, habits, and practices be of that order that you will educate those who are connected with you to make excuses similar to those that you have made for the indulgence of eating the flesh of dead animals?

Back to the Primitive Diet

The Lord intends to bring His people back to live upon simple fruits, vegetables, and grains. He led the children of Israel into the wilderness, where they could not get a flesh diet; and He gave them the bread of heaven. "Man did eat angels' food." But they craved the fleshpots of Egypt, and mourned and cried for flesh, notwithstanding that the Lord had promised them that if they would submit to His will He would carry them into the land of Canaan and establish them there, a pure, holy, happy people, and there should not be a feeble one in all their tribes; for He would take away all sickness from among them.

The Murmuring of Israel

But although they had a plain "Thus saith the Lord," they mourned and wept, and murmured and complained, until the Lord was wroth with them. Because they were so determined to have the flesh of dead animals, He gave them the very diet He had withheld from them....

The Lord could have given them flesh had it been essential for their health, but He who created and redeemed them, led them the long journey in the wilderness to educate and discipline and train them in correct habits. The Lord understood what the influence of flesh eating has upon the human system. He would have a people that would, in their physical appearance, bear the divine credentials notwithstanding their long journey....

One of the great errors that many insist upon is that muscular strength is dependent upon animal food. But the simple grains, fruits of the trees, and vegetables have all the nutritive properties necessary to make good blood. This a flesh diet cannot do....

We are composed of what we eat, and eating much flesh will diminish intellectual activity. Students would accomplish much more in their studies if they never tasted meat. When the animal part of the human agent is strengthened by meat eating, the intellectual powers diminish proportionately. A religious life can be more successfully gained and maintained if meat is discarded, for this diet stimulates into intense activities lustful propensities, and enfeebles the moral and spiritual nature. "The flesh warreth against the spirit, and the spirit against the flesh."

We greatly need to encourage and cultivate pure, chaste thoughts, and to strengthen the moral powers rather than the lower and carnal powers. God help us to awake from our self-indulgent appetites! ...

A Cause of Mortality

Cancers, tumors, and all inflammatory diseases are largely caused by meat eating.

From the light God has given me, the prevalence of cancers and tumors is largely due to gross living on dead flesh. I sincerely and prayerfully hope that, as a physician, you will not forever be blind on this subject, for blindness is mingled with a want of moral courage to deny your appetite, to lift the cross, which means to take up the very duties that cut across the natural appetites and passions....

I have the subject presented to me in different aspects. The mortality caused by meat eating is not discerned; if it were, we would hear no more arguments and excuses in favor of the indulgence of the appetite for dead flesh. We have plenty of good things to satisfy hunger without bringing corpses upon our table to compose our bill of fare....

I have had opened before me the stumbling block which this diet question has been to your own spiritual advancement, and what a stumbling block you have placed in the pathway of others, and all because your own sensibilities were blunted through the selfish gratification of appetite. For Christ's sake look deeper, study deeper, and act in accordance with the light God has been pleased to give you and others on this subject.—Letter 72, 1896.

Appeal to a Minister

It has been clearly presented to me that God's people are to take a firm stand against meat eating. Would God for thirty years give His people the message that if they desire to have pure blood and clear minds they must give up the use of flesh-meat, if He did not want them to heed this message? By the use of flesh-meat the animal nature is strengthened and the spiritual nature weakened. Such men as you, who are engaged in the most solemn and important work ever entrusted to human beings, need to give special heed to what they eat.

Remember that when you eat flesh-meat, you are but eating grains and vegetables secondhand; for the animal receives from these things the nutrition that makes it grow and prepares it for market. The life that was in the grains and vegetables passes into the animal and becomes part of its life, and then human beings eat the animal. Why are they so willing to eat their food secondhand? ...

The thought of killing animals to be eaten is in itself revolting. If man's natural sense had not been perverted by the indulgence of appetite, human beings would not think of eating the flesh of animals.

Do Not Counterwork Reform

We have been given the work of advancing health reform. The Lord desires His people to be in harmony with one another. As you must know, we shall not leave the position in which for the last thirty-five years the Lord has been bidding us stand. Beware how you place yourself in opposition to the work of health reform. It will go forward; for it is the Lord's means of lessening the suffering in our world and of purifying His people.

Be careful what attitude you assume, lest you be found causing division. My brother, even while you fail to bring into your life and into your family the blessing that comes from following the principles of health reform, do not harm others by opposing the light God has given on this subject.

While we do not make the use of flesh-meat a test, while we do not want to force anyone to give up its use, yet it is our duty to request that no minister of the conference shall make light of or oppose the message of reform on this point. If, in the face of the light God has given concerning the effect of meat eating on the system, you will still continue to eat meat, you must bear the consequences. But do not take a position before the people that will permit them to think that it is not necessary to call for a reform in regard to meat eating; because the Lord is calling for reform.

The Lord has given us the work of proclaiming the message of health reform, and if you cannot step forward in the ranks of those who are giving this message, you are not to make this prominent. In counterworking the efforts of your fellow laborers who are teaching health reform, you are out of order, working on the wrong side.—Letter 48, 1902.

An Appeal to Parents

The Lord will cut His work short in righteousness. The earth is corrupted under the inhabitants thereof. Disease of every kind is now afflicting the human family. The misery created by the corruption that is in the world through lust is developing in a startling manner in the commission of crimes of every description. Robbery, murder, sensuality, the cruelty of satanic powers—these and many other evils are seen on every hand. We are surrounded by unseen dangers.

When will those who know the truth take their stand on the side of right principles for time and for eternity? When will they be true to the principles of health reform? When will they learn that it is dangerous to use flesh-meat?

I am instructed to say that if meat eating ever were safe, it is not safe now. Diseased animals are taken to the large cities and to the villages, and sold for food. Many of these poor creatures would have died of disease in a very short time if they had not been slaughtered; yet the carcasses of these diseased animals are prepared for the market, and people eat freely of this poisonous food. Such a diet contaminates the blood and stimulates the lower passions.

Many parents act as if they were bereft of reason. They are in a state of lethargy, palsied by the indulgence of perverted appetite and debasing passion. Our ministers, who know the truth, should arouse the people from the paralyzed condition and lead them to put away those things that create an appetite for flesh-meat. If they neglect to reform, they will lose spiritual power, and become more and more debased by sinful indulgence. Habits that disgust the heavenly universe, habits that degrade human beings lower than the beasts, are practiced in many homes. Let all those who know the truth, say, "Flee fleshly lusts, that war against the soul."

Examples in Rightdoing

Let not any of our ministers set an evil example in the eating of flesh-meat. Let them and their families live up to the light of health reform. Let not our ministers animalize their own nature and the nature of their children. Children whose desires have not been restrained are tempted not only to indulge in the common habits of intemperance, but to give loose rein to their lower passions and to disregard purity and virtue. These are led on by Satan not only to corrupt their own bodies, but to whisper their evil communications to others. If parents are blinded by sin they will often fail of discerning these things.—Manuscript 133, 1902.

Making Dyspeptics

We shall soon reach a time when we must understand the meaning of a simple diet. The time is not far hence when we shall be obliged to adopt a diet very different from our present diet....

We need to study the art of preparing in a simple manner the fruits, grains, and vegetables. We do not need these complex combinations that are provided. As the matter now stands we are in danger of making dyspeptics.—Manuscript 150, 1905.

Eating Too Frequently

Indulging in eating too frequently, and in too large quantities, overtaxes the digestive organs and produces a feverish state of the system. The blood becomes impure, and then diseases of various kinds occur. A physician is sent for, who prescribes some drug which gives present relief but which does not cure the disease. It may change the form of disease, but the real evil is increased tenfold. Nature was doing her best to rid the system of an accumulation of impurities, and could she have been left to herself, aided by the common blessings of heaven such as pure air and pure water, a speedy and safe cure would have been affected.

The sufferers in such cases can do for themselves that which others cannot do as well for them. They should commence to relieve nature of the load they have forced upon her. They should remove the cause. Fast a short time, and give the stomach chance for rest. Reduce the feverish state of the system by a careful and understanding application of water. These efforts will help nature in her struggles to free the system of impurities.—Spiritual Gifts, 4a:133, 134.

The Two-Meal Plan

It is quite a common custom with people of the world to eat three times a day, besides eating at irregular intervals between meals; and the last meal is generally the most hearty, and is often taken just before retiring. This is reversing the natural order; a hearty meal should never be taken so late in the day. Should these persons change their practice, and eat but two meals a day, and nothing between meals, not even an apple, a nut, or any kind of fruit, the result would be seen in a good appetite and greatly improved health.—The Review and Herald, July 29, 1884.

Perseverance in Overcoming

Persons who have indulged their appetite to eat freely of meat, highly seasoned gravies, and various kinds of rich cakes and preserves, cannot immediately relish a plain, wholesome, and nutritious diet. Their taste is so perverted they have no appetite for a wholesome diet of fruits, plain bread, and vegetables. They need not expect to relish at first, food so different from that which they have been indulging themselves to eat. If they cannot at first enjoy plain food, they should fast until they can. That fast will prove to them of greater benefit than medicine, for the abused stomach will find that rest which it has long needed, and real hunger can be satisfied with a plain diet. It will take time for the taste to recover from the abuses which it has received, and to gain its natural tone. But perseverance in a self-denying course of eating and drinking will soon make plain, wholesome food palatable, and it will soon be eaten with greater satisfaction than the epicure enjoys over his rich dainties.—4SG 130, 131.

Pray for Moral Courage

Whenever I have seen children feeding upon flesh-meats, since the light was given me from heaven, I have felt that if the parents only knew what they were doing they would fast and pray for moral courage and God-given wisdom and grace to do right. All who feel their need of His Spirit to educate and discipline self and to properly train their children, will deny self, and take up the cross and follow Jesus.

For certain things fasting and prayer are recommended and appropriate. In the hand of God they are a means of cleansing the heart and promoting a receptive frame of mind. We obtain answers to our prayers because we humble our souls before God. If our appetites clamor for the flesh of dead animals, it is a necessity to fast and pray for the Lord to give His grace to deny fleshly lusts which war against the soul.

Feeding Upon Christ

There should be far less anxiety as to what we shall eat and what we shall drink to gratify our fleshly appetites; but we may well encourage the appetite of the soul, and pray for especial enlightenment upon the word of God, and eat and drink that word. Jesus says, "I am that Bread of Life." ...

We must be constantly meditating upon the word, eating it, digesting it, and by practice, assimilating it, so that it is taken into the life current. He who feeds on Christ daily will by his example teach others to think less of that which they eat and to feel much greater anxiety for the food they give to the soul.

The True Fast

The true fasting which should be recommended to all, is abstinence from every stimulating kind of food, and the proper use of wholesome simple food, which God has provided in abundance. Men need to think less about what they shall eat and drink of temporal food, and much more in regard to the food from heaven, that will give tone and vitality to the whole religious experience.—Letter 73, 1896.

Suggestions for Sanitarium Diet

The patients are to be provided with an abundance of wholesome, palatable food, prepared and served in so appetizing a way that they will have no temptation to desire flesh-meat. The meals may be made the means of an education in health reform. Care is to be shown in regard to the combinations of foods given to the patients. Knowledge in regard to proper food combinations is of great worth, and is to be received as wisdom from God....

We must remember that while there are some who are better for eating only two meals, there are others who eat lightly at each meal, and who feel that they need something in the evening. Food enough is to be eaten to give strength to sinew and muscle. And we are to remember that it is from the food eaten that the mind gains strength. Part of the medical missionary work that our sanitarium workers are to do is to show the value of wholesome food.

Avoid Sudden Changes

It is right that no tea, coffee, or flesh-meat be served in our sanitariums. To many, this is a great change and a severe deprivation. To enforce other changes, such as a change in the number of meals a day, is likely, in the cases of some, to do more harm than good.

There are many to whom the supper hour has been the most cheerful hour of the day. Then it is that all the family, the day's work done, have gathered round the table for social intercourse.

It is plain that two meals a day are better than three. I believe and practice this, but I have no "Thus saith the Lord" that it is wrong for some to eat the third meal. We are not to be as the Pharisees, bound about by set rules and regulations. God's word has not specified any set hours when food should be eaten. We are to be careful not to make laws like the laws of the Pharisees, or to teach for doctrines the commandments of men.

Let your regulations be so consistent that they will appeal to the reason of those even who have not been educated to see all things clearly. As you strive to introduce the renovating, transforming principles of truth into the life practice of those who come to the sanitarium to gain improvement in health, let them see that no arbitrary exactions are laid on them. Give them no reason to feel that they are compelled to follow a course that they do not choose.—Letter 213, 1902.

No Flesh-Meat on Sanitarium Tables

I have been plainly instructed by the Lord that flesh-meat should not be placed before the patients in our sanitarium dining rooms. Light was given me that the patients could have flesh-meat if, after hearing the parlor lectures, they still urged us to give it to them; but that, in such cases, it must be eaten in their own rooms. All the helpers are to discard flesh-meat. But, as stated before, if, after knowing that the flesh of animals cannot be placed on the dining-room tables, a few patients urge that they must have meat, cheerfully give it to them in their rooms....

A Liberal Variety

Let the food be palatably prepared and nicely served. More dishes will have to be prepared than would be necessary if flesh-meat was served. Other things can be provided, so that meats can be discarded. Milk and cream can be used by some.

I make myself a criterion for no one else. There are things that I cannot eat without suffering great distress. I try to learn that which is best for me, and then, saying nothing to anyone, I partake of the things that I can eat, which often are simply two or three varieties that will not create a disturbance in the stomach.

Let us remember that we have had a long time to become accustomed to the health-reform diet. We cannot expect anything else than that in our sanitariums it will be necessary to furnish dishes prepared somewhat differently from those prepared for our own use; for we have learned to relish plain food. It is necessary to plan more liberally for a medical institution than for a private family. Many things must be taken into consideration, and concessions must be made to meet the peculiar needs of the many classes of patients coming to our sanitariums. A straitjacket is not to be put on the appetite suddenly. When you become acquainted with these people, and understand their true condition, prescriptions can be given to meet the individual requirements.—Letter 45, 1903.

Lectures to be Given

In dealing with the patients in our sanitariums, we must reason from cause to effect. We must remember that the habits and practices of a lifetime cannot be changed in a moment. With an intelligent cook, and an abundant supply of wholesome food, reforms can be brought about that will work well, but it may take time to bring them about. A strenuous effort should not be made unless it is actually demanded. We must remember that food which would be appetizing to a health reformer might be very insipid to those who have been accustomed to highly seasoned food.

Lectures should be given explaining why reforms in diet are essential, and showing that the use of highly seasoned food causes inflammation of the delicate lining of the digestive organs. Let it be shown why we as a people have changed our habits of eating and drinking. Show why we discard tobacco and all intoxicating liquor. Lay down the principles of health reform clearly and plainly, and with this, let there be placed on the table an abundance of wholesome food, tastefully prepared; and the Lord will help you to make impressive the urgency of reform, and will lead them to see that this reform is for their highest good. They will miss the highly seasoned food to which they have been accustomed, but an effort must be made to give them food that is so wholesome and so appetizing that they will cease to miss the unwholesome dishes. Show them that the treatment given them will not benefit them unless they make the needed change in their habits of eating and drinking.—Letter 331, 1904.

To a Physician Dying from Overwork and a Meager Diet

Do not put yourself through as you have done, and do not go to extremes in regard to the health reform. Some of our people are very careless in regard to health reform. But because some are far behind, you must not, in order to be an example to them, be an extremist. You must not deprive yourself of that class of food which makes good blood. Your devotion to true principles is leading you to submit yourself to a diet which is giving you an experience that will not recommend health reform. This is your danger.

When you see that you are becoming weak physically, it is essential for you to make changes, and at once. Put into your diet something you have left out. It is your duty to do this. Get eggs of healthy fowls. Use these eggs cooked or raw. Drop them uncooked into the best unfermented wine you can find. This will supply that which is necessary to your system. Do not for a moment suppose that it will not be right to do this.

There is one thing that has saved life—an infusion of blood from one person to another; but this would be difficult and perhaps impossible for you to do. I merely suggest it.

The prayer of faith shall save the sick, and I beseech you to call for the elders of the church without delay. May the Lord help you, is my most sincere prayer.

The Use of Milk and Eggs

We appreciate your experience as a physician, and yet I say that milk and eggs should be included in your diet. These things cannot at present be dispensed with, and the doctrine of dispensing with them should not be taught.

You are in danger of taking too radical a view of health reform, and of prescribing for yourself a diet that will not sustain you.

Again, let nothing come up before you to worry you. Come apart and rest awhile. This you must do. Draw from the Great Physician leaves from the tree of life. Plead in your own behalf, and let others also plead for you. "Let him take hold of My strength, that he may make peace with Me, and he shall make peace with Me."

I do hope that you will heed the words I have spoken to you. It has been presented to me that you will not be able to exert the most successful influence in health reform unless in some things you become more liberal to yourself and to others. The time will come when milk cannot be used as freely as it is now used; but the present is not the time to discard it. And eggs contain properties which are remedial agencies in counteracting poisons. And while warnings have been given against the use of these articles of diet in families where the children were addicted to, yes, steeped in habits of self-abuse, yet we should not consider it a denial of principle to use eggs of hens which are well cared for and suitably fed....

Use Appetizing Foods

Those who take an extreme view of health reform are in danger of preparing tasteless dishes. This has been done over and over again. The food has become so insipid as to be refused by the stomach. The food given the sick should be varied. They should not be given the same dishes over and over again....

Nutritious, Palatable Food Essential

God calls upon those for whom Christ died to take proper care of themselves and set a right example to others. My brother, you are not to make a test for the people of God upon the question of diet; for they will lose confidence in teachings that are strained to the farthest point of extension. The Lord desires His people to be sound on every point in health reform, but we must not go to extremes....

The reason for Dr. -----'s poor health is his overdrawing on his bank stock of health and then failing to replace the amount drawn out by wholesome, nutritious, palatable food. My brother, devote your whole life to Him who was crucified for you, but do not tie yourself down to a meager diet; for thus you misrepresent health reform.

While working against gluttony and intemperance, we are to remember the means and appliances of gospel truth, which commend themselves to sound judgment. In order to do our work in straight, simple lines, we must recognize the conditions to which the human family are subjected.

Wisdom in Teaching

God has made provisions for those who live in the different countries of the world. Those who desire to be co-workers with God must consider carefully how they teach health reform in God's great vineyard. They must move carefully in specifying just what food should and should not be eaten. The human messenger must unite with the divine Helper in presenting the message of mercy to the multitudes God would save.

We are to be brought into connection with the masses. Should health reform be taught them in its most extreme form, harm would be done. We ask them to leave off eating meat and drinking tea and coffee. That is well....

All flesh food should be discarded, but vegetables should be made palatable with a little milk or cream or something equivalent. The poor say, when health reform is presented to them, "What shall we eat? We cannot afford to buy the nut foods." As I preach the gospel to the poor, I am instructed to tell them to eat that food which is most nourishing. I cannot say to them, "You must not eat eggs or milk or cream. You must use no butter in the preparation of food." The gospel must be preached to the poor, and the time has not yet come to prescribe the strictest diet.

The time will come when we may have to discard some of the articles of diet we now use, such as milk and cream and eggs; but my message is that you must not bring yourself to a time of trouble beforehand, and thus afflict yourself with death. Wait till the Lord prepares the way before you.—Letter 37, 1901.

Light Given in Love and Pity

Our gracious heavenly Father sees the deplorable condition of men who, some knowingly but many ignorantly, are living in violation of the laws that He has established. And in love and pity to the race He causes the light to shine upon health reform. He publishes His law and the penalty that will follow the transgression of it, that all may learn and be careful to live in harmony with natural law. He proclaims His law so distinctly and makes it so prominent that it is like a city set on a hill. All accountable beings can understand it if they will. Idiots will not be responsible. To make plain natural law and urge the obedience of it is the work that accompanies the third angel's message, to prepare a people for the coming of the Lord.—Testimonies for the Church 3:161.

* * * * *

For Further Study

Diet and Health:
Counsels on Health, 107-161 (Testimonies for the Church 2:63, 362-364, 368-370, 374, 375, 412-414, 602, 603);
Testimonies for the Church 3:171, 172, 485-489;
Testimonies for the Church 9:153-166;
The Ministry of Healing, 295-336;
Education, 202-206.

Relation of Health Habits to Character:
Counsels on Health, 43-48 (Testimonies for the Church 2:354-359);
Counsels on Health, 64-70, 107-121;
The Ministry of Healing, 130;
Testimonies For The Church 1:487, 488, 618, 619;
Testimonies for the Church 2:404;
Testimonies for the Church 3:162, 163;
Testimonies for the Church 7:199, 257, 258;
Gospel Workers, 230, 241;
Fundamentals of Christian Education, 143, 144, 147.

A Reform Needed:
Counsels on Health, 575-579.

Results of Indulgence of Appetite:
Testimonies for the Church 3:164, 165.

A Simple Diet:
Counsels on Health, 42 (Testimonies for the Church 2:352).

Plainness of Diet a Reason for Daniel's Success:
Testimonies for the Church 4:515, 516.

Diet for Children:
Testimonies for the Church 2:365, 366;
Fundamentals of Christian Education, 20, 143, 150.

An Impoverished Diet:
Counsels on Health, 151, 152 (Testimonies for the Church 2:366-

368);
Testimonies for the Church 2:254;
Gospel Workers, 241.
Liquid Diet Not Best:
Fundamentals of Christian Education, 226, 227;
Testimonies for the Church 3:74.
Extremes in Diet:
Counsels on Health, 153-156;
Testimonies For The Church 1:205;
Testimonies for the Church 2:538.
Healthful Cooking, and Cooking Schools:
Counsels on Health, 135 (Testimonies for the Church 9:161);
Counsels on Health, 143-147 (Testimonies For The Church 1:681-687; Testimonies for the Church 2:370, 373);
Counsels on Health, 443, 450, 451, 551, 552;
Testimonies for the Church 2:537;
Testimonies for the Church 7:112, 113;
Testimonies for the Church 9:112.

Section 16—The Worker's Health

We Belong to God

Our bodies belong to God. He paid the price of redemption for the body as well as for the soul. "Ye are not your own; for ye are bought with a price: therefore glorify God in your body, and in your spirit, which are God's." "The body is not for fornication, but for the Lord; and the Lord for the body." The Creator watches over the human machinery, keeping it in motion. Were it not for His constant care, the pulse would not beat, the action of the heart would cease, the brain would no longer act its part.

The brain is the organ and instrument of the mind, and controls the whole body. In order for the other parts of the system to be healthy, the brain must be healthy. And in order for the brain to be healthy, the blood must be pure. If by correct habits of eating and drinking the blood is kept pure, the brain will be properly nourished.

It is the lack of harmonious action in the human organism that brings disease. The imagination may control the other parts of the body to their injury. All parts of the system must work harmoniously. The different parts of the body, especially those remote from the heart, should receive a free circulation of blood. The limbs act an important part, and should receive proper attention.

God is the great caretaker of the human machinery. In the care of our bodies we must cooperate with Him. Love for God is essential for life and health.... In order to have perfect health our hearts must be filled with love and hope and joy.

I wish to impress upon the minds of physicians the fact that they cannot do as they please with their thoughts and imaginations and at the same time be safe in their calling. Satan is the destroyer; Christ is the restorer. I desire our physicians to fully comprehend this point. They may save souls from death by a right application of the knowledge they have gained, or they may work against the great Master Builder. They may cooperate with God, or they may counterwork His plans by failing to work harmoniously with Him.

Habits of Regularity Important

All physicians should place themselves under the control of the Great Physician. Under His guidance they will do as they should do. But the Lord will not work a miracle to save physicians who recklessly abuse His building. As far as possible, physicians should observe regularity in their habits of eating. They should take a proper amount of exercise. They should be determined to cooperate with the great Master Worker. God works, and man must come into line and work with Him; for He is the Saviour of the body.

Physicians, above all others, need to realize the relation human beings sustain to God in regard to the preservation of health and life. They need to study the word of God diligently, lest they disregard the laws of health. There is no need for them to become weak and unbalanced. Under the guidance of the heavenly authority, they may advance in clear, straight lines. But they must give the most earnest heed to the laws of God. They should feel that they are the property of God, that they have been bought with a price, and that therefore they are to glorify Him in all things.—Manuscript 24, 1900.

Faithful Guardians of Their Powers

Those who put their whole souls into the medical missionary work, who labor untiringly in peril, in privation, in watchings oft, in weariness and painfulness, are in danger of forgetting that they must be faithful guardians of their own mental and physical powers. They are not to allow themselves to be overtaxed. But they are filled with zeal and earnestness, and they sometimes move unadvisedly, putting themselves under too heavy a strain. Unless such workers make a change, the result will be that sickness will come upon them and they will break down.

While God's workers are to be filled with a noble enthusiasm, and with a determination to follow the example of the divine worker, the great Medical Missionary, they are not to crowd too many things into the day's work. If they do, they will soon have to leave the work entirely, broken down because they have tried to carry too heavy a load. My brother, it is right for you to make the best use of the advantages given you of God in earnest efforts for the relief of suffering and for the saving of souls. But do not sacrifice your health.

We have a calling as much higher than common, selfish interests as the heavens are higher than the earth. But this thought should not lead the willing, hardworking servants of God to carry all the burdens they can possibly bear, without periods of rest.

How grand it would be if among all who were engaged in carrying out God's wonderful plan for the salvation of souls, there were no idlers! How much more would be accomplished if everyone would say, "God holds me accountable to be wide-awake, and to let my efforts speak in favor of the truth I profess to believe! I am to be a practical worker, not a daydreamer." It is because there are so many daydreamers that true workers have to carry double burdens.—Letter 291, 1904.

Breaking Under the Strain

I hear of workers whose health is breaking down under the strain of the burdens they are bearing. This ought not to be. God desires us to remember that we are mortal. We are not to embrace too much in our work. We are not to keep ourselves under such a strain that our physical and mental powers shall be used threadbare.

More workers are needed, that some of the burdens may be removed from some of those who are now so heavily loaded down. The Lord wants those who have gained an experience in His service to be educators. We are to be learners in the school of Christ, that we may teach others, and that we may plan wisely for the carrying forward of God's work.—Manuscript 71, 1903.

The Physician to Conserve Strength

Some who have chosen the medical profession are too easily led away from the duties resting upon the physicians. Some by misuse enfeeble their powers, so that they cannot render to God perfect service. They place themselves where they cannot act with vigor, tact, and skill, and do not realize that by the disregard of physical laws they bring upon themselves inefficiency and thus they rob and dishonor God.

Physicians should not allow their attention to be diverted from their work. Neither should they confine themselves so closely to professional work that health will be injured. In the fear of God they should be wise in the use of the strength that God has given them. Never should they disregard the means that God has provided for the preservation of health. It is their duty to bring under the control of reason every power that God has given them.

Of all men the physician should, as far as possible, take regular hours for rest. This will give him power of endurance to bear the taxing burdens of his work. In his busy life the physician will find that the searching of the Scriptures and earnest prayer will give vigor of mind and stability of character.—Manuscript 53, 1907

Spiritual Loss Through Overfatigue

There are those who can successfully carry a certain amount of work, but who become overwearied, fractious, and impatient when there is crowded upon them a larger amount of work than they have physical or mental strength to perform. They lose the love of God out of the heart, and then they lose courage and faith, and the blessing of God is not with them. There are physicians who have lost their spiritual power because they have done double the work that they ought to have done. When men are asked or tempted to take more work than they can do, let them say firmly, I cannot consent to do this. I cannot safely do more than I am doing.—Manuscript 44, 1903

The Minister's Duty to Safeguard Health

God not only desires His servants to have faith in the work of His institutions. He desires them to go further than this. They should realize that God wishes them to be living examples of what it means to be well, physically and spiritually. He wants them to show that the truth has accomplished a great work for them.

Those who assemble in our conferences are not always in a fit state to judge righteously. Many suffer from congestion of the brain. Those who assemble in such meetings should first do all in their

[295] power to place themselves in right relation to God and to health. If the head is congested, let them find out what is wrong. The brain is disturbed because there is something the matter with the stomach. Let them find out what is wrong about their diet. Our bodies are the temples of the Holy Spirit, and if we fail to do all we can to place the body in the very best condition of health, we are robbing God of the honor due to Him from the beings He has created.

If you are called upon to attend a council meeting, ask yourself whether your perceptive faculties are in a proper condition to weigh evidence. If you are not in a proper condition, if your brain is confused, you have no right to take part in the meeting. Are you fractious? Is your temper sweet and fragrant, or is it so disturbed and disagreeable that you will be led to make hasty decisions? Do you feel as though you would like to fight someone? Then do not go to the meeting; for if you go you will surely dishonor God. Take an ax and chop wood or engage in some physical exercise until your spirit is mild and easy to be entreated. Just as surely as your stomach is creating a disturbance in your brain, your words will create a disturbance in the assembly. More trouble is caused by disturbed digestive organs than many realize.

We ought always to eat the most simple food. Often twice as much food as the system needs is eaten. Then nature has to work hard to get rid of the surplus. Treat your stomach properly, and it will do its best....

Whether they acknowledge it or not, God lays upon all human beings the duty of taking care of the soul temple. The body is to be kept clean and pure. The soul is to be sanctified and ennobled. Then, God says, I will come unto him and take up My abode with him. We are responsible for our own salvation, and God holds us accountable for the influence we exert on those connected with us. We should stand in such a position, physically and spiritually, that we can recommend the religion of Christ. We are to dedicate our bodies to God.

God desires His ministers to stand in a high and holy position. Those who open the word of God to others should ask themselves, before they enter the pulpit, whether they have been self-denying, whether their food has been simple, such as the stomach can digest, without beclouding the brain. Please read the first chapter of

Second Corinthians. This entire chapter is a lesson for all believers.—Manuscript 62, 1900.

Strengthening the Mental and Moral Powers

I am instructed to say to our ministers and to the presidents of our conferences: Your usefulness as laborers for God in the work of recovering perishing souls depends much on your success in overcoming appetite. Overcome the desire to gratify appetite, and if you do this your passions will be easily controlled. Then your mental and moral powers will be stronger. "And they overcame him by the blood of the Lamb, and by the word of their testimony."—Letter 158, 1909.

In Warm Climates

In warm, heating climates, there should be given to the worker, in whatever line of work he is to do, less work than in a more bracing climate. The Lord remembers that we are but dust....

The less sugar introduced into the food in its preparation, the less difficulty will be experienced because of the heat of the climate.—Letter 91, 1898.

Gardening and Health

Let men and women work in field and orchard and garden. This will bring health and strength to nerve and muscle. Living indoors and cherishing invalidism is a very poor business. If those who are sick will give nerves and muscles and sinews proper exercise in the open air, their health will be renewed.

The most astonishing ignorance prevails in regard to putting brain, bone, and muscle into active service. Every part of the human organism should be equally taxed. This is necessary for the harmonious development and action of every part.

Many do not see the importance of having land to cultivate, and of raising fruit and vegetables that their tables may be supplied with these things. I am instructed to say to every family and every church, God will bless you when you work out your own salvation with fear and trembling, fearing lest, by unwise treatment of the body, you will mar the Lord's plan for you.

Many act as if health and disease were things entirely independent of their conduct and entirely outside their control. They do not reason from cause to effect, and submit to feebleness and disease as a necessity. Violent attacks of sickness they believe to be special dispensations of Providence, or the result of some overruling, mastering power; and they resort to drugs as a cure for the evil. But the drugs taken to cure the disease weaken the system.

Regular Exercise

If those who are sick would exercise their muscles daily, women as well as men, in outdoor work, using brain, bone, and muscle proportionately, weakness and languor would disappear. Health would take the place of disease, and strength the place of feebleness.

Let those who are sick do all in their power, by correct practice in eating, drinking, and dressing, and by taking judicious exercise, to secure recovery of health. Let the patients who come to our sanitariums be taught to cooperate with God in seeking health. "Ye are God's husbandry, ye are God's building." God made nerve and muscle in order that they might be used. It is the inaction of the human machinery that brings suffering and disease.—Letter 5, 1904.

* * * * *

For Further Study

Duty to Preserve Health:
Counsels on Health, 563-566.
Efficiency Dependent on Health:
Counsels on Health, 193, 194
(Testimonies for the Church 4:264-270);
Counsels on Health, 407
(The Ministry of Healing, 219).
The Price of Health:
Counsels on Health, 595
(Testimonies for the Church 4:408, 409).
Exercise and Diet:

Counsels on Health, 572-574
(Testimonies for the Church 3:489-492).

Results of Inaction With Study:
Counsels on Health, 184-188
(Testimonies for the Church 3:148-152);
Counsels on Health, 20;
Testimonies for the Church 4:94, 95).

Recreation:
Counsels on Health, 197, 198
(Testimonies For The Church 1:514, 515).

Caution Against Exhausting, Not Recuperative, Recreation:
Education, 277, 278.

Regular Hours for Rest:
Counsels on Health, 361.

Occasional Relief for Sanitarium Physicians:
Counsels on Health, 354
(Testimonies for the Church 3:182).

Physical Labor for Students:
Counsels to Parents, Teachers, and Students, 285-293.

Vitalizing Effects of Combined Physical and Mental Labor:
Testimonies for the Church 3:157.

Right Use of Voice Conducive to Health:
Testimonies for the Church 4:404, 405.

Section 17—Medical Missionary Work in the Great Cities

Christ's Labors in Cities and Towns

The Lord is speaking to His people at this time, saying, Gain an entrance into the cities, and proclaim the truth in simplicity and in faith. The Holy Spirit will work through your efforts to impress hearts. Introduce no strange doctrine into your message, but speak the simple words of the gospel of Christ, which young and old can understand. The unlearned as well as the educated are to comprehend the truths of the third angel's message, and they must be taught in simplicity. If you would approach the people acceptably, humble your hearts before God and learn His ways.

We shall gain much instruction for our work from a study of Christ's methods of labor and His manner of meeting the people. In the gospel story we have the record of how He worked for all classes, and of how, as He labored in cities and towns, thousands were drawn to His side to hear His teaching. The words of the Master were clear and distinct, and were spoken in sympathy and tenderness. They carried with them the assurance that here was truth. It was the simplicity and earnestness with which Christ labored and spoke that drew so many to Him.

The Great Teacher laid plans for His work. Study these plans. We find Him traveling from place to place, followed by crowds of eager listeners. When He could, He would lead them away from the crowded cities to the quiet of the country. Here He would pray with them, and talk to them of eternal truths.

The sympathy that Christ ever expressed for the physical needs of His hearers won from many a response to the truths He sought to teach. Was not the gospel message of deepest importance to that company of five thousand people who for hours had followed Him and hung upon His words? Many had never before heard truths such as they listened to on that occasion. Yet Christ's desire to teach them spiritual truths did not make Him indifferent to their physical needs.—The Review and Herald, January 18, 1912.

Medical Evangelism for the Cities

Now is the opportune time to work the cities; for we must reach the people there. As a people we have been in danger of centering too many important interests in one place. This is not good judgment nor wisdom. An interest is now to be created in the principal cities. Many small centers must be established, rather than a few large centers....

Let missionaries be laboring two and two in different parts of all our large cities. The workers in each city should frequently meet together for counsel and prayer, that they may have wisdom and grace to work together effectively and harmoniously. Let all be wide-awake to make the most of every advantage. Our people must gird the armor on and establish centers in all the large cities. The agencies of Satan are active in the field, putting forth efforts to confuse the minds of men and to fill them with vain imaginations, that they may not become interested in the truth....

I have endeavored to arouse our people to labor for the unworked portions of the great missionary field, yet but few seem to respond to the appeals of the Spirit of God. We do not realize the extent to which satanic agencies are at work in these large cities. The work of bringing the message of present truth before the people is becoming more and more difficult. It is essential that new and varied talents unite in the intelligent labor for the people. If the burden of these unworked cities rested upon the hearts of our people as it should, they would arouse to labor as they have not yet done for the souls that are perishing in sin....

The message that I am bidden to bear to our people at this time is, Work the cities without delay, for time is short. The Lord has kept this work before us for the last twenty years or more. A little has been done in a few places, but much more might be done. I am carrying a burden day and night, because so little is being accomplished to warn the inhabitants of our great centers of population of the judgments that will fall upon the transgressors of God's law.—Letter 168, 1909.

The Training of Workers

[301] In every large city there should be corps of organized, well-disciplined workers; not merely one or two, but scores should be set to work. But the perplexing question is yet unsolved, how they will be sustained.

I have been shown that in our labor for the enlightenment of the people in the large cities the work has not been as well organized or the methods of labor as efficient as in other churches that have not the great light we regard as so essential. Why is this? Because so many of our laborers have been those who love to preach (and many who were not thoroughly qualified to preach were set at work), and a large share of the labor has been put forth in preaching.

More attention should be given to training and educating missionaries with a special reference to work in the cities. Each company of workers should be under the direction of a competent leader, and it should ever be kept before them that they are to be missionaries in the highest sense of the term. Such systematic labor, wisely conducted, would produce blessed results.

Something has been done in this line, but too frequently the work has dwindled down, and nothing permanent has been accomplished. There is need now of earnest labor. The young men who go forth in the employ of the General Conference are to understand that they are not merely to preach, but to minister, to act like men who are weighted with solemn responsibility to seek and to save that which is lost.

It should not be the object of the laborer to present a large list of sermons he has preached, but what has he done in the work of saving souls, of training workers? This requires earnest labor in personal effort. It requires that the workers shall be often with God in earnest prayer, and that they seek wisdom through diligent searching of the Scriptures.—Letter 34, 1892.

Difficulties Will Increase

The importance of making our way in the great cities is still kept before me. For many years the Lord has been urging upon us this duty, and yet we see but comparatively little accomplished in our great centers of population. If we do not take up this work in a determined manner, Satan will multiply difficulties which will not be easy to surmount. We are far behind in doing the work that should have been done in these long-neglected cities. The work will now be more difficult than it would have been a few years ago. But if we take up the work in the name of the Lord, barriers will be broken down, and decided victories will be ours.

In this work physicians and gospel ministers are needed. We must press our petitions to the Lord, and do our best, pressing forward with all the energy possible to make an opening in the large cities. Had we in the past worked after the Lord's plans, many lights would be shining brightly that are going out.—Letter 148, 1909.

No Time to Colonize

This is no time to colonize. From city to city the work is to be carried quickly. The light that has been placed under a bushel is to be taken out and placed on a candlestick, that it may give forth light to all that are in the house.

Thousands of people in our cities are left in darkness, and Satan is well pleased with the delay; for this delay gives him opportunity to work in these fields with men of influence to further his plans. Can we now depend upon our men in positions of responsibility to act humbly and nobly their part? Let the watchmen arouse. Let no one continue to be indifferent to the situation. There should be a thorough awakening among the brethren and sisters in all our churches.

For years the work in the cities has been presented before me, and has been urged upon our people. Instruction has been given to open new fields. There has sometimes been a jealous fear lest someone who wished to enter new fields should receive means from the people that they supposed was wanted for another work. Some in responsible positions have felt that nothing should be done without their personal knowledge and approval. Therefore efficient workers have been sometimes delayed and hindered, and the carriage wheels of progress in entering new fields have been made to move heavily.

In every large city there should have been a strong force of workers laboring earnestly to warn the people. Had this been undertaken in humility and faith, Christ would have gone before the humble workers, and the salvation of God would have been revealed.

[303] Let companies now be quickly organized to go out two and two, and labor in the Spirit of Christ, following His plans. Even though some Judas may introduce himself into the ranks of the workers, the Lord will care for the work. His angels will go before and prepare the way. Before this time, every large city should have heard the testing message, and thousands should have been brought to a knowledge of the truth. Wake up the churches, take the light from under the bushel.

Our Delay is Satan's Opportunity

Where are the men who will work and study and agonize in prayer as did Christ? We are not to confine our efforts to a few places. "If they shall persecute you in one city, flee ye to another." Let Christ's plan be followed. He was ever watching for opportunities to engage in personal labor, ever ready to interest and draw men to a study of the Scriptures. He labored patiently for men who had not an intelligent knowledge of what is truth. While we are not awake to the situation, and while much time is consumed in planning how to reach perishing souls, Satan is busy devising and blocking the way.

In view of the many neglected cities from one end of the United States to another, I am free to say that too much labor has been put forth in the plants in a few favored localities. Let not so large an expenditure of means and of time as has been devoted to ----- be given to other places; for it will be used as an evidence that we do not really believe that the end of all things is at hand. Satan knows how to make use of every inconsistency, and he will influence men to point at us and say, "They do not believe the things they teach."—Manuscript 21, 1910.

A Mission in Every City

In every city there should be a city mission, that would be a training school for workers. Many of our brethren must stand condemned in the sight of God because they have not done the very work that God would have them do.

If our brethren will use their God-given ability to warn the cities, angels of God will surely go before them to make the impression upon the hearts of the people for whom they labor. The Lord has many thousands who have never bowed the knee to Baal. Let not our ministers and our physicians fail nor be discouraged.—Letter 56, 1910.

A Mighty Movement

There is no change in the messages that God has sent in the past. The work in the cities is the essential work for this time. When the cities are worked as God would have them, the result will be the setting in operation of a mighty movement such as we have not yet witnessed. God calls for self-sacrificing men converted to the truth to let their light shine forth in clear, distinct rays....

As a people we are not half awake to a sense of our necessities and to the times in which we live. Wake up the watchmen. Our first work should be to search our hearts and to become reconverted. We have no time to lose upon unimportant issues.—Letter 46, 1910.

Cooperation

In this effort in behalf of the cities, we greatly need the cooperation of all classes of laborers. Especially do we need the help that the physician can render as an evangelist. If ministers and physicians will plan to unite in an effort to reach the honest-hearted ones in our cities, the physicians, as well as the ministers, will be placed on vantage ground. As they labor in humility God will open the way before them, and many will receive a saving knowledge of truth.—Manuscript 9, 1910.

Move Forward

The principles of health reform are to be promulgated as a part of the work in these cities. The voice of the third angel's message is to be heard with power. Let the teachings of health reform be brought into every effort made to get the light of truth before the people. Let workers be selected who are qualified to teach the truth wisely in clear, simple lines. Let us not wait before beginning this work until all the way is made clear. Faith says, Move forward. Christ says, "Lo, I am with you alway, even unto the end of the world." Go on, step by step, departing not from that spirit of sanctification through the truth which the presence of the Spirit of God and obedience to the truth will give.—Manuscript 1, 1910.

A Parable of What Should Be

When Dr. Paulson showed me the location that had been secured for sanitarium work at Hinsdale, I was thoroughly pleased; for this place answered to the representations that had been given me of places that would be obtained by our people for sanitarium work outside of the large cities. Time will show that such properties as this can be used to far greater advantage than buildings in Chicago; for the wickedness of Chicago is as the wickedness of Sodom and Gomorrah. It was also represented to me that there were other places near Chicago, but away from the city, which the Lord would have His people secure. There are souls to be reached. The message must be proclaimed. This is the light that has been given to me.

I have been given a representation of the preaching of the word of truth with clearness and power in many places where it has never yet been heard. The Lord would have the people warned; for a great work will be done in a short time. I have heard the word of God proclaimed in many localities outside the city of Chicago. There were many voices proclaiming the truth with great power. That which they proclaimed was not fanciful theories, but the warning message. While the solid truth of the Bible came from the lips of men who had no fanciful theories or misleading science to present, there were others who labored with all their power to bring in false theories regarding God and Christ. And miracles were wrought, to deceive, if possible, the very elect.

I heard the message proclaimed in power by men who had not been educated in -----. Among those who were engaged in the work were young men taken from the plow and from the fields, and sent forth to preach the truth as it is in Jesus. Unquestioning faith in the Lord God of heaven was imparted to those who were called and chosen. "All this," said my Instructor, "is a parable of what should be, and what will be."

Rural Outposts

For the present, some will be obliged to labor in Chicago; but these should be preparing working centers in rural districts, from which to work the city. The Lord would have His people looking about them, and securing humble, inexpensive places as centers for their work. And from time to time larger places will come to their notice, which they will be able to secure at a surprisingly low price.—Manuscript 33, 1906.

Sanitariums and Hygienic Restaurants

God has declared that sanitariums and hygienic restaurants should be established for the purpose of making known to the world His law. The closing of our restaurants on the Sabbath is to be a witness that there is a people who will not for worldly gain, or to please people, disregard God's holy rest day. These restaurants are to be established in our cities to bring the truth before many who are engrossed in the business and pleasure of this world. Many of these are professed Christians, but are "lovers of pleasures more than lovers of God." These are to know that God has a people who fear Him and keep His commandments. They are to be taught how to choose and prepare the simple food that is best suited to nourish the body and preserve the health.—Manuscript 115, 1903.

Danger of Missing the Mark

There is danger, in the establishment of restaurants, of losing sight of the work that most needs to be done. There is danger of the workers' losing sight of the work of soul saving as they carry forward the business part of the enterprise. There is danger that the business part of the work will be allowed to crowd out the spiritual part.

Some good is being done by the restaurant work. Men and women are being educated to dispense with meat and other injurious articles of diet. But who are being fed with the bread of life? Is the purpose of God being fulfilled if in this work there are no conversions? It is time that we called a halt, lest we spend our energies in the establishment of a work that does little to make ready a people for the coming of the Lord.

The only object in the establishment of restaurants was to remove prejudice from the minds of men and women, and win them to the truth. The same effort put forth in circulating our publications, in doing evangelistic work, would tell far more for the saving of souls.

[307]
Personal Work to be Done

Our restaurant workers are not doing the personal work that they should do to bring the truth before those who come for meals. And in some respects impressions are being made on the minds of the workers that are not favorable to a growth in grace.

The food itself will not sanctify the souls of those who serve. Are the words being fulfilled? "For our gospel came not unto you in word only, but also in power, and in the Holy Ghost, and in much assurance; ... so that ye were ensamples to all that believe.... For from you sounded out the word of the Lord ... in every place."

This is the work that God has outlined before us. Is it done? Are there employed in our restaurants workers who have sufficient spiritual strength to stand against the temptations that they will meet in the cities?

Let there be shown more of a desire to receive the Holy Spirit as an instructor, and less of a desire to carry forward in human wisdom a work involving so much.

Our young men and young women are to be put to work where their capabilities will be used to the best account. They are to stand where they can carry on Christ's work of soul saving. They should not be kept in a work in which they are continually on losing ground, a work in which no souls are brought to a knowledge of the truth.

Usefulness Determined by Results

It is not the large number of meals served that brings glory to God. What does this avail if not one soul has been converted, to gladden the hearts of the workers?

The question was asked, What does all the work that has been done amount to? Has it had a sanctifying, hallowing influence upon the minds of the workers, or has it been the means of bringing them into temptations that have destroyed their peace and hope?

Let our ministers and physicians reason from cause to effect. Unless our restaurant work brings favorable spiritual results, let the world do their own serving of tables and let the Lord's people take up a work in which their talents will be put out to the exchangers.

The time has come for the Lord's people to be sure that they are engaged in a work that produces as well as consumes. Those who have united themselves with the church are to situate themselves in such a way that their spiritual power will not diminish, but increase. They are not to place themselves where they will have no opportunity to grow in grace.—Manuscript 84, 1903.

[308]

A Sanitarium Near New York

We need a sanitarium and a school in the vicinity of New York City, and the longer the delay in the securing of these, the more difficult it will become.

It would be well to secure a place as a home for our mission workers outside of the city. It is of great importance that they have the advantages of pure water, free from all contamination. For this reason, it is often well to consider the advantages of locations among the hills. And there should be some land, where fruit and vegetables might be raised for the benefit of the workers. Let it be a mission in as healthful a place as possible, and let there be connected with it a small sanitarium. A place in the city should also be secured where simple treatments might be administered.

Such a home would be a welcome retreat for our workers, where they may be away from the bustle and confusion of the city. The exercise called for in climbing hills is often a great benefit to our ministers, physicians, or other workers who are in danger of failing to take sufficient exercise.

Let such homes be secured in the neighborhood of several cities, and earnest, determined efforts be put forth by capable men to give in these cities the warning message that is to go to all the world. We have only touched, as it were, a few of the cities.

Let men of sound judgment be appointed, not to publish abroad their intentions, but to search for such properties in the rural districts, in easy access to the cities, suitable for small training schools for workers, and where facilities may also be provided for treating the sick and weary souls who know not the truth. Look for such places just out from the large cities, where suitable buildings may be secured, either as gift from the owners, or purchased at a reasonable price by the gifts of our people. Do not erect buildings in the noisy cities.

Securing of Buildings

In every city where the truth is proclaimed, churches are to be raised up. In some large cities there must be churches in various parts of the city. In some places, meetinghouses will be offered for sale at reasonable rates, which can be purchased advantageously. In some important places there will be offered for sale properties that are especially suitable for sanitarium work. The advantages of these should be carefully considered.

In order that some of these places may be secured for our work, it will be necessary carefully to husband the resources, no extravagant outlay being made in any one place. The very simplicity of the buildings that we use will be a lesson in harmony with the truths we have to present. For our sanitarium work we must secure buildings whose appearance and arrangement will be a demonstration of health principles.

Location of Workers

It will be a great advantage to have our buildings in retired locations so far as possible. The healthfulness of the surroundings should be fully considered. Locations should be selected a little out from the noisy cities. Those who labor in the large cities need special advantages, that they may not be called to sacrifice life or health unnecessarily.

I write these things because it has been presented to me as a matter of importance that our workers should so far as possible avoid everything that would imperil their health. We need to exercise the best of judgment in these matters. Feeble or aged men and women should not be sent to labor in unhealthful, crowded cities. Let them labor where their lives will not be needlessly sacrificed. Our brethren who bring the truth to the cities must not be obliged to imperil their health in the noise and bustle and confusion, if retired places can be secured.

Those who are engaged in the difficult and trying work in the cities should receive every encouragement possible. Let them not be subjected to unkind criticism from their brethren. We must have a care for the Lord's workers who are opening the light of truth to those who are in the darkness of error. We have a high standard presented before us.

Every gospel minister should be a friend to the poor, the afflicted, and the oppressed among God's believing people. Christ was always the poor man's friend, and the interests of the poor need to be sacredly guarded. There has too often been a wonderful dearth of Christ's compassion and loving interest in the poor and afflicted. Love, sacred, refined love, is to be exercised in behalf of the poor and unfortunate.—Letter 168, 1909.

Redeeming the Time

The terrible disasters that are befalling great cities ought to arouse us to intense activity in giving the warning message to the people in these congested centers of population while we still have an opportunity. The most favorable time for the presentation of our message in the cities has passed by. Sin and wickedness are rapidly increasing; and now we shall have to redeem the time by laboring all the more earnestly.—Letter 148, 1906.

Seek Rural Homes

To parents who are living in the cities the Lord is sending the warning cry, Gather your children into your own houses; gather them away from those who are disregarding the commandments of God, who are teaching and practicing evil. Get out of the cities as fast as possible.

Parents can secure small homes in the country, with land for cultivation where they can have orchards and where they can raise vegetables and small fruits to take the place of flesh-meat, which is so corrupting to the lifeblood coursing through the veins. On such places the children will not be surrounded with the corrupting influences of city life. God will help His people to find such homes outside of the cities.—Manuscript 133, 1902.

Rural Location for Institutions

As far as possible, our institutions should be located away from the cities. We must have workers for these institutions, and if they are located in the city, that means that families of our people must settle near them. But it is not God's will that His people shall settle in the cities, where there is constant turmoil and confusion. Their children should be spared this; for the whole system is demoralized by the hurry and rush and noise.

The Lord desires His people to move into the country, where they can settle on the land and raise their own fruit and vegetables, and where their children can be brought in direct contact with the works of God in nature. Take your families away from the cities, is my message.—Letter 182, 1902.

Work for the Outcasts

Of late [1899], a great interest has been aroused for the poor and outcast classes; a great work has been entered upon for the uplifting of the fallen and degraded. This in itself is a good work. We should ever have the Spirit of Christ, and we are to do the same class of work that He did for suffering humanity. The Lord has a work to be done for the outcasts. There is no question but that it is the duty of some to labor among them and try to save the souls that are perishing. This will have its place in connection with the proclamation of the third angel's message and the reception of Bible truth. But there is danger of loading down everyone with this class of work because of the intensity with which it is carried on. There is danger of leading men to center their energies in this line when God has called them to another work.

The great question of our duty to humanity is a serious one, and much of the grace of God is needed in deciding how to work so as to accomplish the greatest amount of good. Not all are called to begin their work by laboring among the lowest classes. God does not require His workmen to obtain their education and training in order to devote themselves exclusively to these classes.

The working of God is manifest in a way which will establish confidence that the work is of His devising, and that sound principles underlie every action. But I have had instruction from God that there is danger of planning for the outcasts in a way which will lead to spasmodic and excitable movements. These will produce no really beneficial results. A class will be encouraged to do a kind of work which will amount to the least in strengthening all parts of the work by harmonious action.

The gospel invitation is to be given to the rich and the poor, the high and the low, and we must devise means for carrying the truth into new places and to all classes of people. The Lord bids us, "Go out into the highways and hedges, and compel them to come in, that My house may be filled." He says, "Begin in the highways; thoroughly work the highways; prepare a company who in unity with you can go forth to do the very work that Christ did in seeking and saving the lost."

Christ preached the gospel to the poor, but He did not confine His labors to this class. He worked for all who would hear His word—not only the publican and the outcasts, but the rich and cultivated Pharisee, the Jewish nobleman, the centurion, and the Roman ruler. This is the kind of work I have ever seen should be done. We are not to strain every spiritual sinew and nerve to work for the lowest classes, and make that work the all in all. There are others whom we must bring to the Master, souls who need the truth, who are bearing responsibilities, and who will work with all their sanctified ability for the high places as well as for the low places.

The work for the poorer classes has no limit. It can never be got through with, and it must be treated as a part of the great whole. To give our first attention to this work, while there are vast portions of the Lord's vineyard open to culture and yet untouched, is to begin in the wrong place. As the right arm is to the body, so is the medical missionary work to the third angel's message. But the right arm is not to become the whole body. The work of seeking the outcasts is important, but it is not to become the great burden of our mission.—Manuscript 3, 1899

Safeguard the Youth

Great care should be taken in working for the outcasts. Neither young men nor young women should be sent into the lowest places of our cities. The sight of the eyes and the hearing of the ears of young men and women should be kept from evil. There is much that the youth can do for the Master. If they will watch and pray and make God their trust, they will be prepared to do various kinds of excellent work under the supervision of experienced laborers.—Manuscript 33, 1901.

[313]

Difficulties Overcome

In visions of the night I was shown the difficulties that must be met in the work of warning the people in the cities; but in spite of difficulties and discouragements, efforts should be made to preach the truth to all classes....

The Lord desires His people to arise and do their appointed work. The responsibility of warning the world rests not upon the ministry alone. The lay members of the church are to share in the work of soul saving. By means of missionary visits and by a wise distribution of our literature, many who have never been warned may be reached. Let companies be organized to search for souls. Let the church members visit their neighbors and open to them the Scriptures. Some may be set to work in the hedges, and thus, by wise planning, the truth may be preached in all districts.

With perseverance in this work, increasing aptitude for it will come, and many will see fruit of their labors in the salvation of souls. These converted ones will, in turn, teach others. Thus the seed will be sown in many places, and the truth be proclaimed to all.—The Review and Herald, January 25, 1912.

* * * * *

For Further Study

Medical Missionary Work in Cities:
Counsels on Health, 549-553; (Testimonies for the Church 7:110-114).

The Work in the Cities:
Testimonies for the Church 7:34-36.
The Work in Greater New York:
Testimonies for the Church 7:37-39;
Testimonies for the Church 9:137-151.
Special Work in Centers of Travel:
Counsels on Health, 500, 501.
Sanitariums as City Outposts:
Counsels on Health, 554-556.
City Churches to Conduct Treatment Rooms:
Counsels on Health, 468 (Testimonies for the Church 6:113).
City Missions:
Counsels on Health, 443, 444 (Testimonies for the Church 9:112, 113).
Rescue Work Often Superficial and Unsatisfactory:
Testimonies for the Church 8:184, 185.
The Health-Food and Restaurant Work:
Counsels on Health, 471-496 (Testimonies for the Church 7:54-57, 60, 115-120, 121-126, 128, 129, 132-137).

Section 18—Extent of the Work

Co-workers With Christ

One who believes in Jesus Christ as a personal Saviour is to be a co-worker with Him, bound up with His heart of infinite love, cooperating with Him in works of self-denial and benevolence. He to whom Christ has revealed His pardoning grace will, in practicing the works of Christ, find himself linked up with Christ. God calls upon those for whom He has made such an infinite sacrifice, to take their position as laborers together with Him in developing the gracious operations of God's divine benevolence.

Christ has withdrawn Himself from the earth, but His followers are still left in the world. His church, consisting of those who love Him, are to give in word and action, in their unselfish love and benevolence, a representation of Christ's love. They are to be the means, by practicing self-denial and bearing the cross, of implanting the principle of love in the hearts of those who are unacquainted with the Saviour by experimental knowledge.

The Purpose of Churches

Upon all who believe, God has placed the burden of raising up churches, for the express purpose of educating men and women to use their entrusted capabilities for the benefit of the world, employing the means He has lent for His glory. He has made human beings His stewards. Gladly and generously they are to use the means in their possession for the advancement of righteousness and truth. They are to employ His entrusted talents in building up His work and enlarging His kingdom.

Ministers as Medical Missionaries

Our churches, large and small, are not to be treated in such a way that they will be helplessly dependent upon ministerial aid. The members are to be so established in the faith that they will have an intelligent knowledge of medical missionary work. They are to follow Christ's example, ministering to those around them. Faithfully they are to fulfill the vows made at their baptism, the vow that they will practice the lessons taught in the life of Christ. Through sanctification of the truth as it is in Jesus they are to plant in hearts the living principles of saving faith. They are to work together to keep alive in the church the principles of self-denial and self-sacrifice, which Christ, His divinity clothed with humanity, followed in His medical missionary work. It is imparting the knowledge of Christ's love and tenderness that gives efficiency to missionary operations.

An Army of Workers

The Lord Jesus desires the members of His church to be an army of workers, laboring for Him according to their varied capabilities, and carrying out the principles of self-denial and self-sacrifice, preserving that love for God which drew them away from the world and which will draw them together, away from separate confederacies, from distant, detached parties. The work is to be one grand, harmonious whole in Christ Jesus. The faith that works by love and purifies the soul is the holy, uplifting, sanctifying agency which is to soften and subdue jarring human nature. The love of Christ is to constrain the believers, causing them to blend in harmonious action at the cross of Calvary. As they live the principles which separated them from the world, they will be bound to one another by the sacred cords of Christian love.

Work the Works of Christ

With grace in their hearts believers are to work the works of Christ, placing themselves, soul, body, and spirit, on His side, as His human hand, to impart His love to those who are out of the fold. Believers are to associate together in Christian fellowship, regarding one another as brothers and sisters in the Lord. They are to love one another as Christ loved them. They are to be lights for God, shining in the church and in the world, receiving grace for grace as they impart to others. Thus they are constantly kept in spiritual nearness to God. They reflect the image of Christ.

Sanctified love is diffusive, refusing to be bound by the home or the church. It seeks to save perishing souls. Every heart that has felt the love of a sin-forgiving Saviour finds itself allied to every other Christian heart. True believers will unite with one another in working for souls ready to perish. Let not our ministers expend time and energy in laboring for those who know the truth. Let them instead seek for those outside the fold, and each should stimulate the other to earnest action in well-defined, sanctified efforts to save the poor souls who are perishing in their sins.

A Living Church

When our churches will fulfill the duty resting upon them, they will be living, working agencies for the Master. The manifestation of Christian love will fill the soul with a deeper, more earnest fervor to work for Him who gave His life to save the world. By being good and doing good Christ's followers expel selfishness from the soul. To them the most costly sacrifice seems too cheap to give. They see a large vineyard to be worked, and they realize that they must be prepared by divine grace to labor patiently, earnestly, in season and out of season, in a sphere which knows no boundaries. They obtain victory after victory, increasing in experience and efficiency, extending on all sides their earnest efforts to win souls for Christ. They use to the best advantage their increasing experience; their hearts are melted by the love of Christ.

Opportunities

All can labor for the salvation of those who are out of the ark of safety. When church members stand pledged to the service of God, pledged to do missionary work, when they take hold of the work unselfishly because they love the souls for whom Christ has died and are desirous of uniting with the great Medical Missionary, the Lord will come very near to them to instruct them. Life is full of opportunities for practical missionaries. Every man, woman, and child can sow each day the seeds of kind words and unselfish deeds.

A Thousand Streams

We shall see the medical missionary work broadening and deepening at every point of its progress, because of the inflowing of hundreds and thousands of streams, until the whole earth is covered as the waters cover the sea. Our ministers are displeasing God by their feeble efforts to let the truths of His word shine forth to the world. Nothing so strengthens the churches as to see the work progressing in other portions of the vineyard. When the ministers understand the great blessing to be derived from laboring for those who know not the truth, they will leave the churches, after impressing upon them the importance of devising plans and methods whereby they can do within their borders the same kind of work that the ministers of the gospel are doing in the regions beyond.

Lifework a School

The world is not a croquet ground, on which we are to amuse ourselves; it is a school where we are to study earnestly and thoroughly the lessons given in the word of God. There they may learn how to receive and how to impart. There they may learn how to seek for souls in the highways and byways of life. How earnestly the games of this world are engaged in! If those who engage in them would strive as earnestly for the crown of life which fadeth not away, what victories they would gain! They would become medical missionaries, and they would see how much they could do to relieve suffering humanity. What a blessing they would be! What we need is practical education. Ministers and people, practice the lessons Christ has given in His word, and you will become Christlike in character.—Manuscript 32, 1901.

Truth to Be Presented in Many Ways

The church of Christ is dependent on Him for her very existence. Only through Him can it gain continued life and strength. The members are to live constantly in the most intimate vital relationship with the Saviour. They are to follow in His steps of self-denial and sacrifice. They are to go forth into the highways and byways of life to win souls to Him, using every possible means to make the truth appear in its true character before the world.

The truth is to be presented in various ways. Some in the higher walks of life will grasp it as it is presented in figures and parables. As men labor to unfold the truth with clearness that conviction may come to their hearers, the Lord is present as He promised to be. As they go forth on their mission, teaching all things whatsoever Christ has commanded, the promise will be fulfilled, "Lo, I am with you alway, even unto the end of the world." Those who are honest in heart will see the importance of the truth for this time, and will take their place in the ranks of those who are keeping and teaching the commandments.—Letter 223, 1905.

How to Reveal Christ

There is a great work to be done. How shall we reveal Christ? I know of no better way ... than to take hold of the medical missionary work in connection with the ministry. Wherever you go, there begin to work. Take an interest in those around you who need help and light. You may stand and preach to those here who know the truth; you may preach sermon after sermon to them, but they do not appreciate it. Why? Because they are inactive. Everyone who is able to go out and work should bring to the foundation stone, not hay, wood, or stubble, but gold, silver, and precious stones.—The General Conference Bulletin, 1901, Extra No. 18.

A New Element

A new element needs to be brought into the work. God's people must receive the warning, and work for souls right where they are; for people do not realize their great need and peril. Christ sought the people where they were, and placed before them the great truths in regard to His kingdom. As He went from place to place, He blessed and comforted the suffering and healed the sick. This is our work. God would have us relieve the necessities of the destitute. The reason that the Lord does not manifest His power more decidedly is because there is so little spirituality among those who claim to believe the truth.—Letter 42, 1898.

Opportunities for All

"And they went forth, and preached everywhere, the Lord working with them, and confirming the word with signs following."

The words spoken to the disciples are spoken to us also. None need think that the day for working as the apostles worked is past. Men and women can today work as Christ has given them example. To all will come opportunities to minister to sin-sick souls and to those in need of physical healing. Physical healing is a science of heavenly birth, bound up with the gospel commission.—Manuscript 16, 1904.

Will Revive the Churches

Get the young men and women in the churches to work. Combine medical missionary work with the proclamation of the third angel's message. Make regular, organized efforts to lift the church members out of the dead level in which they have been for years. Send out into the churches workers who will live the principles of health reform. Let those be sent who can see the necessity of self-denial in appetite, or they will be a snare to the church. See if the breath of life will not then come into our churches.—Testimonies for the Church 6:267.

Be Practical Missionaries

In every place the sick may be found, and those who go forth as workers for Christ should be true health reformers, prepared to give those who are sick the simple treatments that will relieve them, and then pray with them. Thus they will open the door for the entrance of the truth. The doing of this work will be followed by good results. Our Sabbath-keeping families should keep their minds filled with helpful principles of health reform and other lines of truth, that they may be a help to their neighbors. Be practical missionaries. Gather up all the knowledge possible that will help to combat disease. This may be done by those who are diligent students.

But few can take a course of training in our medical institutions. But all can study our health literature and become intelligent on this important subject.—Manuscript 19, 1911.

Work for Children and Youth

The Lord has appointed the youth to be His helping hand. If in every church they would consecrate themselves to Him, if they would practice self-denial in the home, relieving their careworn mother, the mother could find time to make neighborly visits, and, when opportunity offered, they could themselves give assistance by doing little errands of mercy and love. Books and papers treating on the subject of health and temperance could be placed in many homes. The circulation of this literature is an important matter; for thus precious knowledge can be imparted in regard to the treatment of disease—knowledge that would be a great blessing to those who cannot afford to pay for a physician's visits.—Testimonies for the Church 7:64, 65.

In Time of Persecution

As religious aggression subverts the liberties of our nation, those who would stand for freedom of conscience will be placed in unfavorable positions. For their own sake they should, while they have opportunity, become intelligent in regard to disease, its causes, prevention, and cure. And those who do this will find a field of labor anywhere. There will be suffering ones, plenty of them, who will need help, not only among those of our own faith, but largely among those who know not the truth. The shortness of time demands an energy that has not been aroused among those who claim to believe the present truth.—Counsels on Health, 506.

The Appeal of Unpromising Fields

The instruction the Lord has given me is that a field should not be shunned because it has objectionable features. This world was seared and marred by the curse, but still Christ came to it. He, the Son of the most high God, was made flesh, and dwelt among us. He willingly left His high command to take His place at the head of a fallen race, becoming poor, that through His poverty we might be made rich.—An Appeal for the Medical Missionary College, pages 11, 12.

Self-Supporting Effort

The Macedonian cry is coming from every quarter. Shall men go to the "regular lines" to see whether they will be permitted to labor, or shall they go out and work as best they can, depending on their own abilities and on the help of the Lord, beginning in a humble way and creating an interest in the truth in places in which nothing has been done to give the warning message?

The Lord has encouraged those who have started out on their own responsibility to work for Him, their hearts filled with love for souls ready to perish. A true missionary spirit will be imparted to those who seek earnestly to know God and Jesus Christ, whom He hath sent. The Lord lives and reigns. Young men, go forth into the places to which you are directed by the Spirit of the Lord. Work with your hands, that you may be self-supporting, and as you have opportunity proclaim the message of warning.—Letter 60, 1901.

Medical Missions in Every City

Intemperance has filled our world, and medical missions should be established in every city. By this I do not mean that expensive institutions should be established, calling for a large outlay of means. These missions are to be conducted in such a way that they will not be a heavy drain on the cause; and their work is to prepare the way for the establishment of present truth. Medical missionary work should have its representative in every place in connection with the establishment of our churches. The relief of bodily suffering opens the way for the healing of the sin-sick soul.—Manuscript 88, 1902.

Advantages of Small Schools

The Lord is certainly opening the way for us as a people to divide and subdivide the companies that have been growing too large to work together to the greatest advantage. And this dividing should be done, not only that the students may have greater advantages, but that the teachers may be benefited, and life and health spared. To establish another school will be better than further enlargement of the school at -----. Let another locality have the advantage of one of our educational institutions. Secure for it the best talent, and guard against the dangers of an overcrowded school.—Letter 253, 1908.

Many Training Schools

Let forces be set at work to clear new ground, to establish new centers of influence, wherever an opening can be found. Rally workers who possess true missionary zeal, and let them go forth to diffuse light and knowledge far and near. Let them take the living principles of health reform into the communities that to a large degree are ignorant of these principles....

[323] After a time, as the work advances, schools will be established in many cities, where workers can be quickly educated and trained for service. The students and their teachers can go out with our publications and spread the truth by means of the printed page. Desirable places can be secured for meetings to be held, and here the people can be invited to gather. Let those who are fitted for the work, the young and middle-aged, act a disinterested, unselfish part in laboring for the fields white for the harvest that are yet unworked.—Manuscript 11, 1908.

Sanitariums Connected With Schools

In every place where schools are established we are to study what industries can be started that will give the students employment. Small sanitariums should be established in connection with our larger schools, that the students may have opportunity to gain a knowledge of medical missionary work. This line of work is to be brought into our schools as part of the regular instruction.—Letter 25, 1902.

Many Small Sanitariums

It is that thirsting souls may be led to the living water that we plead for sanitariums, not expensive, mammoth sanitariums, but homelike institutions, in pleasant places.

Never, never build mammoth institutions. Let these institutions be small, and let there be more of them, that the work of winning souls to Christ may be accomplished. It may often be necessary to start sanitarium work in the city, but never build a sanitarium in a city. Rent a building, and keep looking for a suitable place out of the city. The sick are to be reached, not by massive buildings, but by the establishment of many small sanitariums, which are to be as lights shining in a dark place. Those who are engaged in this work are to reflect the sunlight of Christ's face. They are to be as salt that has not lost its savor. By sanitarium work, properly conducted, the influence of true, pure religion will be extended to many souls.

From our sanitariums trained workers are to go forth into places where the truth has never been proclaimed, and do missionary work for the Master.—Letter 17, 1905.

Opportunities to Purchase Sanitarium Properties

I have just read again your letter of April 25, 1905, and will try to write something in reply. I shall not be able to write a long letter, for the mail goes at noon today.

I wish to say that I do not see any objections to securing the buildings mentioned. The light given me is that buildings suitable for our work will be offered to us at a price far below their cost, making it possible for us to secure them. This has been the case in our experience in establishing sanitarium work in southern California, and it will be the case in other countries. Advantage should be taken of these opportunities to establish and extend gospel medical missionary work; for time is short, and we must sow the seeds of health-reform principles.

When an opportunity presents itself to purchase at a low price buildings in which our work may be carried on, let us take advantage of these opportunities. Had this been done by the leaders of the medical work in -----, there would now be many, many plants in our cities in America, cities that have not yet been enlightened by the truth upon health reform. Therefore forbid not those who desire to extend medical missionary work in some other part of Australia. Adelaide is a long way from Sydney. A sanitarium there would not interfere with the work of Wahroonga Sanitarium.

There should be sanitariums near all our large cities. Advantage should be taken of the opportunities to purchase buildings in favorable locations, that the standard of truth may be planted in many places.

I have been instructed that we are not to delay to do the work that needs to be done in health-reform lines. Through this work we are to reach souls in the highways and the byways. I have been given special light that in our sanitariums many souls will receive and obey present truth. In these institutions men and women are to be taught how to care for their own bodies, and at the same time how to become sound in the faith. They are to be taught what is meant by eating the flesh and drinking the blood of the Son of God. Said Christ, "The words that I speak unto you, they are spirit, and they are life."

[325]
Sanitariums to Educate

Our sanitariums are to be schools in which instruction shall be given in medical missionary lines. They are to bring to sin-sick souls the leaves of the tree of life, which will restore to them peace and hope and faith in Christ Jesus. Forbid not those who have a desire to extend this work. Let the light shine forth. All worthy health productions will create an interest in health reform. Forbid them not. The Lord would have all opportunities to extend the work taken advantage of....

In every large city there should be a representation of true medical missionary work. The principles of genuine health reform are to be brought out in clear lines, in our health publications, and in lectures delivered to the patients in our sanitariums. In every city there are men and women who would go to a sanitarium were it near at hand, who would not be able to go to one a long way off. There are many who will be convicted and converted, who now appear indifferent. I look at this matter in a very decided light.

Let many now ask, "Lord, what wilt Thou have me to do?" It is the Lord's purpose that His method of healing without drugs shall be brought into prominence in every large city through our medical institutions. God invests with holy dignity those who go forth in His power to heal the sick. Let the light shine forth farther and still farther, in every place to which it is possible to obtain entrance. Satan will make the work as difficult as possible, but divine power will attend all truehearted workers. Guided by our heavenly Father's hand, let us go forward improving every opportunity to extend the work of God.

We shall have to labor under difficulties, but because of this, let not our zeal flag. The Bible does not acknowledge a believer who is idle, however high his profession may be.—Letter 203, 1905.

Not as a Business Speculation

During the past few months I have been exceedingly busy, writing out the instruction given me as the Lord's witness and messenger. Often I have written ten pages before others were up in the morning. I have been obliged to bear urgent messages to many persons....

The Lord knows all the perils that surround us at this time. He knows our necessities. He knows the strength that we need in order to uphold the truth in its elevated, holy character, and He will supply all our need. We are not to be depressed by any trials that may come.

I wish to say to you that if God opens the way for the brethren in other parts of Australia to purchase property that may be used for sanitarium work, such as the place that Brother ----- has written about, forbid them not. Utter not one word of remonstrance. There are many cities to be worked, and medical missionary work is not to be confined to a few centers.

For a long time the Battle Creek Sanitarium was the only medical institution conducted by our people. But for many years light has been given that sanitariums should be established near every large city. Sanitariums should be established near such cities as Melbourne and Adelaide. And when opportunities come to establish the work in still other places, never are we to reach out the hand and say: No, you must not create an interest in other places, for fear that our patronage will be decreased.

If sanitarium work is the means by which the way is to be opened for the proclamation of the truth, encourage and do not discourage those who are trying to advance this work.

Faith Needed

May the Lord increase our faith and help us to see that He desires us all to become acquainted with His ministry of healing and with the mercy seat. He desires the light of His grace to shine forth from many places. We are living in the last days. Troublous times are before us. He who understands the necessities of the situation arranges that advantages should be brought to the workers in various places, to enable them more effectually to arouse the attention of the people. He knows the needs and the necessities of the feeblest of His flock, and He sends His own message into the highways and the byways. He loves us with an everlasting love....

The Light to Shine

In our sanitariums the truth is to be cherished, not banished or hidden from sight. The light is to shine forth in clear, distinct rays. These institutions are the Lord's facilities for the revival of pure, elevated morality. We do not establish them as a speculative business, but to help men and women to follow right habits of living.

Christ, the great Medical Missionary, is no longer in our world in person. But He has not left the world in darkness. To His subjects He has given the commission, "Go ye into all the world, and preach the gospel to every creature," "teaching them to observe all things whatsoever I have commanded you: and, lo, I am with you alway, even unto the end of the world." The great questions of Bible truth are to enter into the very heart of society, to reform and convert men and women, bringing them to see the great necessity of preparing for the mansions that Christ told His disciples He would prepare for those that love Him....

A United Work

Our work is to gain a knowledge of Him who is the way, the truth, and the life. We are to interest people in the subjects that concern the health of the body, as well as in the subjects that concern the health of the soul. Believers have a decided message to bear to prepare the way for the kingdom of God. The will of the Lord is to be done on earth. We have not one moment to spend in idle speculation. "Prepare ye the way of the Lord, make His paths straight," is the message that we are to proclaim. Amidst all the confusion that now fills the world, a clear, decided message is to be heard.

Some will be attracted by one phase of the gospel, and some by another. We are instructed by our Lord to work in such a way that all classes will be reached. The message must go to the whole world. Our sanitariums are to help to make up the number of God's people. We are not to establish a few mammoth institutions; for thus it would be impossible to give the patients the messages that will bring health to the soul. Small sanitariums are to be established in many places.

Be Vigilant

Satan will introduce every form of error in an effort to lead souls away from the work to be accomplished in these last days. There needs to be a decided awakening, in accordance with the importance of the subjects we are presenting. The conversion of souls is now to be our one object. Every facility for the advancement of God's cause is to be put into use, that His will may be done on earth as it is done in heaven. We cannot afford to be irreligious and indifferent now. We must take advantage of the means that the Lord has placed in our hands for the carrying forward of medical missionary work. Through this work infidels will be converted. Through the wonderful restorations taking place in our sanitariums, souls will be led to look to Christ as the Great Healer of soul and body.—Letter 233, 1905.

Move With Understanding

Let those who contemplate the establishment of a sanitarium be subject to the molding and fashioning of the Spirit of God. Such men will not misrepresent Christ in the character building. Let all who are in positions of trust use the holy oil of grace in spirit, in word, and in action. Let them do thorough work in purifying the soul temple, that they may have an understanding of the work that they contemplate undertaking, and that they may be able to sow seeds of truth in many hearts. In one hand they are to carry the gospel for the relief of sin-burdened souls, and in the other hand they are to carry remedies for the relief of physical suffering. Thus they will be true medical missionaries for God.—Manuscript 41, 1902.

Fulfilling God's Plans

I am instructed to tell our people that it will be necessary for them to give all that they can spare of their means for the establishment of sanitariums that will do the work which the Lord says must be done. These sanitariums are to be under the supervision of men who are controlled by the Holy Spirit, men who will carry out, not their own plans, but the plans of God....

We are to cooperate with the Lord Jesus in the great work of presenting the truth for this time to the people of the world. We need health, we need fortitude; we need a pure, unadulterated faith in the gospel message. We need to study the book of Revelation, especially the important messages that are to be borne to our world. When, if not now, are these messages to be given?

Now and ever we are to stand as a distinct and peculiar people, free from all worldly policy, unembarrassed by confederacy with those who have not wisdom to discern the claims of God so plainly set forth in His law.—Letter 110, 1902.

Securing Help From the Wealthy

We have many interests to be developed. We have come into possession of institutions in various places. In southern California we have three sanitariums that have proved to be a great blessing to many. Through the providence of God we shall continue to come into possession of institutions in various places. We must extend our influence as widely as possible....

There are wealthy men who have in trust the Lord's money, and we have a perfect right to ask them to help us in our missionary work. We have a work to be carried on in all parts of the world, and must have means. Will not some of these wealthy men come to our help? The scripture we have read [Isaiah 60:1.] encourages us to believe that they will. There are some who would consider it a privilege.—Manuscript 113, 1908.

Our Needs to Be Presented

We are to do special work for those who are in high positions of trust. The Lord calls upon those to whom He has entrusted His goods, to use in His service their talents of intellect and of means. Some will be impressed by the Holy Spirit to invest the Lord's means in a way that will advance His work. They will fulfill His purpose by helping to create centers of influence in our large cities. Our workers should represent before these men a plain statement of our needs. Let them know what we need in order to help the poor and needy, and to establish the work on a firm basis.—Manuscript 79, 1900

Plants in Foreign Fields

When those in charge of the medical missionary work realize that plants must be made in many places, God's work will be carried forward even in the hardest fields. When men see that it is necessary to establish the medical missionary work in America, can they not see that the same work is needed in new fields, where there is nothing to give character to the work?

To send missionaries into a foreign field to do missionary work, unprovided with facilities and means, is like requiring bricks to be made without straw.

Let God's servants act like wise men, remembering that the work in every part of the world is to assist the work in every other part. "Be ye not unwise, but understanding what the will of the Lord is." ...

Workers in new places where there may not be one believer in present truth should be furnished with means for helping the needy. They meet with many who are sick and in need of help. As they relieve their temporal necessities, the way opens for them to speak of the Saviour and His precious truth. These workers must be given facilities for preparing the way of the Lord and making straight in the desert a highway for our God. Let our publishing houses help by gifts of books and papers, and let our sanitariums furnish facilities for the care of the sick....

Those who go into new fields to use the breaking-up plow in preparing the soil for the sowing of the seed of truth are to be encouraged, prayed for, sustained. It is the Lord's desire that every worker sent into new fields shall be furnished with means and facilities for the successful accomplishment of His work. They are to receive help and encouragement from those in the home field, that they may have courage to overcome the difficulties that they meet in their work.—Letter 92, 1902.

Health Institutions in Many Lands

God has qualified His people to enlighten the world. He has entrusted them with faculties by which they are to extend His work until it shall encircle the globe. In all parts of the earth they are to establish sanitariums, schools, publishing houses, and kindred facilities for the accomplishment of His work.

The closing message of the gospel is to be carried to "every nation, and kindred, and tongue, and people." Revelation 14:6. In foreign countries many enterprises for the advancement of this message must yet be begun and carried forward. The opening of hygienic restaurants and treatment rooms, and the establishment of sanitariums for the care of the sick and the suffering, is just as necessary in Europe as in America. In many lands, medical missions are to be established to act as God's helping hand in ministering to the afflicted.

Christ cooperates with those who engage in medical missionary work. Men and women who unselfishly do what they can to establish sanitariums and treatment rooms in many lands will be richly rewarded. Those who visit these institutions will be benefited physically, mentally, and spiritually—the weary will be refreshed, the sick restored to health, the sin-burdened relieved. In far-off countries, from those whose hearts are by these agencies turned from the service of sin unto righteousness, will be heard thanksgiving and the voice of melody. By their songs of grateful praise a testimony will be borne that will win others to allegiance and to fellowship with Christ.—Counsels on Health, 215.

Go Forward

When I think of the history of our work during the past ten years I can but say, See what the Lord hath wrought. Mercifully He has been working to shed light upon the pathway of His people. In spite of the hindrances that have been met with in the work, we need not feel sadness, except as we see a failure on the part of God's people to follow their Leader step by step....

The work in the cities is the essential work for this time, and is now to be taken hold of in faith. When the cities are worked as God would have them, the result will be the setting in operation of a mighty movement such as we have not yet witnessed. May the Lord give wisdom to our brethren that they may know how to carry forward the work in harmony with His will. With mighty power the cry is to be sounded in our large centers of population: "Behold, the Bridegroom cometh; go ye out to meet Him."

Every Agency to be Set in Operation

The ordained minister alone is not equal to the task of warning the world. God is calling not only upon ministers, but also upon physicians, nurses, canvassers, Bible workers, and other consecrated laymen of varied talents who have a knowledge of present truth, to consider the needs of the unwarned cities. There should be one hundred workers actively engaged in personal missionary work where now there is but one. Time is rapidly passing. There is much work to be done before satanic opposition shall close up the way. Every agency must be set in operation, that present opportunities may be wisely improved.

[332]

The Lord is calling upon the men and women who have the light of truth for this time to engage in genuine, personal missionary work. Especially are the church members living in the cities to exercise, in all humility, their God-given talents in laboring with those who are willing to hear the message that should come to the world at this time. There are great blessings in store for those who fully surrender to the call of God. As such workers undertake to win souls for Jesus, they will find that many who never could be reached in any other way will respond to intelligent personal effort.

A working church is a living church. Church members, let the light shine forth. Let your voices be heard in humble prayer, in witness against the intemperance, the folly, and the amusements of this world, and in the proclamation of the truth for this time. Your voice, your influence, your time—all these are gifts from God, and are to be used in winning souls to Christ. Visit your neighbors, and show an interest in the salvation of their souls. Arouse every spiritual energy to action. Tell those whom you visit that the end of all things is at hand. The Lord Jesus Christ will open the door of their hearts, and will make lasting impressions upon their minds.

Strive to arouse men and women from their spiritual insensibility. Tell them how you found Jesus, and how blessed you have been since you gained an experience in His service. Tell them what blessing comes to you as you sit at the feet of Jesus and learn precious lessons from His word. Tell them of the gladness and joy that are found in the Christian life. Your warm, fervent words will convince them that you have found the pearl of great price. Let your cheerful, encouraging words show that you have certainly found the higher education. This is genuine missionary work, and as it is done, many will awake as from a dream.

Listen to the voice of Jesus as it comes sounding down along the line to our time, addressing the professed Christian who stands idle in the marketplace: "Why stand ye here all the day idle? ... Go ye also into the vineyard." Work while it is day; for the night cometh, in which no man can work....

A Time of Overwhelming Interest

Soon strife among the nations will break out with an intensity that we do not now anticipate. The present is a time of overwhelming interest to all living. Rulers and statesmen, men who occupy positions of trust and authority, thinking men and women of all classes, have their attention fixed upon the events taking place about us. They are watching the strained, restless relations that exist among the nations. They observe the intensity that is taking possession of every earthly element, and they realize that something great and decisive is about to take place, that the world is on the verge of a stupendous crisis.

A moment of respite has been graciously given us of God. Every power lent us of Heaven is now to be used in working for those perishing in ignorance. There must be no delay. The truth must be proclaimed in the dark places of the earth. Obstacles must be met and surmounted. A great work is to be done, and to those who know the truth for this time, this work has been entrusted.

As a Lamp that Burneth

I am instructed to speak words to our people that will give them courage to do diligently the work that shall come to them in this their day of opportunity. I am instructed to urge the necessity of personal consecration, and the sanctification of the whole being to God. Let each one inquire, Lord, what wouldst Thou have me to do, that the vigilance of Christ may be seen in my life, that His example may be followed by me, that I may speak sincere words, which will help souls in darkness? Oh, how I long to see church members clothed with their beautiful garments, and prepared to go forth to meet the Bridegroom! Many are expecting to sit down to the marriage supper of the Lamb, who are unprepared for the coming of the King. They are like the blind; they do not seem to discern their danger.

The Lord calls upon you, oh, church that has been blessed with the truth, to give a knowledge of this truth to those who know it not. From one end of the world to the other must the message of Christ's soon coming be proclaimed. The third angel's message—the last message of mercy to a perishing world—is so precious, so glorious. Let the truth go forth as a lamp that burneth. Mysteries into which angels desire to look, which prophets and kings and righteous men desired to know, the church of God is to make known.

A Call to Greater Self-Denial

It is our privilege to see the work of God advancing in the cities. Christ is waiting, waiting, for places to be entered. Who are preparing for this work? We shall not say that we are destitute of laborers. There are some workers, and for this we are glad. But there is a greater, a far greater work to be done in our cities. Far greater self-denial is to be practiced in order that the word of life may be carried from place to place and from house to house.

More and more, men and women are going forth with the gospel message. We thank God for this. But we need a greater awakening. We slide back into self-indulgence; we do not exercise to the utmost the virtues that Christ has promised if we ask in faith. That which we receive from Christ we must give to others. Just as surely as we receive, so surely must we give. None who receive the grace of Christ can keep it to themselves. As soon as Christ becomes an abiding presence in the heart, we shall not be able to see souls perishing in ignorance of the truth and be at rest. We shall make any sacrifice that we may reach them; and none of us are so poor that we cannot make daily sacrifices for Christ.

The influence of the work we are doing will be felt through all eternity. If we will work in harmony with one another and with heaven, God will demonstrate His power in our behalf as He did for the disciples on the Day of Pentecost. Those days of preparation, in which the disciples prepared themselves by prayer and a putting away of all disunion, brought them into such close relation to God that He could work for them and through them in a marvelous manner. Today God desires to accomplish great things through the faith and works of His believing people. But we must stand in right relation to Him, that when He speaks to us we may hear and understand His voice.

Let not unbelief come in; for God's work is to go from city to city, from country to country. The plans of the enemies of God may be laid to defeat His work; but have faith that Jehovah will remove all obstructions to its progress. Talk faith, work in faith, and advance in faith. Obstacles will be removed as we lay hold of the promises of God. Let the Lord's people go forward, and their hearts will be made strong.

What is the promise to those living in these last days?—"Turn you to the stronghold, ye prisoners of hope: even today do I declare that I will render double unto thee.... Ask ye of the Lord rain in the time of the latter rain; so the Lord shall make bright clouds, and give them showers of rain."—The Review and Herald, November 17, 1910.

* * * * *

For Further Study

Into All the World:
Counsels on Health, 215-220
(Testimonies for the Church 7:51-60).

Breadth of Medical Missionary Work Not Understood:
Counsels on Health, 509, 510
(Testimonies for the Church 8:203, 204).
Warning Against Centralization:
Counsels on Health, 223-227
(Testimonies for the Church 7:99-102);
Testimonies for the Church 8:204, 205.
Jerusalem Centers to Be Scattered:
Counsels on Health, 299, 300.
Centers in All Cities:
Counsels on Health, 214
(Testimonies for the Church 8:204, 205).
Relation of Schools to Sanitariums:
Counsels on Health, 242, 243, 301, 54;
Testimonies for the Church 9:178.
Unselfish Interest for All Parts of the Field:
Testimonies for the Church 8:170, 171.
Prosperous Institutions to Help Others:
Counsels on Health, 220
(Testimonies for the Church 7:59, 60);
Counsels on Health, 308-3;
Testimonies for the Church 8:136-144).
Many to Be Quickly Trained:
Counsels on Health, 394, 395, 397.
Self-Supporting Workers:
The Ministry of Healing, 154-156, 479-48;
Testimonies for the Church 7:23, 24, 227, 254;
The Acts of the Apostles, 18.
Gospel of Health to Be Given Its Place:
Testimonies for the Church 6:327.